Worship Matters

A United Methodist Guide to Ways to Worship

Volume I

Edited by
E. Byron Anderson

DISCIPLESHIP RESOURCES

PO BOX 340003 • NASHVILLE, TN 37203-0003
www.discipleshipresources.org

Cover design by Sharon Anderson

Book design by Kym Whitley

ISBN 978-0-88177-279-1

Library of Congress Catalog Card No. 98-96831

Second printing: 2007

Contents

ABBREVIATIONS

All references to the official resources of The United Methodist Church listed below appear in parentheses in the articles.

BOD	=	*The Book of Discipline of The United Methodist Church—1996*
MV	=	*Mil Voces Para Celebrar: Himnario Metodista*
UMBOW	=	*The United Methodist Book of Worship*
UMH	=	*The United Methodist Hymnal*

Introduction

THE UNITED METHODIST CHURCH FACES MANY CHALLENGES today. The shape, practice, and style of worship ranks high on the list of our concerns, because worship is the single most public event in the church's life. The church expresses these concerns in the form of various polarizations. We express and create tensions between those perceived to be "high church sacramentalists" over against "low church preachers." There are conflicts between "traditionalists" and advocates of "contemporary" liturgical and musical styles, as well as between those concerned with theological orthodoxy and those more concerned with social-cultural relevance. There is stress between growth experts who argue for a communal homogeneity—whether of age, musical taste, economic status, or personal need—and those who call our attention to the increasing racial diversification and globalization of our churches. The list continues to grow. As it does so, United Methodist pastors, preachers, worship leaders and planners find cause to explore the particular gifts and graces of United Methodist worship, particularly as represented in the basic worship resources of the church: *The United Methodist Hymnal* and *The United Methodist Book of Worship.*

These conflicts are not the only reasons to give renewed attention to United Methodist worship. For more than half a century, we could safely assume a stable, relatively homogeneous, church community, with churches planted at every crossroad or train stop across the country. We could also assume that our churches would continue to grow as our children grew, married, joined the church, had their own children (in some order of these events), and as their children repeated the pattern. For a variety of reasons, this is not the case today in many of our churches. The church has changed, as has the religious sensibility of the country. We know that today the largest number of unchurched people is not across either ocean but in our own back yards. The mission field is on our doorsteps. We also know that many people of all ages, but especially youth and young to middle-aged adults are seeking places and practices that will give meaning to their lives. North-American Christianity today, especially United Methodism, provides a quickly changing landscape in which to explore a tradition of worship.

In many ways, it is our very awareness of this changing landscape and of the missionary context in which we live that places the questions of the shape, practice, and style of worship before us. Although the mission field

E. BYRON ANDERSON

Assistant Professor of Worship, Christian Theological Seminary, Indianapolis, Indiana

Worship Matters: A United Methodist Guide to Ways to Worship (Volume I) © 1999 Discipleship Resources. Used by permission.

There are a number of consequences in recovering this historic and ecumenical pattern. Through it we discover the possibilities for a common worship that reaches across denominational lines. One sign of this is the extensive sharing of resources in recent worship books, evidenced in the copyright acknowledgments of the *Book of Worship: United Church of Christ;* the *Book of Alternative Services of the Anglican Church of Canada;* the Presbyterian *Book of Common Worship;* as well as in our own United Methodist *Book of Worship.* At the same time, this sharing has opened a significant, though often subtle, liturgical creativity as the particular theological concerns of each denomination are brought to bear on these patterns. On the one hand, we discover in the midst of these resources the close relationship between doctrine and worship. On the other hand, even as we move toward shared basic patterns and practices of worship, we discover that unity does not require uniformity. These basic patterns enable us to be united even as we embrace a diversity of theological expression—even within one tradition.

Another consequence of this shared work is the way in which these basic patterns provide a new opportunity for *guided freedom.* Guided freedom accomplishes two things: It reminds us that freedom without form brings chaos. But it also reminds us that form without freedom brings an unthinking *ritualism.*[7] By way of analogy, we can compare the guided freedom of the basic patterns of worship to the performance of the blues. In playing the blues, what happens in the various melody lines, in the interaction between bass and treble at the piano, or in the interaction between various instruments, depends on a basic pattern and progression of harmonies that keep repeating. While this repeating pattern regulates the improvisation that occurs above and within it, it is also this repeating pattern that makes the improvisation possible in the first place. If each musician has to constantly think about or reinvent the pattern, improvisation will be limited; the music will not "happen." The pattern must be so much a part of the musicians, like the beating of the heart or the regular inhaling and exhaling of the lungs, that they do not have to think about it but can "play" it. At the same time, the pattern provides something upon which the diverse instrumental voices can build harmony and play off one another; without the pattern, there is only a discordant juxtaposition of voices, speaking at or over one another.

In the perceived conflict between form and freedom—often set up as the conflict between "high church" and "low church," sometimes as a conflict between "sacramental" and "evangelical" traditions—the basic patterns of United Methodist worship lead us to see that the gift of our work of worship as United Methodists lies somewhere between the two, requiring that it be both sacramental and evangelical. As pastor and liturgist Robert Hovda suggested some years ago, the two poles of form and freedom have become the idols of various worship traditions.[8] On the one hand, some have made an idol of the book—that is, of form—and have come to believe that nothing in the book or the tradition is dispensable from the liturgy. On the other hand, some have made an idol of freedom, arguing that everything is dispensable or, at most, optional. The first leads to ritualism or magic. The second leads to chaos or susceptibility to the idiosyncrasies of individual preachers, musicians, and liturgists. As we dig into, think about, and explore these patterns, we discover that guided freedom can be a gift consistent with our United Methodist heritage. We also discover how important these patterns are to both the formation and expression of our Christian faith.

critical reflection on Scripture, tradition, and experience. At the same time, our reflection must account for the realities of our practices in particular places and times. In this, the *how* and *why* of United Methodist worship must answer more than the pragmatic question, What works? It also must answer the question, What is this work doing?

In preparing these volumes, we understand reflection and action to be mutual partners, joined hand in hand, for the work of worship. Volume I provides basic perspectives on worship for the emerging missionary context in North America, emphasizing the importance of worship in making, nurturing, and sending disciples. Volume II provides a practical guide for planning and implementing vital and faithful worship, emphasizing the materials of worship. Both volumes support the work of worship with the basic United Methodist patterns and practices. Both volumes address the importance and materials of United Methodist worship. Worship *matters*!

INTRODUCTION TO VOLUME I

This first volume of *Worship Matters* develops, in three parts, basic theological and liturgical perspectives on United Methodist worship. Part One explores the relationship between theology, liturgy, and worship. Part Two examines the connections between theology, culture, and worship. Part Three gives attention to some questions about the people leading worship and the work of planning worship. Because of this emphasis on people and planning, local churches are permitted, as stipulated on page 2 in this book, to make photocopies of the articles for use with local church worship committees, leaders, and planning teams.

PART ONE: PERSPECTIVES ON THEOLOGY, LITURGY, AND WORSHIP

The articles in the first part set out the place of worship at the heart of and as a means for (re-)shaping the life and ministry of United Methodist congregations. They explore normative principles in shaping and evaluating United Methodist worship and interpret the basic pattern of worship for the Lord's Day, in both its simplicity and complexity, as found in *The United Methodist Hymnal, Mil Voces Para Celebrar: Himnario Metodista,* and *The United Methodist Book of Worship*. Articles in this section also explore the work of worship as the work of the whole congregation, arguing for the importance of reclaiming the centrality of baptism and the Lord's Supper (Eucharist) for congregational life and ministry.

PART TWO: PERSPECTIVES ON THEOLOGY, CULTURE, AND WORSHIP

The second part begins by exploring how the church has used cultural forms in the praise of God, offering guidelines in the selection and use of various cultural forms. Subsequent articles explore the ways in which the patterns of United Methodist worship permit a response to the particular cultural needs and styles of the local church. Some of these articles also explore the questions and contributions of feminist, African American, Asian American, and Hispanic American worship practices in relationship to the basic United Methodist worship patterns.

FORMATION AND EXPRESSION

The patterns of Christian worship both form and express our faith. Unfortunately, our current context, concerned with the expression of individual desire and experience, emphasizes the expressive power of worship over its formative power. In our distrust of ritual, we let go of an important gift to the church. This is not to deny the clear expressive power of Christian worship; psalms, hymns, and spiritual songs were sung because people believed and felt that they had something to sing about and someone to sing to. Rather, it is to reclaim an understanding reflected in early Christian writers, such as John Chrysostom and Cyril of Jerusalem—both bishops of the church in the late fourth century—who understood the importance of the ritual action and repeated practice of Christian worship in the formation of Christian people.

Today, learning theorists, neurologists, and ritual anthropologists similarly argue that repeated actions in place and time, whether with individuals, objects, or gestures, form people with particular kinds of memories, abilities, and relationships. For example, psychologist Erik Erikson argues in his work on the human life cycle that repeated visual experience with patterns and categories teach an infant to recognize the face of the mother. This experience, Erikson suggests, provides a foundational experience of the holy—experience necessary for the development of trust and faith.[9]

By examining and reclaiming the historic, ecumenical patterns and practices of Christian worship—as we will do in the various articles in this volume and in the next—we give renewed attention to the ways in which worship forms us. In other words, we begin to see that the repeated patterns and practices of Christian worship *over time* shape us in ways of being with God and one another. In the repeated patterns and practices of Christian worship, we are formed and fashioned into the values and vision of the gospel.[10] In the habit of worship, it becomes possible, in part, for us to remain in relationship to God and one another through the varying conditions of our lives and the inconsistencies of our feelings and moods.

Even as our work of worship guides and frees us, it forms and expresses our ongoing response to the *evangel* (good news) of God in Jesus Christ. Animated by the presence and power of the Holy Spirit, we lift our hearts and hands, minds and voices that the world may feel and hear and see "love's ecstatic height, the glorious joy unspeakable, the beatific sight" (*UMH,* 88).[11] We take up our work of worship and adoration in particular times and places, in the changing character of language, space, gesture, and symbol, with hymns, psalms, and spiritual songs. In this work we are free to worship "without fear" and are formed for service "in holiness and righteousness" (Luke 1:74-75).

OVERVIEW

The two volumes of *Worship Matters—A United Methodist Guide to Ways to Worship* (Volume I) and *A United Methodist Guide to Worship Work* (Volume II)—have a common starting point: Worship *matters* because it is at the heart of and vital to the work of the local church as it makes, nurtures, and sends disciples in ministry to the world. Although Volume I is more theological in its approach and Volume II is more practical, both draw upon the close relationship between theology and practice. The work of planning worship must build upon informed and

In the conflict form and freedom.. basic patter United Meth worship lead u to see that the gift of our work of worship as United Methodists lies somewhere between the two.

PART THREE: PERSPECTIVES ON DOING THE WORK OF WORSHIP

The articles in the third part anticipate the practical issues addressed more fully in Volume II. The first two articles explore the role of the presider and the roles of deacons and other assisting ministers in worship. Two articles address the question of who should receive Holy Communion and the extension of Communion to those who cannot attend Sunday worship. One article examines the relationship between liturgical architecture and worship. Two articles explore the role and use of art and other media in worship, while the final article deals with the power of sign, symbol, and gesture to encourage full and active participation in worship beyond words alone.

The challenges and tensions in United Methodist worship offer an invitation to a renewed and in-depth exploration of why and how we worship. We hope this volume provides a means by which you can accept this invitation.

ENDNOTES

1 From *The Book of Discipline of The United Methodist Church—1996,* ¶1112.3. Copyright © 1996 by The United Methodist Publishing House. Used by permission.

2 From "The Order for Consecrations and Ordinations," © 1979 by Board of Discipleship, The United Methodist Church; © 1992 by The United Methodist Publishing House; from *The United Methodist Book of Worship,* p. 690. Used by permission.

3 From "An Order of Sunday Worship Using the Basic Pattern," © 1985, 1989, 1992 by The United Methodist Publishing House; from *The United Methodist Book of Worship,* p. 16. Used by permission.

4 See *John Wesley's Prayer Book: The Sunday Service of the Methodists in North America,* with introduction, notes, and commentary by James F. White (Akron, OH: O.S.L. Publications, 1991).

5 See *Baptism, Eucharist and Ministry: Faith and Order Paper No. 111* (Geneva: World Council of Churches, 1982); *Covenanting Toward Unity: From Consensus to Communion: A Proposal to the Churches From the Consultation on Church Union* (Princeton, NJ: Consultation on Church Union, 1985); and *Churches in Covenant Communion: The Church of Christ Uniting* (Princeton, NJ: Consultation on Church Union, 1989).

6 From "Forth in Thy Name, O Lord," by Charles Wesley, in *The United Methodist Hymnal* (Nashville, TN: The United Methodist Publishing House, 1989), 438.

7 *Ritualism* is a category Erik H. Erikson used to describe the maladaptive possibilities of ritualization—a category best described in terms of neuroses and obsessive-compulsive behaviors. He explored this in *The Life Cycle Completed: A Review* (New York, NY: W. W. Norton & Company, 1985), pp. 43–82.

8 See *Strong, Loving and Wise: Presiding in Liturgy,* by Robert W. Hovda (Collegeville, MN: The Liturgical Press, 1980).

9 See especially *The Life Cycle Completed: A Review,* by Erik H. Erikson (New York, NY: W. W. Norton & Company, 1985), pp. 43–48, and *Stages of Faith: The Psychology of Human Development and the Quest for Meaning,* by James W. Fowler (San Francisco, CA: Harper & Row, Publishers, 1981), pp. 119–21.

10 For a more extensive treatment of these themes, see *Worship Come to Its Senses,* by Don E. Saliers (Nashville, TN: Abingdon Press, 1996) and *Liturgy and the Moral Self: Humanity at Full Stretch Before God: Essays in Honor of Don E. Saliers,* edited by E. Byron Anderson and Bruce T. Morrill, S.J. (Collegeville, MN: The Liturgical Press, 1998).

11 From "Maker, in Whom We Live," by Charles Wesley, in *The United Methodist Hymnal* (Nashville, TN: The United Methodist Publishing House, 1989), 88.

The *how* and *why* of United Methodist worship must answer more than the pragmatic question, What works? It must also answer the question, What is this work doing?

PERSPECTIVES ON THEOLOGY, LITURGY, AND WORSHIP

leaders in the postmodern world is to see our order, liturgy, doctrine, and discipline as gifts and means of grace, and to use these with gratitude, confidence, and competency born of the Spirit.

FOR FURTHER READING

For the Life of the World: Sacraments and Orthodoxy, by Alexander Schmemann (Crestwood, NY: St. Vladimir's Seminary Press, 1973).

Planning Blended Worship: The Creative Mixture of Old and New, by Robert Webber (Nashville, TN: Abingdon Press, 1998).

Worship & Daily Life: A Resource for Worship Planners, introduction by Doris Rudy (Nashville, TN: Discipleship Resources, 1999).

Worship as Theology: Foretaste of Glory Divine, by Don E. Saliers, edited by Ulrike Guthrie (Nashville, TN: Abingdon Press, 1994).

Worship Come to Its Senses, by Don E. Saliers (Nashville, TN: Abingdon Press, 1996).

ENDNOTES

1 From "A Service of Word and Table I," © 1972, 1980, 1985, 1989 by The United Methodist Publishing House; from *The United Methodist Hymnal,* p. 10. Used by permission.

2 From "Constitution on the Sacred Liturgy (Sacrosanctum Concilium)" in *The Documents of Vatican II,* edited by Walter M. Abbott, S.J. (New York, NY: The America Press, 1966), p. 142.

3 From *The Book of Discipline of The United Methodist Church—1996,* ¶62, p. 68. Copyright © 1996 by The United Methodist Publishing House. Used by permission.

4 This is the subtitle of Don E. Saliers' book, *Worship as Theology: Foretaste of Glory Divine* (Nashville, TN: Abingdon Press, 1994).

5 The primary task of United Methodist congregations consists of four interrelated components: inviting people to God, helping them commit themselves to God, nurturing them in Christian faith, and sending them out into the world as Christ's disciples (see *BOD,* p. 115).

6 Reprinted by permission from "What Resources Are Available to Assist Catechumenal Ministers?" by Karen Ward, in *Welcome to Christ: A Lutheran Introduction to the Catechumenate,* p. 57 (emphasis added). Copyright © 1997 Augsburg Fortress.

7 See "Ordering Congregational Life Around the Means of Grace," on pp. 43–50 in this volume.

8 I am indebted to Robert Webber for this insight, which he included in his "Renew Your Worship!" seminars.

9 From "Constitution on the Sacred Liturgy (Sacrosanctum Concilium)" in *The Documents of Vatican II,* edited by Walter M. Abbott, S.J. (New York, NY: The America Press, 1966), p. 144.

10 From "Baptismal Covenant I," © 1976, 1980, 1985, 1989 by The United Methodist Publishing House; from *The United Methodist Hymnal,* p. 37. Used by permission.

11 From "By Water and the Spirit: A United Methodist Understanding of Baptism" in *The Book of Resolutions of The United Methodist Church—1996,* p. 725. Copyright © 1996 by The United Methodist Publishing House. Used by permission.

Worship at the Heart of the Congregation's Ministry System

DANIEL T. BENEDICT, JR.

Worship Resources Director, The General Board of Discipleship, Nashville, Tennessee

RECOVERY OF THE FULLNESS AND DYNAMISM OF CHRISTIAN public worship as the congregation's central faith practice is crucial as we enter the new millennium. This is not to make an exclusive claim for worship separate from other practices of the congregation. Rather, it is an assertion that in worship *God encounters the community of faith* through its use of the means of grace, initiating and sustaining the church's ministry of welcoming and transforming people for discipleship in all of life. As the church employs the means of grace in public worship, God acts to constitute and form the church for the life of the world.

In this article, we look at worship in broad outline and leave detailed discussion of the various aspects of worship to subsequent articles. Here we will aim to articulate clearly the centrality of worship in relation to God's action in the congregation's whole life and witness.

A VISION OF WORSHIP

What comes to mind when we think about worship, or when we speak about "going to church"? At least the following come to mind: hymn singing, reading Scripture, preaching, inviting people to Christian discipleship, baptism and confirmation, offering gifts, Holy Communion, and scattering into the world. Without these actions, we can hardly imagine the meaning of the word *church.*

This is not to say that other processes and activities, such as small-group meetings and Christian education, outreach and witness, stewardship and social ministry are not important—even essential. It is to say that, in the hearts of most congregational leaders, the centrality of worship is not in question. Most leaders are convinced that worship is vital to the weekly schedule of church activities. "Whatever else they may do or not do in congregational life, the people participate regularly in weekly worship," we say. Pastors live and breathe for Sunday morning worship.

However, it is evident that in many United Methodist congregations people and leaders worship week to week without a vision for the theological, missional, and pastoral centrality of worship. Worship, when viewed as an important part of the *programmatic life* of the congregation, leads to one result. Worship, when envisioned as the heart of the congregation's *spiritual life*—its relationship to God—leads to quite another result.

The people of Butler Memorial United Methodist Church know that what happens in worship on Sunday and what happens in their daily

Worship Matters: A United Methodist Guide to Ways to Worship (Volume I) © 1999 Discipleship Resources. Used by permission.

When viewed this way, Christian public worship is central to the church as a missionary people resident in a hurting and hoping world. It forms us in a life. It reorients us to who we are as people baptized into Jesus Christ. Here, as Robert Webber points out, church is neither a school (as we thought in the seventeenth and eighteenth centuries), nor a revival tent (as we thought in the nineteenth and early twentieth centuries),[8] nor an activity and social service center (as we have thought for much of this century). Instead, vital and faithful Christian worship touches the whole person and engages the whole faith community in rehearsing, enacting, singing, experiencing, trusting, and committing to the great story of God's saving action in Jesus Christ.

Worship is not mere ritual, repeating lifeless checklists of prayers, readings, and movements. Ritual in the sense used here is an *outward engagement* with the living God, using the means of grace that convert and order the church's *inward experience*. Such ordering of experience is central to congregational life and is God's own engagement with us that forms and reforms the church week by week.

CHRIST'S ROYAL PRIESTHOOD

Worship as I am describing it represents a seismic shift from worship as a form of North-American consumerism and entertainment to worship as a "full, conscious, and active participation"[9] in Christ's priestly work for the redemption of the world. When people are baptized, the congregation welcomes them, saying, "Through baptism you are…made to share in Christ's royal priesthood" (*UMH*, p. 37).[10] The image of priesthood is drawn directly from 1 Peter 2:9, in which Peter affirms the unique character and work of the baptized.

Through baptism all Christians are initiated into the liturgical life of the holy catholic church and the communion of saints, as we say in the Apostles' Creed. "By Water and the Spirit: A United Methodist Understanding of Baptism" states: "Baptism brings us into union with Christ, with each other, and with the church in every time and place."[11] The ministry system of the congregation is always more than the local and the contemporary; it is always linked to and enriched by the communion of saints and the rich textures of the faith of those who have been made to share in Christ's royal priesthood. Through the congregation's discipline, gathered worship shapes and propels the scattered disciples to be a holy priesthood joined to Christ and proclaiming "the mighty acts of him who called [them] out of darkness into his marvelous light" (1 Peter 2:9).

RITUAL PRACTICE AS CRUCIBLE AND CONTEXT

Ritual actions are the crucible in which faith is forged; and the metal of discipleship is alloyed with the power of the Holy Spirit. The word *ritual* derives from the word *rite,* meaning "a formal procedure, custom, or habit." A ritual act is a simple action that may or may not involve words. The Holy Spirit uses ritual actions to open up the eyes of the mind and heart. The usefulness of ritual practices—the means of grace—in the hands of the Spirit lies in the juxtaposition of words, space, people, story, sound, movement, music, and ordinary things such as water, oil, bread, and cup. Ritual actions are repeated actions; and they are usually recognizable because they have been repeated.

Antipathy to ritual actions arises when it appears that the repetition does not "connect" us with anything, and so it becomes a mere formality, a dead ritual. Liturgical scholars and anthropologists call this "ritual failure." "Ritual success" comes when the ritual action connects us to past experiences of faith—God's story in Scripture—and to ever-new circumstances of living and growing faith.

For example, children love the ritual of bedtime. Most children have a playful but solemn sense of order about their bedtime ritual. It is a time for telling or reading a story; talking about a "just thought of it, Dad, why did…?" question; the good-night prayer up close; blankets tucked in around the neck; a kiss on the forehead; and lights out. The bedtime ritual gives continuity to daily life, orders the end of the day, deepens the child-parent relationship, and serves as a prelude to sleep.

For the church, the time we celebrate and try to make sense of is God's time. We keep time with Christ using ordinary actions and things in light of the sacred story. By our ritual practices, we claim the promises of God for ourselves and for the world. Even the gathering of the congregation each Sunday is a ritual practice. That act, even if no further actions or words are used, is a powerful sign of a participation in something that orders all of the week that follows. The crucial thing is to practice rituals in ways that succeed both in bringing us "home" again and in sending us forth transformed and reconnected to God in Christ by the power of the Spirit.

Ritual practice, in this broad sense, is necessary for us because of our persistent amnesia: We forget who we are, whom we live for, and why. In the crucible of faithful ritual practice, God "remembers" us and we, together, are caught up in the drama of the dying and rising of Christ and our union with him in baptism. We worship the risen Christ, who meets us in worship. Far from being disconnected from life and being lost, the full range of our human experience during the week past is remembered, offered, shaped, and organized in and by the rituals of gathering around Christ in Word and Sacrament.

In ritual action, the fire of the Spirit continually interprets our day-to-day experience. In the drama of public Christian worship, we know anew that "whether we live or whether we die, we are the Lord's" (Romans 14:8). The Greek word used in "Do this in remembrance of me" is *anamnesis,* which means "remember." Ritual practice is a gift for those who have poor memories! By it we come "home" each week and are converted from strangers to friends and followers of the risen Lord.

Ritual practices and the liturgical texts of services are gifts from God. They are not burdensome constraints or fences to keep leaders and congregations corralled but, rather, catapults for transformation and service. If the order of the church expressed in its doctrine and liturgy is seen as a constricting and constraining fence, worshipers will soon try to jump the fence to "freedom."

If, however, rites and ritual texts are seen as marking a gracious enclosure where life can be found in wonder, love, and praise, the church's practices of Word and Sacrament will shape us with the realism Peter expressed in answer to Jesus' question: "Do you also wish to go away?" Peter answered: "Lord, to whom can we go? You have the words of eternal life" (John 6:67-68). Rites are not about chafing under burdensome constraint; they are about entering into eternal life for the life of the world! (John 20:30-31).

This is a critical issue in the spiritual formation of elders and deacons as leaders of worship. The great opportunity before United Meth…

Liturgical life is not simply about doing "religiou… things; it is about takin… life God gi… lifting it… thanks… brea… an… th…

How Shall We Worship?

2

L. EDWARD PHILLIPS

Associate Professor of Historical Theology, Garrett-Evangelical Theological Seminary, Evanston, Illinois

THE WORSHIP COMMITTEE IS MEETING FOR THE FIRST TIME. The chairperson asks the pastor, "What are we supposed to accomplish with this committee?"

The pastor answers, "Our goal is to facilitate good worship for our church."

The chairperson presses on, "How will we know when we have done that? The idea of 'good worship' seems a little vague to me."

The pastor suggests, "Let's poll this committee to find out what our expectations of 'good worship' might be."

One man responds, "I like worship that uses the old traditional hymns, such as 'Blessed Assurance.'"

Another person suggests, "But our teenagers want gospel songs they can clap their hands to! Remember how much they liked the Christian rock music performed by that touring youth choir?"

A teenager joins in, "I didn't like that at all! I find it embarrassing when my church tries to do that stuff."

A woman comments, "I think we should always say the Lord's Prayer."

Another woman asks, "But do we have to say it every Sunday? I like it when the pastor just makes up the prayer."

Someone else suggests, "Isn't worship supposed to give us something to think about?"

The teenager speaks up again, "I think we need to focus on social issues such as hunger or homelessness."

The man who spoke first comments again, "But let's not forget that we need to focus more on personal conversion."

The chairperson of the committee concludes by commenting, "I think we are headed for trouble here."

Scenarios such as this one are played out in numerous United Methodist churches. We know that worship is important, and we want it to be good; yet we have many diverse and incompatible ideas of what "good" worship should include. Some people prefer what we call traditional worship that gives us a strong sense of continuity with our tradition, using traditional hymns, prayers, and creeds. Other people, however, prefer what we call contemporary worship, which uses novelty and popular music styles to generate and maintain interest. We might characterize this tension between traditional and contemporary

Worship Matters: A United Methodist Guide to Ways to Worship (Volume I) © 1999 Discipleship Resources. Used by permission.

expression as the dynamic relationship between *structure* and *freedom,* with traditional worship emphasizing structure, and contemporary worship emphasizing freedom.

The role of expectation in worship, however, points to another dynamic that is often overlooked: Worship also has a *telos* (purpose) that finds expression in a particular pattern or *ethos* (character).

PATTERNS IN UNITED METHODIST WORSHIP

There are a variety of worship patterns that have been influential within Methodism over the last century or so, each with its own distinctive purpose and character.

THE REVIVAL/SEEKER-SERVICE PATTERN

At the beginning of the nineteenth century, most Methodists preferred a simple service made up of prayers, Scripture readings (one chapter from the Old Testament and one from the New Testament), and preaching. A few years later, this changed as a new revivalism spread among the Methodists, first in the form of the camp meeting, and later in a style of revival popularized by Charles G. Finney.

Finney took a practical business approach to revivals. He believed that the business of revivals was to solicit conversions by any means that might be useful. It did not matter to him if his methods flouted tradition or even appeared crass, as long as they worked. He devised a style of conducting revivals that he called new measures, which included such innovations as protracted meetings during the weekdays, using visiting evangelists to preach the message, "anxious benches" for those seeking conversion, and choirs and song leaders with musical instruments to lead the music. Everything in the revival was aimed at producing a heartfelt response in the congregation.

The pattern for a Finney revival was to begin with preliminaries. These would include rousing songs and testimonies, introductions of visitors and the newly saved, prayers for a successful meeting, and special music sung by the choir or a soloist. These preliminaries were conducted by the pastor and the song leader, and they served the purpose of warming up the audience for the visiting evangelist.[1] The evangelist usually read a Scripture lesson (a few verses at most) and then began the "message." It was a "message" rather than a "sermon," because the line of communication was clearly from the speaker to the audience.

The message was typically anecdotal. It began with humorous stories and gradually became more and more melodramatic. The payoff came at the conclusion when the evangelist gave the "altar call" (also called the "harvest" or "invitation"). At this time those who had been moved by the message were invited to come forward while the choir sang a song, to kneel at the front of the church, and to pray for a conversion experience.

This three-fold pattern—preliminaries, message, and altar call—was a dramatically different style of church service and was very effective in producing results. Thousands of people were brought into Methodist congregations through revivals. Indeed, the pattern was so successful that it began to be used for Sunday morning worship, even when there was no revival meeting going on. Finney himself was not particularly interested in worship as such. The telos of his revivals was to produce conversions. Nevertheless, Finney's revival pattern soon became a standard pattern for worship, and Methodist churches began to have choirs, song leaders, anecdotal message-style sermons, and altar-call invitations—a revival ethos for a revival telos.

Few United Methodist churches today have regular revivals of the sort that Finney advocated. Nevertheless, many churches that have developed contemporary "seeker services" use this pattern with few modifications. Seeker services also begin with preliminaries that include professional music by soloists and small ensembles, often accompanied by pre-recorded music to ensure high quality. Skits or other methods may be used to present Scripture, but these, too, are done with great attention to good performance.

The message tends to be motivational, using simple, clear stories and illustrations. Instead of a heavy-handed altar call, the seeker service has a more gentle invitation: People are encouraged to come to a meeting for inquirers, or perhaps to join a small interest group focusing on their needs. But the strong emphasis on polished performance aimed at audience response links the contemporary seeker service ideologically to the old-fashioned revival, with a similar telos of personal response and an ethos that emphasizes stage performance.

THE SUNDAY SCHOOL/CREATIVE WORSHIP PATTERN

The second pattern to leave its imprint on Methodist worship is the Sunday school assembly. Similar to the revival, the Sunday school movement began to grow in the nineteenth century and became a regular feature of church life well before the end of the century. Unlike the revival, with its professional evangelist and song leaders, the Sunday school was largely a lay movement. The pattern for worship in the Sunday school was the assembly. A layperson serving as superintendent would call the gathering of children to order, usually with a rousing song and opening prayer. There might be a few general announcements before the children and adult leaders were dismissed to their classes.

Following the class sessions, the assembly reconvened. There would be more rousing music, such as "Onward Christian Soldiers," during which children might march around the assembly room in procession. The superintendent took attendance, introduced visitors, and took up the collection. Children recited the Scripture memory verse of the day. Someone may have shared a short devotional reading or recited a poem on a theme of the day, such as "Mother's Day" or "Mission Sunday." Finally, there would be a closing prayer to dismiss the assembly. Large-city congregations might have a Sunday worship service after Sunday school, but for the small, rural congregations that had only a preaching service once or twice a month, the lay-led Sunday school would be the regular weekly service.

If the revival aimed at the gut to produce an emotional response, the telos of the Sunday school assembly was education. Therefore, memorization of Scripture, catechisms, and creeds found a place along with participatory skits, programs, and songs in order to grow a deepening religious faith. Unlike the slick professionalism of the revival, the ethos of the Sunday school assembly consisted of rowdy processions, readings, and performances of programs by children.

The telos and ethos of the Sunday school assembly are manifested in worship today in a variety of "creative" styles of worship. Such worship services use various interactive means to educate the congregation about theological or social issues. For example, I recently participated

We know that worship is important, and we want it to be good; yet we have many diverse and incompatible ideas of what "good" worship should include.

in a service in which the congregation was asked to gather and hold hands in a circle during the prayers to symbolize our turning to God for guidance, and then to face outward for a dismissal to symbolize our going out to serve in the world. The prayer itself was a printed litany that mentioned various social justice concerns of the congregation and larger community. We found reading the litany awkward since we were trying to hold hands with fellow worshipers. The fact that this was awkward was actually worked into the liturgy as the leader explained: "We sometimes find it difficult to keep in touch with our neighbors and to focus our attention on God."

The telos of "creative worship," as in the case of the Sunday school assembly, is to educate. The ethos is didactic, participatory, and wordy, with lengthy (usually printed) prayers, responsive readings, and congregational responses. This is quite different from the revival or the seeker service, which treats the congregation like an audience that needs to be moved emotionally.

THE AESTHETIC WORSHIP PATTERN

The third worship pattern is what I call the aesthetic pattern. It also began to develop in Methodist churches in the nineteenth century as a reaction against the coarseness of frontier worship and the emotionalism of revivals. This style of worship fit well with larger city churches, which were inspired by the Gothic Revival architecture of the late-nineteenth century, especially those that could afford well-decorated buildings (stained glass and pointed arches!) as well as good musical instruments and musicians.

Aesthetic worship values classical hymns, formal anthems, and robed choirs and preachers. Churches began to use printed orders of worship for the whole congregation, first in the hymnals and then in worship bulletins in larger churches. Consequently, aesthetic worship began to employ neatly printed prayers and creeds, which typically used the poetical Elizabethan English of the *Book of Common Prayer*.

Aesthetic worship is structured and dignified rather than spontaneous and emotional. It suited American Methodism as it began to see itself as a national church rather than as a frontier movement. Aesthetic worship lives on today in churches that continue to use the classical hymns and prayers of the church. These churches also typically employ terminology such as *choral introit, invocation, offertory anthem,* and so forth. Worship bulletins use language that connotes stability and social class. The telos of aesthetic worship is to elevate cultural sensibility and stability through an ethos of aesthetic integrity, dignity, and high social standing.

THE WORD AND TABLE PATTERN

The fourth pattern of worship is Word and Table. This pattern goes back to the earliest centuries of the Christian church, when Christians had a weekly Sunday service of both preaching and the Lord's Supper. The oldest description of this pattern comes from Justin Martyr, and dates from around 150 C.E. (Common Era). According to Martyr, the Christians gathered together for worship at a designated meeting place, and someone read lessons from the Old Testament and the writings of the apostles. Afterward, the pastor preached a sermon based on the lessons.

Following the sermon, someone led the congregation in prayers of intercession for the needs of the world and then concluded with a sign of peace. Next came the offertory, which included the bread and wine the congregation would use for the Lord's Supper. The pastor then offered a lengthy prayer of thanksgiving over the bread and wine, which concluded with a resounding "Amen!" from the congregation. The pastor and helpers distributed the bread and wine to the congregation, saving some to take to those who could not attend because of illness.

This worship pattern from the early church is virtually identical to the Basic Pattern of Worship that we find today in *The United Methodist Hymnal* (p. 2). This is not accidental. Over the last forty years, those who are leaders in renewing United Methodist worship resources have drawn their models from the New Testament and the early church. The telos of the Word and Table pattern is to form the worshiping congregation as the people of God; as, for example, expressed by these words from the Great Thanksgiving: "By your Spirit make us one with Christ, one with each other, and one in ministry to all the world" (*UMBOW*, p. 38).[2]

The ethos of the Word and Table pattern is "universal liturgy." These words need some explaining. *Universal* is another word for *catholic,* as in the Apostles' Creed when we affirm our belief in the "holy catholic church." This denotes an understanding of the church that includes Christians throughout history as well as all Christians today. When the church gathers in worship, it does so with all the saints, past and present. *Liturgy* means "work of the people" or "public service," and in this context "worship service."[3] Moreover, as we do our "worship work" before God, God works through the Holy Spirit to change and empower us. The ethos of the Word and Table pattern stresses the transformative, active work of worship that God uses to form women and men into the body of Christ.

But the ethos of Word and Table is more than austere service; it intends celebration. Our service of God is meant to be our joy; therefore, we have a symbolic party: the Lord's Supper. In its most basic outline, the pattern here is: God speaks God's Word through Scripture and preaching, and we respond with offering, thanksgiving, and celebration—Word and Table. When we worship this way, we behave as the people of God.

UNDERSTANDING OUR EXPECTATIONS FOR WORSHIP

Whenever United Methodists plan worship (as in the opening scenario of this article), these four patterns—revival (seeker service), Sunday school (creative worship), aesthetic (traditional worship), and Word and Table—all come to mind. This is why our expectations for worship are so diverse. However, if worship planners are unaware of the telos and ethos guiding each of the four patterns, they often will wind up putting together services with elements that are at cross-purposes.

A particular worship committee might take elements of the Word and Table pattern and twist them into a revival pattern by dropping the Lord's Supper and adding an "Invitation to Christian Discipleship." They might also put in a "Call to Worship," which uses didactic, "creative-worship" language to educate the congregation about the "theme of the day." Let's use Mother's Day as an example. After a formal choral introit by the chancel choir, the worship leader begins the "Call to Worship" by asking the congregation, "Why are we here today?" To which the congregation responds, "We are here to honor our mothers and to acknowledge that God is like a mother to us all."

> **If worship planners are unaware of the telos and ethos guiding each of the four patterns, they often will wind up putting together services with elements that are at cross-purposes.**

This kind of approach may work smoothly, but then again, it may not. The congregation will find all the parts of the service "worship-like," since each part comes from a worship pattern, but people will not find the experience as a whole very satisfying as a service of worship. This is because it is nearly impossible to have a revival, a Sunday school meeting, and an aesthetic and inspiring, artistic performance at the same time! The telos and ethos of the different worship patterns inevitably clash. Worship planners who aspire to instill one overarching telos and ethos in congregational worship (such as a "traditional" worship service) will have a more satisfied congregation because the worship has a coherence of telos and ethos.

In all honesty, if a church's goal is to get more people through the doors of the sanctuary, a seeker service is likely to be the most successful because it is designed to do just that. On the other hand, congregations with a large number of members who care about issues of social justice will be drawn to the didacticism of "creative worship." Large and aging "First Church" congregations will likely prefer "traditional worship."

THE STRUCTURED FLEXIBILITY OF WORD AND TABLE

Yet few of our established congregations are this monolithic. If worship planners are to succeed in facilitating "good" worship, they need an overarching telos and ethos for worship that can blend the best aspects of the various patterns without creating a clash of elements. The *structured flexibility* of the Word and Table pattern is capable of providing just this sort of overarching purpose and character. The revival/seeker-service pattern reminds us that worship needs to move our hearts; this means that worship must be enchanting and emotionally engaging. The Word and Table pattern has the capacity to move us emotionally and to elicit response. Indeed, it has built into it an invitation to "come forward": the invitation to Holy Communion.

The Sunday school pattern reminds us that the laity play a role in liturgical leadership and that worship is meant to instruct us in the Christian life. The Word and Table pattern provides for all sorts of lay-liturgical ministries, such as readers, prayer leaders, and Communion servers. Furthermore, this pattern stresses that the whole congregation is responsible for "doing" the worship service, rather than sitting as a passive audience.

"Traditional worship" reminds us that worship deserves our best artistic efforts because God deserves our best service. Word and Table promotes a simple elegance in pattern and prayer. It also reminds us that tradition reaches back farther than the last one hundred years; it includes the whole history of the church—even "all the company of heaven" (*UMBOW,* p. 36).[4]

Furthermore, the Word and Table pattern is able to avoid the weaknesses of the other patterns: the individualism of the revival pattern, the consumer mentality of the seeker service, the unwieldy didacticism of the Sunday school assembly, the wordiness of creative worship, the class bias of aesthetic worship, and the nostalgia of traditional worship.

How shall we worship? The Word and Table pattern found in *The United Methodist Hymnal,* and supported by the resources in *The United Methodist Book of Worship,* offers the best answer. It is not merely one option among many; with its structured flexibility aimed at forming us into the body of Christ in our service of God, it is the most holistic and faithful pattern available to us.

FOR FURTHER READING

Blended Worship: Achieving Substance and Relevance in Worship, by Robert E. Webber (Peabody, MA: Hendrickson Publishers, 1996).

Protestant Worship: Traditions in Transition, by James F. White (Louisville, KY: Westminster John Knox Press, 1989).

Reaching Out Without Dumbing Down: A Theology of Worship for the Turn-of-the-Century Culture, by Marva J. Dawn (Grand Rapids, MI: William B. Eerdmans Publishing Company, 1995).

ENDNOTES

1 To this day, many churches in the southern United States of America have three large chairs on a platform behind the pulpit—one for the pastor, one for the song leader, and one for the evangelist.

2 From "A Service of Word and Table I," © 1972 by The Methodist Publishing House; © 1980, 1985, 1989, 1992 by The United Methodist Publishing House; from *The United Methodist Book of Worship,* p. 38. Used by permission.

3 For a more extended discussion of liturgy as work, see the introduction to Volume II of *Worship Matters,* on pp. 5–11.

4 From "A Service of Word and Table I," © 1972 by The Methodist Publishing House; © 1980, 1985, 1989, 1992 by The United Methodist Publishing House; from *The United Methodist Book of Worship,* p. 36. Used by permission.

The Word and Table pattern... with its structured flexibility aimed at forming us into the body of Christ in our service of God,... is the most holistic and faithful pattern available to us.

3

HOYT L. HICKMAN

*Worship Consultant,
Nashville, Tennessee*

The Basic Pattern of Worship

THE KEY TO *THE UNITED METHODIST HYMNAL* IS PAGE 2, THE Basic Pattern of Worship. The key to *The United Methodist Book of Worship* is pages 13–15, the same Basic Pattern with an introduction. The primary function of both these books is to provide resources and guidance for fleshing out this Basic Pattern to meet the diverse needs of United Methodist congregations.

The previous article described diverse patterns of worship found among United Methodist congregations, but behind this diversity there is a unity. The Basic Pattern attempts to express this unity, while affirming a wide range of diversity in orders and styles of worship. Most United Methodist worshiping congregations, even if they are not using the official *Hymnal* and *Book of Worship,* follow some version of this pattern most of the time.

This pattern is a guide as well as a description. Read the introduction to the Basic Pattern, on pages 13–14 in the *Book of Worship*. Notice how the Basic Pattern is rooted in Scripture and is seen, for instance, in the Emmaus story (Luke 24:13-35). Note the underlying assumption that our worship is an *encounter*. It is not simply talking and singing *about* God, but meeting and communing *with* the living God through the risen Christ in the power of the Holy Spirit.

Intimate and personal though this encounter can be, I am not alone with God when I join the family of Christ in worship. Other people surround and support me. The living presence of the whole body of Christians of all times and all places joins and upholds those visibly present. We are reminded that we are part of a universe whose whole history is an act of worship in which the continuing call of the Creator is answered by the continuing response of the creation.

The Pentecost story in Acts 2 reminds us that we worship an inclusive God, who enables us to reach out to and welcome people who do not speak our language—our literal language, our patterns of thought, or our language of musical and visual styles. People can worship God in whatever is their own heart-language. The Spirit can speak a new word that enables us to do new and daring things. The Spirit is also the spirit of truth, who has already spoken in Scripture and has been speaking to Christians through the ages and around the world: "God is spirit, and those who worship him must worship in spirit and truth" (John 4:24). We are to "test the spirits to see whether they are from God" (1 John 4:1).

Worship Matters: A United Methodist Guide to Ways to Worship (Volume I) © 1999 Discipleship Resources. Used by permission.

As we reflect on the Basic Pattern, hard questions emerge out of its descriptive sentences. As we struggle with these questions, we can thread our way through the controversies over types and styles of worship and be effective while keeping our integrity. We can be relevant and authentic. We can worship "in spirit and truth."

Let's take a closer look at the elements of the Basic Pattern.

ENTRANCE

Congregational worship, like human assemblies in general, begins with gathering and opening exchanges. The Basic Pattern calls this the Entrance, but other names also can be given to it. It consists of two parts, each of which is important and should be planned with great care.

Gathering, the first part of the entrance, is what happens as the people are coming together. They come for different reasons, with diverse personal needs and cultural backgrounds. First-time visitors need to be able to find the place of worship, find convenient parking, find their way to the sanctuary or other worship space as well as to facilities such as restrooms and childcare. As people encounter one another, some feel the need to socialize, while others feel the need to go promptly to their seats for quiet reflection or inner composure. Some want to be greeted and meet people, while others are more cautious. It is important to be sensitive to these diverse needs and to make appropriate provision for them. If a congregation cannot meet everyone's needs, it needs to discern the sorts of people it is especially called to reach and serve and to give their needs priority.

We gather *in the Lord's name.* Like the disciples walking toward Emmaus, we have been joined by the risen Christ. Unlike them, some of us are expecting an encounter with Christ. Like them, others are not, and for them such an encounter will be a surprise.

The visual environment can significantly support worship and make a powerful first impression on the visitor. Some, who are looking for a church that "looks like a church," need familiar symbols such as stained glass and a cross to signify that they are gathering in the Lord's name. Unchurched seekers who work for a corporation may be more willing to come to a building without Christian symbols that looks like a corporate headquarters and a room that looks like an auditorium. Those who have been hurt in some other church may need a building and a room that silently say, "This is definitely not the church that hurt you." What meets the needs of a newcomer may not meet that same person's needs after several years as a worshiper.

How do we meet all these conflicting needs? There is no one answer. There are many answers, one of which may be best in your situation. The Basic Pattern does not tell you what to do, but it does say: "Pay close attention to the gathering. What happens there is important."

The second part of the Entrance consists of opening acts by the gathered congregation and its leaders—typically greetings, praise and prayer, with music and other arts employed in various ways. Greetings should make it clear that we have gathered in the Lord's name. Then, as the disciples on the Emmaus road poured out their hearts to Christ and so opened their hearts for what was to come, we open up to God in Christ with expressions of what is on our hearts.

This can take many forms. A Christian congregation meeting secretly in a time of persecution, when they dare not gather for long or make much noise, may go abruptly from the gathering to the sharing of Word

Worship is an *encounter.* It is not simply talking and singing *about* God, but meeting and communing *with* the living God through the risen Christ in the power of the Holy Spirit.

and Sacrament. Many congregations today have simply a greeting or call to praise in the Lord's name, an opening hymn or song of praise, an opening prayer, and perhaps an act of praise by the choir. Others have a more extended praise and prayer service. This may be mostly a succession of songs, choruses, or hymns that are led in a very informal manner. It may be a more formal and bulletin-oriented service of morning worship (adapted from the Anglican Morning Prayer), which became popular in the mid-twentieth century and is still commonly called the "traditional service."

As often happens in human encounters, we may not be ready for "full disclosure" right away. Early in the service may be too soon for confession of sin, extended prayer, or affirmation of faith. These are judgment calls for pastors and congregations to make with sensitivity.

Some go further and advocate a seeker service that is not only *seeker-sensitive* but *seeker-targeted*—that is, primarily addressed to the needs of those who may not be ready to pray or praise or affirm faith. Those present are given the passive role of audience while the gospel is presented in music and drama and teaching by Christians up front on a platform. The service is *about* God and our human condition but does not take the form of explicit interchange *with* God.

This can be a legitimate form of evangelism, but it will not meet the worship needs of an ongoing congregation. It may serve a useful purpose if conducted side by side with weekly worship, but it should not be confused with worship. Serious questions must be dealt with: Will it be hard to move people as they grow in grace from a seeker-targeted service into weekly worship? If we gradually transform a seeker-targeted service into worship that is an explicit encounter with God, do we then need from time to time to start new seeker-targeted services or congregations? The fact is that the majority of what are called seeker services today are not seeker-targeted services but seeker-sensitive congregational worship services and should be planned and evaluated as such.

Determining the form and style of this opening part of the worship service involves much more than seeing what "works." The primary question is, What are the nonnegotiable essentials of authentic worship? There should be no place for praise, prayer, or other acts of worship that communicate false teaching—no matter how effectively. If over time they express only certain aspects of the gospel and ignore others, they need to be supplemented so that the whole gospel is expressed. If nothing is expressed in the cultural or ethnic heart-language of segments of the congregation, or of the population the congregation is called to include, then the acts of worship need to become more inclusive. If we are aware of the church of all times and all places that invisibly joins the worshiping congregation, we shall want to widen our inclusiveness and use more treasures from the praise and prayer of the universal church.

PROCLAMATION AND RESPONSE

When the disciples on the road to Emmaus had poured out their hearts to the risen Christ, he opened the Scriptures to them and "interpreted to them the things about himself in all the scriptures" (Luke 24:27). The primary purpose of this great central part of congregational worship is to open the Scriptures to the people and lead them into the mind and heart of Christ. There are many ways in which this can be done, but we typically do this in a call-and-response pattern in which proclamation alternates with response.

The congregation is challenged to listen for God's word calling to them as Scripture passages are proclaimed. Usually an individual reads from the Scriptures, but there are other options. Passages may be read dramatically, acted out by several people, or set to music. The proclamation may be enhanced with background music, visuals, or dance. The point is to let Scripture speak in all its power to the people so that they may find in it God's word.

In United Methodist understanding, Scripture, tradition, experience, and reason are the sources and criteria of Christian doctrine. Of these, Scripture is primary. For Scripture to be opened to the people in its wholeness, it is important that a generous portion be proclaimed at each service. Over time, what is proclaimed should cover the basic story and teachings of Scripture. Anything less calls into question our belief in the primacy of Scripture.

This can be done in various ways. The three-year Revised Common Lectionary is a tool for doing this (see *UMBOW*, pp. 227–37); however, following the Lectionary is not an end in itself. Other plans may be devised for full and balanced coverage of the Scriptures. What is important is the goal. We live in an age of scriptural illiteracy, when only a minority of regular worshipers (let alone seekers!) read the Bible at home or are enrolled in Bible-study classes. The only Scripture that many worshipers will encounter all week is what they hear in congregational worship. The people are being spiritually malnourished if the pastors simply "ride their hobbyhorses," using only the parts of Scripture that the pastors are familiar with and like.

Lectionary users should not be enslaved to it but exercise freedom and imagination. It is not necessary to use three readings every Sunday, especially if a long reading is used. It is seldom a good idea to preach from all three. Preaching need not be from the Gospel but may be from one of the other readings, perhaps thinking of the Lectionary in terms of a nine-year preaching cycle. The passage to be preached may be moved, if necessary, to the place immediately before the sermon. From time to time, a preacher sensitive to the needs (not necessarily the wants) of the people may feel called to read and preach a passage not in the Lectionary.

Scripture readings may alternate with responses of praise—a psalm, an anthem, a hymn, an alleluia or other praise chorus. (It should be noted that the Lectionary offers the psalm not as a reading but as a response to the first reading.) The hearts of the two disciples walking to Emmaus burned within them as the risen Christ opened to them the Scriptures, and these praises can express the burning of our hearts today. Responses of praise enable the people to be more active, attentive listeners to the Word. They give an effective call-and-response rhythm to the proclamation of the Word, provided they are not so numerous that they put substantial distance between the reading and preaching of the Word.

On the walk to Emmaus, Christ not only quoted from the Scriptures but also interpreted them in relation to himself and to the situation in which the disciples found themselves. The challenge to a preacher today is to do this for the people gathered in worship. It is hard to bring together the world of the Bible, the world of the preacher, and the worlds of the congregation. Preachers who proclaim their preconceived opinions on no more authority than "it seems to me" or a snippet of a text (pretext?) torn out of its biblical context are not really connecting people with the world of the Bible. Preachers who do not relate the message (even if biblical) to the worlds in which the people live are also failing.

People can worship God in whatever is their own heart-language.

We can meet this interpretive challenge in various ways. There is no need to argue over whether to call the proclamation a sermon, homily, message, or lay speaking. It can be a traditional sermon, a dramatized first-person monologue, a dialogue, or a panel. It can be prefaced by a short dramatization of a contemporary life situation. It can include quotation of poetry or readings from any source. Scripture can be both proclaimed and interpreted in a cantata. The possibilities are as great as the challenge.

Since the proclamation seeks to lead people into the mind and heart of Christ, the proclamation often ends with an explicit invitation to Christian discipleship. Even when this is not explicit, proclamation by its very nature calls for a response. People may come forward and make an act of Christian commitment such as baptism, confirmation, reaffirmation of faith, reception into The United Methodist Church, or reception by transfer into a local congregation. Any of these acts involves a major act of commitment, not only by the candidates and their parents or sponsors but by the whole congregation. As such, these acts require more preparation than a single worship service or sermon can provide. People may also be invited to come forward in commitment to a particular project or cause.

How can the congregation make a response of commitment and faith when no one comes forward? This happens in most congregations at most services. Surely a response of commitment and faith is needed at every service. This can be simply a closing hymn; but is that enough?

If affirmation of faith, concerns and prayers, and offering have not taken place earlier, they are fitting responses to the Word. The Apostles' Creed, traditionally used when someone comes forward for baptism, can remind us of the faith into which we were baptized, even when there is no baptism. Prayer will mean more if people have some way of contributing their specific prayer requests. If the offering is a response to the Word, it more effectively signifies our larger offering to God of all that we have and all that we are.[1] The sequence of invitation-confession-pardon-peace-offering is both powerful and biblical (Matthew 5:23-24).

THANKSGIVING AND COMMUNION

Up to this point, the basic pattern of the service is the same whether or not Holy Communion is to be celebrated. But we have not yet spoken of two crucial elements in Christian worship: thanksgiving and communion. These are most fully expressed in Holy Communion—the Service of the Table, as distinct from the Service of the Word that has preceded it. It is a meal—a token meal, a holy meal, but nevertheless a meal. It is eating and drinking with the risen Christ and the universal church. It calls to mind Jesus' actions not only when he instituted the Lord's Supper but also at the supper in Emmaus three days later. As at Emmaus, it led to the moment when the disciples recognized the risen Christ, who had been walking with them on the road, so it leads to the moment when the Risen Presence that has been with us becomes most focused and intimate.

Holy Communion consists of four actions: taking, blessing (giving thanks), breaking, and giving. They are what Jesus did when feeding the hungry multitudes, when instituting the Lord's Supper, and when eating supper in Emmaus. This is what we traditionally do at meals, especially solemn or festive meals.

Since the first and third actions are brief and preliminary to the second and fourth, we may group the four actions into two. The taking and blessing are the *thanksgiving*. The breaking and giving are the *communion*.

The thanksgiving is a sublime form of bringing the meal from the kitchen to the dining table and saying a blessing before we partake. The food and drink are brought to the Lord's Table, or uncovered if already in place. Then the presiding minister, acting as representative of Christ the Host, says the blessing. The blessing, which we call the *Great Thanksgiving,* but which has other names as well, can take various forms and be done in diverse styles. It can be read or memorized from the *Hymnal* or *Book of Worship* or some other resource, it can be prepared by the presider, or it can be prayed spontaneously. It can be fulsome, with congregational responses, like the ones on pages 9–11 and 27–30 in *The United Methodist Hymnal.* It can be brief and without responses, like the ones on pages 52–53 and 80 in *The United Methodist Book of Worship.* Whatever the form, the content is two-fold. We first recall God's mighty acts in creation and covenant; remember the life and ministry of Jesus Christ, including the institution of the Lord's Supper; and, joining ourselves to Christ's self-giving, offer ourselves in praise and thanksgiving. Then we invoke the Holy Spirit upon us and upon what we are about to eat and drink, praying that we may partake of the Lord's Supper with all its benefits.

This blessing is traditionally followed by the Lord's Prayer, which serves as a bridge between thanksgiving and communion. It is the most sublime prayer, soaring as high as words can go. It takes us to the very threshold of the communion that is beyond words.

The communion begins as the presiding minister, still functioning as visible representative of Christ the Host, breaks the bread as a hostly gesture of invitation to partake and as the opening act of distributing the bread to the people. This may be accompanied by raising the cup in a gesture of invitation. This may be done in silence, or words (such as 1 Corinthians 10:16b-17 with the bread, and verse 16a with the cup) may accompany the action. (See *UMH,* p. 11.)

The climax of the service is giving the bread and cup to the people and their partaking in Holy Communion with God in Christ and with the whole family of Christ in every time and place. Eating and drinking together in all human societies is a primordial act of bonding. *Communion* is translated from the New Testament Greek word *koinonia,* which can also be translated "community," "sharing," "fellowship," or "participation," but goes beyond any of these. Among ancient Greek-speaking peoples it was a favorite term for the most intimate marital relationship. The giving of the bread and cup can be done in various ways, but what is crucial is that it be done in whatever way most effectively expresses the sublime power of what is happening.

Holy Communion is not celebrated at the majority of weekly services in United Methodist congregations. The Basic Pattern indicates that at such services thanks are given for God's mighty acts in Jesus Christ, but it is open and flexible about how and where in the service this is to be done. It also says nothing specific about any form of Communion. In the most literal reading of the Basic Pattern, there may be a prayer at this point in the service similar to the Great Thanksgiving (but shorter and without reference to the Lord's Supper), followed by the Lord's Prayer and then perhaps by a time of silent communion with God (see *UMBOW,* pp. 550–55).

Alternatively, the main time of prayer earlier in the service may regularly include thanksgiving for what God has done in Christ and may conclude with the Lord's Prayer. This thanksgiving should not be confused with thanksgivings for particular recent blessings, though these also should have

Over time, what is proclaimed should cover the basic story and teachings of Scripture. Anything less calls into question our belief in the primacy of Scripture.

an important place. Care may be taken to emphasize throughout the service that our worship is a constant communion with God through the risen Christ in the power of the Holy Spirit. What is essential is that our worship include *thanksgiving* for the greatest and most enduring of God's blessings, with clear awareness of the *communion* that is God's gift in Christ.

SENDING FORTH

Finally, the people stand and are sent forth to active ministry in the world. A dismissal with blessing is spoken to the people. *Dis-missal* literally means "forth-sending." A recessional or other closing hymn may add a further note of sending forth, as may instrumental music. During the people's going forth, their informal sharing with one another before scattering—what someone has called "the benediction of friendly voices"—continues to renew their communion with one another as well as with God.

FOR FURTHER READING

The United Methodist Book of Worship (Nashville, TN: The United Methodist Publishing House, 1992). See especially pages 13–32.

Worshiping With United Methodists: A Guide for Pastors and Church Leaders, by Hoyt L. Hickman (Nashville, TN: Abingdon Press, 1996).

ENDNOTES

1 See "How to Make the Offering a Vital Part of Worship," on pp. 148–54 in Volume II of *Worship Matters.*

Keeping Worship Focused on Christ

C. MICHAEL HAWN

*Associate Professor of Church Music,
Perkins School of Theology,
Southern Methodist University,
Dallas, Texas*

JESUS CHRIST HAS BEEN THE CENTER OF CHRISTIAN WORSHIP since the early days of the faith following Christ's ascension. Throughout the centuries, the Christian community has maintained Christ's centrality through the sacraments, a Christian understanding of time, the use of a lectionary, the organization of hymnals and worship books, and the Basic Pattern of Worship. Each of these practices will be examined below.

SACRAMENTS

The primacy of the sacraments of the church—baptism and the Lord's Supper—reflects the centrality of Christ in worship. Each sacrament derives its significance from actions modeled for us by Christ: his baptism by John in the Jordan River and the various meals that Christ shared with the multitudes, the disciples, and those who were with him following his resurrection.

THE CHRISTIAN YEAR

From the conception of Christianity, the development of the Christian Year has depended on the centrality of the Resurrection. Beginning with the change from sabbath gatherings to assembling on the day of Christ's resurrection (the first day of the week), events in Christ's life shaped the basic structure of the Christian Year during the first four centuries C.E. (Common Era). These events include the annual celebration of Easter (or the Christian Passover), the season of Eastertide (or the week or weeks following Easter), and the gradual development of the season of Lent as a preparation for baptism and the Feast of Feasts. Later observances include the celebration of Epiphany and Christmas and, finally, Advent, an observance that takes place only in the Western church. Christ's birth, ministry, passion, resurrection, and ascension provide the fundamental structure that shapes (to greater or lesser degrees) the annual cycles of Christian worship in the various liturgical traditions.

THREE-YEAR LECTIONARY

Since the deliberations of the Roman Catholic Church during the Second Vatican Council in the mid-1960's, the Synoptic Gospels have been the basis of the three-year Lectionary—the Gospel of Matthew for

Worship Matters: A United Methodist Guide to Ways to Worship (Volume I) © 1999 Discipleship Resources. Used by permission.

Year A, the Gospel of Mark for Year B, and the Gospel of Luke for Year C. The Gospel of John is prominent on Christmas Day, during Holy Week and Easter, and on other specific Sundays. While there have been adjustments to these readings, as well as to the Epistle lessons, psalms, and passages from the Old Testament that accompany them, the fundamental organizational principle of the modern three-year Lectionary for every Christian tradition has been the Synoptic Gospels, those accounts that tell us the most about the life and ministry of Christ.

HYMNAL STRUCTURE AND EMPHASIS

The organization of modern hymnals represents the sung faith of the Christian church and reflects the significance of Jesus Christ for worship. Historically, there have been three prominent organizational structures for hymnals. One has been based on the Christian Year, followed by selections on the ministry of the church, the sacraments, and eschatology. A second organizational principle is that of the creed, a Trinitarian structure with a strong christological center. A third organizational approach is that of structuring the hymnal by the basic flow (or *ordo*) of worship. Some Reformed hymnals vary the patterns above by beginning with a complete sung Psalter, followed by variations on one or more of the three structures. The first two are more common among mainline denominations. Option two, based on the creed, is the overarching structure of *The United Methodist Hymnal*. Once again, we see that the life and ministry of Christ are central to the structure of the hymnal and the sung faith of the church.

THE BASIC PATTERN OF WORSHIP

Even the Basic Pattern of Worship, found in *The United Methodist Hymnal* (page 2), reflects the pivotal role of Christ's life. There is evidence that the early church heard a selection from the law or prophets and the apostles during the proclamation of the Word.[1] Following the response to the Word, the early church celebrated the Eucharist, a ritual that is almost a *sine qua non* within various Christian faith communities, albeit in varying ways and at differing intervals. Following the Second Vatican Council, many Christian worship traditions reaffirmed their interest in this basic worship pattern including the significance of the Gospel reading and the celebration of Communion, practices that are rooted in the life of Jesus Christ.

THE SOURCE OF THE PROBLEM

Given the variety of ways that Christ has been central to worship in the Christian community—the sacraments, the Christian Year, the Lectionary, the structure of hymnals, the basic order of worship following Vatican II—it is a paradox that on a given Sunday in many congregations, the gospel (good news) of Jesus Christ is sometimes neglected or stifled by a host of other activities and emphases. The lack of appearance of Christ's good news in much worship today is primarily the result of two factors: (1) the minimization of those structures outlined above that would guarantee a focus on Christ's life and ministry; and (2) the substitution of other civic, denominational, and/or social emphases for the proclamation of the gospel.

In the case of the first factor, some feel that these historical structures are too traditional, inflexible, or irrelevant to the needs and tastes of today's parishioners. Others claim that these old rituals are dead and that new paradigms are needed to reach the unchurched. The older forms have lost their meaning, the argument continues, and people visiting worship for the first time have no idea what is going on. Therefore, the traditional structures that have undergirded much of our worship and centered it on Jesus Christ have begun to fall into disuse among some fellowships.

Before responding defensively to such criticism, we should acknowledge that much of our ritual has become dead, a state that Jaroslav Pelikan calls "traditionalism."[2] Tradition is a living, vibrant, and ever-evolving inheritance from the communion of the saints. Traditionalism is a pale imitation of tradition or is a frozen relic that once was living but now resides in a museum.

Perhaps some worship leaders have allowed to atrophy the heritage of worship traditions such as those described above. The life of the One from whom these traditions evolved is no longer celebrated weekly, but is remembered when it suits our needs. Those enabling these traditions have either lost an understanding of their power or have failed to communicate the meaning embodied in them. It is no wonder that for some our worship has become a liturgical museum.

There are those who choose to remove from worship the structures that have kept Christ central rather than to examine and energize them, realizing that every age must rediscover the meaning of these structures in its own time. Neglecting these structures is to separate ourselves from the roots of our faith; to leave us adrift on the tides of current fad and fancy; and, in the most extreme cases, to neglect the One from whom we take our name at baptism, the name *Christian*.

Closely related to the neglect of traditional structures is the substitution of other emphases for the message of Christ. These emphases may be well-meant and may have noble aims, but one must always ask if they are central to worship and those acts that demonstrate that we are among Christ's followers—washing at the font, hearing and proclaiming Christ's message, and eating together at Christ's Table. Lester Ruth has indicated that we are letting other agendas shape the way we pray.[3] Many hold that the way we pray shapes the way we believe.[4] Rather than substituting civic, denominational, and social agendas for Christ in worship, the validity of each potential agenda should be measured by the gospel. If indeed the emphasis remains relevant, it should be placed within the context of the good news. It may be that there are worthy causes that should receive attention in venues outside worship. Those that remain within worship will be strengthened as they draw from the deep wells of the gospel for validity and relevance to worship.

MAINTAINING THE FOCUS OF WORSHIP ON CHRIST

Based on the analysis provided above, I offer the following strategies for maintaining the focus of worship on the life and ministry of Jesus Christ.

ENLIVENING THE SACRAMENTS

Baptism is a singular event within the Christian experience, an event that binds all Christians together. It is centered in the witness of Christ's life, including his own baptism by John (Matthew 3:13-17) and his command to baptize in the name of the Father, Son, and Holy Spirit (Matthew 28:19). "Christ constitutes the church as his Body by the power of the Holy Spirit (1 Corinthians 12:13, 27)"[5]; therefore, baptism incorporates people into the

> The life of the One from whom these traditions evolved is no longer celebrated weekly, but is remembered when it suits our needs. Those enabling these traditions have either lost an understanding of their power or have failed to communicate the meaning embodied in them.

church—the body of Christ.[6] Baptism is an event that shapes the rest of our Christian experience. From that moment forward, each time we witness another's baptism, we celebrate the church—Christ's body—as a growing, living, and regenerating organism.

Rather than being performed in a perfunctory manner, baptism is a celebration. Celebrations require preparation. In this case, the person being baptized, the family, and the congregation need to be informed of the significance of this event. A young person or adult coming to be baptized needs significant time for instruction in order to participate in the life of the community.[7] Sponsors or godparents are tangible symbols of the congregation's care. The sacrament should be performed with the joy that greets the birth of a child; for, indeed, that person is receiving a new birthday. Appropriate sections of the rite might be spoken by church leaders or others significant to the baptism or the family. Rather than rushing an infant into and out of worship, one should not be embarrassed by the crying of a child in the service. At the birth of an infant, the sound of crying is a blessing—a sign of life and health. Water should be used abundantly. As often as possible, the celebration of the Eucharist should follow baptism.

Celebrate rather than merely observe the Lord's Supper. While there is a long history of observing the Lord's Supper as an act of personal penitence, newer rites focus on a celebration of the mighty acts of God, a risen Christ, and on the power of the Holy Spirit to unite all those gathered into one with the broader church, past and present. This is indeed a celebration. It may be helpful to relate the leadership of the Lord's Supper with an act of hospitality experienced by people who would join you for dinner in your home. As a host, you carefully prepare the table. You welcome your guests to your table. You bless the food and enjoy the bond of friendship that unites you around the table.

Drawing from this metaphor, consider preparing the Lord's Table within the context of the service with a joyful procession. Use an actual loaf of bread and serve it to the people. As minister, use a celebratory tone in your voice and explore a range of vocal inflections. Encourage the people to speak or sing the acclamations joyfully. As a representative of Christ at the Table, stress the joy of the Body gathered into one, especially during the Easter season or any time outside of Lent and Holy Week. A vital sacramental life is pivotal to keeping worship focused on Christ.

MARKING TIME WITH CHRIST

Various faith traditions stress to a lesser or greater degree the Christian Year. I will focus on two points relative to the topic of this article: (1) Provide a focus on Holy Week, the Triduum (three days from Good Friday through Easter Sunday), and Easter comparable to what is done for Christmas. (2) Guide your congregation through seasons of preparation for the Christmas and Easter cycles.

There seems to be a trend among many churches to celebrate the incarnation of Christ extensively while limiting the celebration of Easter to just a few days. Not only did an observance of Easter eclipse by far the observance of Christmas for many centuries, but it also provided the primary rationale for celebrating the Incarnation. The reverse appears to be true in many situations. Perhaps we give more weight to Christmas than to Easter because the church is influenced by commercial interests, a sign of the increasing cultural captivity of the church.

One may overcome in part this sense of cultural captivity by involving congregations in seasons of preparation before these major feasts of the Christian experience. Once again, it may run counter to current cultural expectations to emphasize the discipline of Lent, but plumbing the spiritual depths of Lent may lead to a more joyful Easter.

TELLING THE STORY AGAIN

Biblical literacy seems to be on the decline. Historically, corporate worship depended on a healthy devotional life. The use of the Lectionary guarantees that the Gospels will be covered regularly in corporate worship and that readings can be available for parishioners to use for personal devotions. It is common to hear that pastors have lectionary study groups. Perhaps laypeople also need to have the option of preparing for worship by having a study group based on lectionary passages that will be used. A pastor may be enriched by the perspectives that her or his parishioners offer in this study.

In one congregation, the pastor meets with a volunteer group who come together to share their insights on passages that will be used in corporate worship within the next two weeks. Each month the group changes. Not only has the pastor found new understandings from the ideas shared by the laypeople, but also has found it helpful in making preaching more relevant to the lives of the people. Additional benefits include a renewed emphasis on biblical study. Some congregations list the lectionary readings for the coming weeks or month, inviting members to prepare for worship by reading the texts in advance.

SINGING THE WHOLE STORY

It has been commonly recognized that singing shapes belief.[8] United Methodists have inherited a tradition of singing a balanced and more complete gospel. It is easy to sing only what is familiar or what provides immediate emotional gratification. Each era of congregational song has embedded within its verbal and musical message a particular spirituality. Maintaining a historically diverse range of congregational song helps to sustain a variety of theological emphases within our sung faith.

Some practical suggestions for preserving a focus on Christ would be to choose one sung congregational selection each Sunday that expresses a Trinitarian perspective, another that focuses on the life and ministry of Jesus Christ as appropriate to the Gospel lesson, and a third congregational song on a theme appropriate to the flow of the service or theme emphasized. Musical styles should be varied, ranging from the songs of the saints to recent expressions of faith.

SUNDAY AS A DAY OF RESURRECTION

Essential to keeping the focus of worship on Jesus Christ is to regain the spirit of the early Christian church in which all Sundays were, first and foremost, days to celebrate the Resurrection. The basic structure of worship was designed to hear and proclaim the story of faith, share the sacred meal, and, especially on Easter Sunday, wash and welcome through baptism those who were to become a part of Christ's body.

In today's culture, where miracles are in doubt and science seems to provide an explanation for everything, the wonder of the Resurrection reality may be on the wane. A symptom of this is the lack of emphasis

The embodiment of Christ's resurrection reality in the life of each congregation... is potentially a miracle full of wonder. If Christ is to remain the focus of our faith and worship, we must learn how to take the tried and true and make it live today.

on the hope for the future unity of the church and Christ's return as an agent in the fulfillment of time. Unless the acclamation "Christ has died; Christ is risen; Christ will come again" (*UMBOW,* p. 38)[9] becomes a part of our liturgical and theological vocabulary, we will remain content with worship that focuses on our present comfort more than the cosmic reality of the central event of our faith—the Resurrection.

CONCLUSION

For some people, the centrality of Christ in worship is a problem because their experiences are not rooted in the signs of the saints, but float on the breeze of the existential and ephemeral. The methodology is old, that is, tried and true. The embodiment of Christ's resurrection reality in the life of each congregation, however, is potentially a miracle full of wonder. If Christ is to remain the focus of our faith and worship, we must learn how to take the tried and true and make it live today. Forsaking the methods of our heritage—the sacraments; the Christian Year; the order of worship; the diversity of the sung word; the ordered, intentional proclamation of Scripture—in the hope of finding a more exciting alternative to tradition will lead ultimately to a rootless faith that quickly withers. We need to discover our worship roots again for the first time.

FOR FURTHER READING

By Water and the Spirit: Making Connections for Identity and Ministry, by Gayle Carlton Felton (Nashville, TN: Discipleship Resources, 1997).

Liturgy Made Simple, by Mark Searle (Collegeville, MN: The Liturgical Press, 1981).

What Are the Essentials of Christian Worship? by Gordon Lathrop (Minneapolis, MN: Augsburg Fortress Publishers, 1996).

ENDNOTES

1 See, for example, a description of early Christian worship in *Documents of Christian Worship: Descriptive and Interpretive Sources,* by James F. White (Louisville, KY: Westminster John Knox Press, 1992), pp. 185–86.

2 See *The Vindication of Tradition,* by Jaroslav Pelikan (New Haven, CT: Yale University Press, 1984), p. 65.

3 See "Lex Agendi, Lex Orandi: Toward an Understanding of Seeker Services as a New Kind of Liturgy," by Lester Ruth, in *Worship,* Volume 70, Number 5 (Collegeville, MN: Order of Saint Benedict, 1996), pp. 386-405.

4 See *Doxology: The Praise of God in Worship, Doctrine and Life,* by Geoffrey Wainwright (New York, NY: Oxford University Press, 1980), p. 224. He discusses the history and significance of *lex orandi* and *lex credendi* in depth in Chapters VII and VIII.

5 From "By Water and the Spirit: A United Methodist Understanding of Baptism" in *The Book of Resolutions of The United Methodist Church—1996,* p. 724. Copyright © 1996 by The United Methodist Publishing House. Used by permission.

6 See *By Water and the Spirit: Making Connections for Identity and Ministry,* by Gayle Carlton Felton (Nashville, TN: Discipleship Resources, 1997), p. 21.

7 For an in-depth consideration of a period of instruction, see *Come to the Waters: Baptism & Our Ministry of Welcoming Seekers & Making Disciples,* by Daniel T. Benedict, Jr. (Nashville, TN: Discipleship Resources, 1996).

8 See *Introducing a New Hymnal: How to Improve Congregational Singing,* by James Rawlings Sydnor (Chicago, IL: G.I.A. Publications, 1989), p. 114.

9 From "A Service of Word and Table I," © 1972 by The Methodist Publishing House; © 1980, 1985, 1989, 1992 by The United Methodist Publishing House; from *The United Methodist Book of Worship,* p. 38. Used by permission.

Ordering Congregational Life Around the Means of Grace

DANIEL T. BENEDICT, JR.

*Worship Resources Director,
The General Board of Discipleship,
Nashville, Tennessee*

JACKIE TEMPLETON, AN INQUISITIVE MEMBER OF THE confirmation preparation group, asks Pastor Stone, "Why are we called United Methodists?" Pastor Stone replies with an explanation about the *Book of Discipline* and how United Methodists systematically make reports, keep formal records, and have a discipline of itinerating pastors who go where the bishop sends them. Neither Jackie nor Pastor Stone feels satisfied with his response.

What is the distinctive heritage of United Methodists when it comes to the practice of congregational life? Around what focus should congregational life be shaped or reshaped as we move consciously into the missionary context of the third millennium? The 1996 General Conference sensed the urgency of such questions when it declared that congregational life and mission are to be oriented toward making disciples of Jesus Christ (*BOD*, p. 114).

THE MEANS TO FULFILLING THE MISSION

This article contends that the *means of grace,* as practiced "methodically" in early Methodism, are basic to a Wesleyan way of traditioning and forming disciples in our congregations in the midst of today's emerging missionary context. More specifically, this article holds that there must be a balance of those means used in worship and those used in small groups and personal disciplines. This distinction will be clearer as we move more deeply into the various means of grace listed by John Wesley in the General Rules and in his other writings.

The means of grace are those practices that enable disciples to keep their appointments with God so that God has opportunity to empower them for discipleship. As the saying goes, "What has your attention has you!" The means of grace are practices by which we give our attention to God so that God has us! For the purposes of this article, the term *means of grace* includes both the "works of mercy" and the "works of piety," as outlined in the General Rules of the early Methodist Societies:

> Wherever this [desire to flee from the wrath to come, and to be saved from sin] is really fixed in the soul it will be shown by its fruits.... By doing no harm... By doing good... By attending upon all the ordinances [means of grace] of God; such are:
> The public worship of God.
> The ministry of the Word,

Worship Matters: A United Methodist Guide to Ways to Worship (Volume I) © 1999 Discipleship Resources. Used by permission.

either read or expounded.
The Supper of the Lord.
Family and private prayer.
Searching the Scriptures.
Fasting or abstinence.
(*BOD,* ¶62, pp. 70–72)[1]

Note three things about this description. First, the fruits of discipleship are practices—patterns of doing by which we enact faith, hope, and love. Second, the works of mercy are represented by "by doing no harm" and "by doing good." Third, the means of grace proper—the works of piety or the "ordinances"—are listed in a particular order. First, Wesley lists those to be employed in corporate worship: public worship, the ministry of the Word, and the Lord's Supper. He follows by listing those to be used in small groups or in personal discipline: family and private prayer, Bible study, and fasting. We will explore the third observation later.

THE FULLNESS OF THE GIFT

David Lowes Watson contends that when Methodism fails to make disciples according to the tradition of the means of grace (doing the works of mercy and the works of piety), it is susceptible to the hawkers of "spiritual amphetamines."[2] Espousing the mission of making Christian disciples will remain a vague platitude in congregational life until spiritual leaders order and shape congregational practices around the means of grace. When leaders practice the means of grace in their own lives and in their leadership of the congregation's life, welcoming, forming, supporting, and deploying disciples will become central to the very life of the congregation.

One reason we unintentionally hawk spiritual amphetamines when we intend to serve nourishing food is that we fail to recognize and maintain the full dynamic of grace. Henry H. Knight sees a vital and necessary interplay between the *identity* means of grace and the *presence* means of grace.[3] The identity means of grace are those practices that connect us to the character and mission of God embodied in the biblical narrative. The presence means of grace are those practices that connect us to the presence of God. For example, Scripture reading and the church's hymns and written prayers help us to stay on track with a faithful sense of the true God rather than our own fabrication of who God is. By contrast, extemporaneous prayer, rousing gospel choruses and praise songs, and silence help us to sense the nearness and reality of God in lived experience. We need both to remain on an even keel in our living together as disciples. We will return to these understandings of the means of grace as we move through this article.

We should not equate United Methodist congregations of today with the Methodist Societies of eighteenth-century England. Early Methodism was a movement within the larger context of the Anglican Church; however, The United Methodist Church is now roughly equivalent to the Anglican Church of Wesley's day. The Methodist Societies were vocational communities, and those called into a Society were expected to keep the discipline of the community. If they did not, they were expelled. Churches such as The United Methodist Church or the Episcopal Church do not expel people, though they may censure them or restrict them on grounds of grave sin. Therefore, I am not suggesting that leaders impose the General Rules and use of the means of grace on every member or seeker as a *condition* of membership.[4] I am proposing that the means of grace be the primary way we focus on Christ, both publicly and privately, and that leaders consistently and passionately offer and urge, by word and example, the use of the means of grace by all as gift and pathway for a dynamic redemption.

THE TASK OF ORDERING CONGREGATIONAL LIFE

The means of grace are central to the pastoral task of leadership. Ordained elders are chosen, ordained, and appointed to lead congregations in Service, Word, Sacrament, and Order.[5] Most pastors, assisted by deacons, take Service, Word, and Sacrament with great seriousness. With equal gravity, pastors seek to *order* the life of the congregation in conformity with the *Book of Discipline*. However, they do so generally by keeping an eye on the latest management (more recently, leadership) thinking and by paying more attention to the *organizational* parts than to the part about our doctrinal standards and theological task.

The consequences of leaders focusing on the organization of the church rather than on the Christian life and discipleship is poignantly symbolized in E. Stanley Jones' confession of his own experience. As a teenager attending a revival, he responded to the invitation to heed the gospel. However, he did not have a conversion experience until two years later. Reflecting on that experience, he wrote: "I fumbled for the latchstring of the Kingdom of God, missed it...[and] took church membership as a substitute."[6] How many people hear the call of Christ and settle for church (organizational) membership because congregational life fails to focus on the Christian life and the identity and presence of God to be known and experienced through the means of grace?

What if leaders—pastors and those who share in leading the community of faith—were to focus on creating settings in which the people could experience God by using the means of grace? What if leaders were to work to ensure that every member and seeker had the opportunity and encouragement to hear the Word of God proclaimed, to partake of the Lord's Supper, and to learn and exercise all the disciplines that form and sustain discipleship?

OUR WESLEYAN HERITAGE OF ORDERING COMMUNAL LIFE

John Wesley was methodical in ensuring that the Methodist Societies supported people in struggling to center their lives on the love of God and neighbor. He understood profoundly the forces that dissipated that love. The early Methodists aimed at abandoning a way of life that was rooted in the values of the wider society. The reason for the abandonment was their perception that the culture subverted discipleship and faith. Methodism emerged as a "missionary movement" within the church to reform the nation, but first it had to recover the communal fullness of the means of grace for every participant in the movement.[7]

Our celebrated but largely unpracticed Methodist heritage is one of accountability to a discipline counter to the reigning culture, while at the same time living in that culture as Christian disciples. As important as public worship is, the hold the culture has upon people is such that this grip cannot be broken short of participation in a fully communal context where we watch over each other in love.

The *means of grace*, as practiced "methodically" in early Methodism, are basic to a Wesleyan way of traditioning and forming disciples in our congregations in the midst of today's emerging missionary context.

THE MEANS OF GRACE AS COMMUNAL RESISTANCE

Our "methodical" Methodist heritage is rooted in the means of grace as a dynamic system for welcoming, forming, supporting, and deploying disciples in service to God and neighbor. By using the means of grace, the early Methodists had an outward *form* that knit them together in a web of *accountable* and *liturgical* grace and positioned them to anticipate and receive the power of godliness (2 Timothy 3:5).

- "Accountable grace" (my term) was available in small groups (classes and bands) in which seekers and believers were expected to participate consistently in order to watch over each other in love.
- "Liturgical grace" (my term) was available through a system of ecclesial practices, both corporate and personal: "the ministry of the Word, either read or expounded; the Supper of the Lord; family and private prayer; searching the Scriptures; fasting or abstinence" (*BOD,* ¶62, pp. 71–72).[8] The aim was an ordering of communal life through use of the means of grace.

To treat the means of grace piecemeal, to pick and choose from among them, or to use them as a private venture borders on settling for dry bones. When the means of grace are viewed as interactive—as a *system*—they become a means of vital faith development:[9] The Lord's Supper, Scripture, preaching, the written prayers of the church, devotional writings, and hymns are means that present and orient us to God's *identity*. These means of grace, on their part, hedge against an *enthusiasm* that mistakes the self and its feelings for the will and presence of God. Furthermore, disciplined community and Christian conferencing (small-group life), and extemporaneous prayer, fasting, and the general means of grace (watching, self-denial, exercising the presence of God, taking up one's cross) all nurture faith in the immediate *presence* of God. The means of grace that foster God's presence, on their part, protect against a *formalism* that claims too much for the church and confuses God's action with our activities—with doing liturgy "right."

PATTERNING EXPERIENCE TO THE PRESENCE AND IDENTITY OF GOD

The practical result of full and consistent use of the means of grace is the patterning of experience and the shaping of the affections. This patterning and shaping aim at and lead to a recovery of the image of God, to having the mind of Christ, and to loving as God loves in our daily lives. In other words, patterning and shaping result in a life of meaningful discipleship, an apostolic engagement with the world in daily life.

Congregational leaders have the primary responsibility for putting structures in place that encourage all of the people to use the means of grace. The aim is to ensure that the people are consistently and reliably formed in the practice of the presence and identity of God, and in faithful living and loving in the world.

We should be deeply grateful for the broad emphasis on "spirituality" in Protestant circles over the last two decades. However, our Wesleyan vision of spirituality calls us to avoid a tendency toward individualized experience. Wesleyan spirituality is a communal solution to the forces that dissipate the love and life of God among us. United Methodist congregational leaders are called through ordination or election to order the congregation's life using the full range of the means of grace so that the congregation's life and structure support people on a communal journey toward the love of God and neighbor.

While Wesley was steeped in Christian antiquity and practiced the disciplines of the ascetic and monastic traditions, he held that Christian perfection was a "reasonable hope" for every Christian. Striving for perfection did not require leaving home and occupation.[10] Most of our congregations today have a long way to go to be Methodist in vision and in practice in the way Wesley recommended. What would happen if congregational leaders became skilled and focused in shaping communities that nurture faith and counteract dissipation as people seek to live and work as disciples in the world?

WORSHIP AS "THICK" USE OF THE MEANS OF GRACE

Christian worship should be the most concentrated ("thick") expression and experience of the means of grace. Pastors and other worship leaders bear the responsibility for planning and presiding in worship in ways that ensure that the congregation is consistently formed and catechized by the fullness of the good news of God's identity and presence in Jesus Christ. The faithful and imaginative proclamation of the biblical narrative, bringing candidates to the font to share in Christ's dying and rising, and gathering the people at the Table to recall God's mighty action and to receive Christ anew constitute and distinguish the church as Christ's people.

These practices are the most concentrated expression of the means of grace for which spiritual leaders are responsible. It is in worship that the good news of the gospel is heard and tasted—or not at all. It is in worship that the identity and presence of God is known and experienced—or not at all. When we look at the use of the means of grace as a system, we can say that in worship God gives birth to and shapes the life of a people of faith for the conversion and salvation of the world. Through the church's singing and dancing God's praise, through reading and proclaiming of God's story in Scripture, through initiating people in baptism and returning again and again to the Table of forgiveness and unity, God calls, claims, and commissions a people for lives of discipleship and mission. Worship continually nourishes the mind and heart of the church, with the identity of the triune God guarding it against the self-deception of "enthusiasm."

However, the emphasis on worship must always be seen within the larger vision of the congregation's ministry system and the full range of the means of grace. Worship can never be a special domain set apart from the whole ministry system of the congregation. Small groups for mutual oversight and Christian conferencing—as well as continued practice of the personal disciplines of prayer, fasting, abstinence, and reflection—nurture Christians in the presence of God and guard against the inattentiveness of formalism.[11]

Worship cannot be relied on to the exclusion of what I call the *presence* means of grace. The faithful practice of gathering (*ecclesia:* "big church") for Word and Sacrament forms and grounds Christian living in the identity of God and anticipates and welcomes the presence and power of God for obedient discipleship. The consistent practice of meeting in small groups (*ecclesiolae:* "little churches") for mutual oversight

To treat the means of grace piecemeal, to pick and choose from among them, or to use them as a private venture borders on settling for dry bones. When the means of grace are viewed as interactive—as a *system*—they become a means of vital faith development.

(for watching over each other in love) and for the personal disciplines of Scripture reading, prayer, study, and ministry in daily life engages disciples with God's presence. And as these disciples meet in small groups and practice the personal disciplines, they rely precisely on the identity God gives them in Word and Sacrament.

TOWARD LITURGICAL PRACTICES THAT ORDER CONGREGATIONAL LIFE AROUND THE MEANS OF GRACE

Ordering the life of the congregation faithfully around the means of grace is critical to the task of spiritual leadership. As a spiritual leader in the congregation, consider making the following moves:

- *Refuse to settle for quick solutions and slogan-oriented approaches to faith development.* Root your conceptual framework for leadership in a Wesleyan understanding of the means of grace. Too many of our churches operate out of a "hothouse" approach that aims at "touching lives" but fails to offer "good soil" in which Christian disciples can grow and be sustained for ministry in daily life. Persevere in the trust that Christians can grow and be sustained for discipleship when the means of grace are solidly employed. Refuse to peddle spiritual amphetamines!

- *Focus on the apostolic task of making disciples.* The current popular focus on seekers is a much-needed corrective to attentiveness to those who already belong and are settled in patterns of dissipation. In the end, a near exclusive "seeker" focus will fail if congregations are not able to balance the work of "pre-conversion" with the task of "conversion and continuing conversion." Relevance must lead to roots if there is to be good fruit. Balance pre-catechesis with ongoing catechesis. Aim at going all the way to the making of disciples.

- *Give priority to the means of grace over organization and programs.* If this means streamlining structure and organization, be courageous and do it!

- *Initiate "little churches in the big church" (ecclesiolae in ecclesia) as a basic structure for congregational life.* While it would be a mistake to require every person to be in a small group for accountability, make the possibility of "watching over each other in love" available to everyone—members and inquirers alike.[12] Ensure that the *identity* means of grace and the *presence* means of grace are kept in balance through strong corporate worship and small groups.

- *Change from "membership orientation" to Christian initiation as the focus for reaching out and receiving people into the church.* In most circumstances, membership orientation (or making church members) is short-sighted on two counts: First, most people today are not looking for a denominational organization to belong to, but are searching for God and for meaning in their lives. On this score, many of the new "evangelical" churches are ahead of United Methodists! They have their finger on the pulse of the longings of the human heart. Second, at the heart of any understanding of the means of grace is the Baptismal Covenant, in which God joins us to Christ our head, and we pledge to trust in Christ and to serve him "in union with the church." On this count, the RCIA (Rite of Christian Initiation of Adults) of the Roman Catholics has it right when it invites people to join in a public journey of faith and life with the church. The resources in the Christian Initiation series are designed to assist United Methodist leaders in making this shift to a public journey of faith and life.[13]

- *Plan liturgical celebrations with expectancy and high quality.* Nowhere are the means of grace so concentrated as in the gathered assembly on the Lord's Day. Bring substance to worship by using the means of grace.
- *Be vigilant in seeing grace as God's dynamic activity.* Both cold formalism and hot enthusiasm result in loss; formalism loses a dynamic sense of the living God, and enthusiasm relinquishes objectivity about our need and sin, as well as of God's holiness. John Wesley sought to keep the balance when he preached: "In using all means, seek God alone."[14]

Congregational leaders are called to order the life of the congregation to the presence and identity of God through the means of grace. It is time to be finished with addiction to gimmicks and fads. The time has come to order the congregation's life by using time-tested means of grace to help ordinary people find and love God and learn how to love and serve their neighbor.

FOR FURTHER READING

Covenant Discipleship: Christian Formation Through Mutual Account-ability, by David L. Watson (Nashville, TN: Discipleship Resources, 1991).

Forming Christian Disciples: The Role of Covenant Discipleship and Class Leaders in the Congregation, by David L. Watson (Nashville, TN: Discipleship Resources, 1991).

The Presence of God in the Christian Life. John Wesley and the Means of Grace, by Henry H. Knight III (Lanham, MD: The Scarecrow Press, 1992).

ENDNOTES

1 From *The Book of Discipline of the United Methodist Church—1996,* ¶62, pp. 70–72. Copyright © 1996 by The United Methodist Publishing House. Used by permission.

2 See "Aldersgate Street and the General Rules: The Form and the Power of Methodist Discipleship," by David Lowes Watson, in *Aldersgate Reconsidered,* edited by Randy L. Maddox (Nashville, TN: Kingswood Books, 1990), p. 45.

3 See Chapters IV and V in *The Presence of God in the Christian Life: John Wesley and the Means of Grace,* by Henry H. Knight III (Lanham, MD: The Scarecrow Press, 1992).

4 Covenant Discipleship groups, as contemporary versions of the Methodist class meetings, are not mandatory for all members of The United Methodist Church. Rather, they are vocational groups open to all who sense the call of God to be saved from their sins and live lives of worship, devotion, compassion, and justice under the guidance of the Holy Spirit. In the Societies of Wesley's Methodism, those who committed to being part of the Society joined with "a desire to flee from the wrath to come, and to be saved from their sins." (From *The Book of Discipline of the United Methodist Church—1996,* ¶62, p. 70. Copyright © 1996 by The United Methodist Publishing House. Used by permission.) One did not even have to have faith to start the journey! One did have to have the desire and intention to be saved from sin on the most basic and practical grounds. For more detail, see David L. Watson's book, *Covenant Discipleship: Christian Formation Through Mutual Accountability* (Nashville, TN: Discipleship Resources, 1991).

5 See the Ordinal in *The United Methodist Book of Worship* (Nashville, TN: The United Methodist Publishing House, 1992), p. 672. (See also *BOD,* ¶303.2.) Licensed local pastors, while not ordained to Word, Sacrament, and Order, are appointed with responsibility for these works of leadership. While deacons are not ordained to order the life of the congregation, they are ordained to service in ways that link the congregation's life to works of mercy; they also assist elders in calling people to doing the works of piety.

6 From *A Song of Ascents: A Spiritual Autobiography,* by E. Stanley Jones, p. 26. Copyright © 1968 by Abingdon Press. Used by permission.

7 See "Aldersgate Street and the General Rules: The Form and the Power of Methodist Discipleship," by David Lowes Watson, in *Aldersgate Reconsidered,* edited by Randy L. Maddox (Nashville, TN: Kingswood Books, 1990), p. 46.

8 From *The Book of Discipline of the United Methodist Church—1996,* ¶62, pp. 70–72. Copyright © 1996 by The United Methodist Publishing House. Used by permission.

What would happen if congregational leaders became skilled and focused in shaping communities that nurture faith and counteract dissipation?

9 In his book, *The Presence of God in the Christian Life: John Wesley and the Means of Grace* (Lanham, MD: The Scarecrow Press, 1992), Henry H. Knight III shows how the means of grace interact as a system. He also explores how the means of grace can be used to counteract the forces that dissipate the vitality of the Christian life.

10 See *The Presence of God in the Christian Life: John Wesley and the Means of Grace,* by Henry H. Knight III (Lanham, MD: The Scarecrow Press, 1992), p. 96.

11 See *The Presence of God in the Christian Life: John Wesley and the Means of Grace,* by Henry H. Knight III (Lanham, MD: The Scarecrow Press, 1992), pp. 29–49, for a substantial treatment of formalism and enthusiasm.

12 David Lowes Watson has written several books to help congregations start and maintain Covenant Discipleship groups. See *Covenant Discipleship: Christian Formation Through Mutual Accountability* (Nashville, TN: Discipleship Resources, 1991), *Class Leaders: Recovering a Tradition* (Nashville, TN: Discipleship Resources, 1998), and *Forming Christian Disciples: The Role of Covenant Discipleship and Class Leaders in the Congregation* (Nashville, TN: Discipleship Resources, 1991).

13 The Christian Initiation series consists of five resources published by Discipleship Resources. These include *Come to the Waters: Baptism & Our Ministry of Welcoming Seekers & Making Disciples* (1996), by Daniel T. Benedict, Jr.; *Gracious Voices: Shouts & Whispers for God Seekers* (1996), by William P. McDonald; *By Water and the Spirit: Making Connections for Identity & Ministry* (1997), by Gayle Carlton Felton; *Accompanying the Journey: A Handbook for Sponsors* (1997), by Lester Ruth; and *Echoing the Word: The Ministry of Forming Disciples* (1998), by Grant Sperry-White. *Come to the Waters* provides an overarching view of the catechumenate (the process of Christian initiation) suitable for United Methodists.

14 See "Sermon XVI: The Means of Grace," by John Wesley, in *The Works of John Wesley,* Volume V (Grand Rapids, MI: Zondervan Publishing House, n.d.), p. 201.

Reclaiming the Centrality of Baptism

GAYLE CARLTON FELTON

*Consultant and Writer
for Worship Resources,
The General Board of Discipleship,
Nashville, Tennessee*

"REMEMBER YOUR BAPTISM AND BE THANKFUL" (*UMH*, p. 37).[1] These simple but powerful words have been repeated many times in United Methodist churches since they were printed as the climax of our service of reaffirmation of the Baptismal Covenant. These words are an expression of our church's recovery of the significance of divine grace as offered to us in "this gift of water" (*UMH*, p. 36),[2] the sacrament of baptism. Some United Methodists continue to be puzzled about how they might "remember" something that happened to them when they were infants. Others are confused about why it is baptism for which we are thankful.

United Methodism has been striving for decades to recover its identity and its mission. We are a large and diverse denomination, characterized by pluralism in theological and liturgical matters. Yet we cannot serve God and the people of God without an appreciation for who we are and what we are to be doing. Reclaiming the centrality of baptism is one of the most potent ways by which United Methodists can come to know their God-given personhood and ministry.

One of the reasons that this is so is that baptism is closely connected with every aspect of our faith. Baptism reveals to us the nature and purpose of the triune God. Baptism proclaims our human nature as creatures in need of divine grace. Baptism is a part of the divinely ordained process of salvation. Baptism is a sacrament of the church, the community of faith. Baptism is a liturgical act with water and Word. Baptism commissions and empowers us for service.

BAPTIZED BY WATER AND THE SPIRIT

The United Methodist Church now has an official interpretive statement on the significance of baptism, which was adopted by the only body that can speak for the whole church: the General Conference. Entitled "By Water and the Spirit: A United Methodist Understanding of Baptism," the statement can be found in *The Book of Resolutions of The United Methodist Church—1996*, pp. 716–35 (hereafter, *BOR*).[3] This statement is the product of a lengthy process of study, debate, revision, and prayer. Let us explore its major themes.

The opening section of "By Water and the Spirit" ("A Report of the Baptism Study Committee," *BOR*, pp. 716–19) attempts to survey the

Wesleyan practice and theology of baptism and how that heritage was shaped in the North-American context. John Wesley was both an Anglican priest and an evangelical revivalist. He held in tension the sacramental theology of his Anglican Communion and the evangelical emphasis on personal conversion. That is why Wesley was able to affirm both the "regenerating grace of infant baptism" (sacramentalism) and the need for "personal decision and commitment to Christ" (evangelicalism) (*BOR,* pp. 716–17).[4]

In the environment of colonial and frontier America, Wesley's followers tended to emphasize evangelicalism at the expense of sacramentalism. Both baptism and the Lord's Supper continued to be important in American Methodism; indeed, some of the most intense controversies in early American Methodist circles involved the availability of the sacraments. Still, it is undeniably true that more emphasis was placed on conversion, the act of free human will to choose Christ as Savior and Lord.

Unfortunately, by the late nineteenth and early twentieth centuries, all of the predecessor denominations of United Methodism were heavily influenced by the prevailing cultural presumption of the natural goodness and capacity of human beings. This resulted in a lessened stress on the need for conversion. As the Wesleyan family of churches moved into the twentieth century, it pulled apart the two aspects of its founder's theology—evangelicalism and sacramentalism—and largely lost both of them!

By the 1960's, as part of a broader rediscovery of the importance of Wesley, the church began to revitalize its theology and practice of the sacraments. This movement has climaxed in the sacramental rites in *The United Methodist Hymnal,* published in 1989. The very placing of these rites at the front of the *Hymnal* is an intentional indication of their significance. The work of a committee to study baptism, authorized by the General Conference, culminated in 1996 with the adoption of "By Water and the Spirit," in which the two-fold Wesleyan heritage of sacramentalism and evangelicalism is reclaimed.

The next section of "By Water and the Spirit" is entitled "We Are Saved by God's Grace" (*BOR,* pp. 719–21). Here human beings are portrayed as out of appropriate relationship with God because of the misuse of their freedom of will. Our sinfulness has separated us from God, alienated us from one another, and violated our stewardship of the natural world. From this tragic situation we can be rescued only by the actions of God.

The God of the Bible takes the initiative to come to God's people—through the covenant community of Israel in the Old Testament (Hebrew Bible), and through the event of Jesus Christ, who establishes the new covenant community of the Christian church in the New Testament. Deliverance from the bondage of sin and the brokenness of estrangement is possible only when we respond in repentance and faith, accepting God's gracious offer of reconciliation. God has chosen to make divine grace available to us in a variety of ways and through a diversity of means. The sacraments of baptism and Eucharist are sign-acts that function as special means of grace.

The longest portion of "By Water and the Spirit" is titled "Baptism and the Life of Faith" (*BOR,* pp. 722–32). Baptism is portrayed as the sign of the new covenant, as circumcision is the sign of the old. Our rituals are named "Services of the Baptismal Covenant" because they celebrate our covenant relationship with God, a relationship in which both parties make promises and undertake responsibilities. Baptism with water is also the celebration of the gift of the Holy Spirit, God's active presence in our lives. The laying on of hands as part of the ritual is the biblical symbol of the anointing of the Spirit.

The use of water, whether by immersion, pouring, or sprinkling connotes cleansing and forgiveness, death to sin, and new spiritual life in Christ. Baptism is the act of the church; through it new people are initiated and incorporated into the community of faith. Baptism signifies the beginning of a lifelong process of increasing Christlikeness. This holiness always includes both the personal and social dimensions of life.

United Methodists join with the vast majority of Christians throughout the centuries who believe that people of all ages are appropriate subjects for baptism. In anticipation of their being nurtured in the faith and accepting for themselves God's gift of salvation, infants receive the sacrament and are claimed as God's own. The validity of infant baptism does not rest on any capacity of the infants themselves; it rests on the action of Christ through the church. We are loved and accepted by God when we can do nothing to save ourselves. This is true regardless of our age.

In baptism, God's side of the covenant is established. Because God is faithful, this can never be nullified and will never need redoing. In contrast, the human side of the covenant relationship must be accepted by profession of faith, confirmation, and reaffirmation at appropriate times throughout life. Our apprehension of the covenant is largely dependent on the nurturing, shaping, and instruction that we receive. The parents (or other responsible adults) of baptized children, with the help of the community of faith, have the privilege and duty of forming these children as Christians.

Because baptism is part of a process of salvation, it may not be appropriate for children for whom there is no expectation that they will be nurtured as Christians. And, despite the teaching of the church, there may be some parents who choose not to have their children baptized. Of course, these children are still enfolded by God's love, and the church is charged to seek ways to minister to them and their families. Just as baptism is not essential for salvation (because God can act outside of the means God has established for us to use), so baptism is not sufficient for salvation.

The covenant has two sides. Our response of faith must accept God's gift of grace. For people who are baptized as infants, this response is celebrated in the service that the church calls confirmation. Here individuals who have attained sufficient maturity to be morally accountable publicly profess their faith in Christ and intention to live as Christ's disciples. In acknowledgment of this profession, the church as the body of Christ confirms these disciples through the power of the Holy Spirit. Confirmation is best understood as the first of a series of reaffirmations of faith that Christians will experience as they continue their lives of discipleship. Ritual opportunities for such reaffirmations are available in our *Hymnal* (pp. 50–53) and *Book of Worship* (pp. 111–14).

Because baptism is related to all aspects of the Christian faith, it has significance in our understanding and practice of other rites of the church as well. The sacrament of Holy Communion is ideally celebrated at each occasion of baptism, regardless of the age of the one baptized, so as to express the uniting of a new person with the community of faith. However, the United Methodist tradition has avoided making baptism a prerequisite for receiving Communion, in the belief that God's grace may act to convert, forgive, and sanctify even those who have not yet become a part of the church.[5]

United Methodism has been striving for decades to recover its identity and its mission.... Reclaiming the centrality of baptism is one of the most potent ways by which United Methodists can come to know their God-given personhood and ministry.

All ministry of Christians has its foundation in baptism. To be baptized is to be set upon the task of working with God toward the redemption of the world. God calls and the church ordains some people to professional vocations of leadership in the community of faith. This ordained ministry should be understood as an extension or specialization of the baptismal ministry of all Christians.

The only kind of marriage that the church offers is Christian marriage; this needs to be made clear in prenuptial counseling as well as in the service itself. Our ability to make faithful covenants with each other is grounded in our prior covenant relationship with God in baptism. Just as Christians marry as baptized people, so they die and have their mortal bodies laid to rest as baptized people. Our true identity and authentic ministry—in life and in death—are realized as we understand ourselves as people claimed and commissioned by God in our baptism.

IMPLICATIONS OF BAPTISM FOR THE CHURCH

Now that we have considered the church's official statement on baptism, it is time to ask, What are the practical implications of our theology and practice of baptism as United Methodist Christians?

One implication should certainly be a renewed emphasis on the responsibility of every pastor to "earnestly exhort" Christian parents to have their infant children baptized. Reluctance of parents is usually the consequence of misunderstanding the meaning of the sacrament. Pastors must preach, teach, and counsel their congregations not only on baptismal occasions but also as a continual focus of their ministry. The baptism of an infant should be understood by all as a part of the process of salvation, which will continue throughout the decades of the individual's life.

A closely related implication involves the teaching ministry of the church in all of its aspects. Appreciating the significance of baptism and living the baptized life requires that people of all ages be taught the United Methodist understanding of the sacrament. This will include understanding the difference between sacrament and ordinance; between infant and believer's baptism; between reaffirmation and "rebaptism"; between divine grace and human response—in short, between a theology of baptism that focuses on God's action and one that focuses on human action. Such teaching is the responsibility of the pastors and others on the professional staff of the church; of the teachers and leaders in Sunday school, vacation Bible school, music ministry, and small groups; of families; and, ultimately, of the entire congregation. No matter the age of an individual at baptism, she or he will never be able to apprehend the richness and profundity of her or his Christian identity and ministry without an ongoing process of nurture that is both intentional and intense.

Enhancing the congregation's self-understanding is another implication of United Methodist baptismal theology. A local congregation is a community of faith and a segment of the larger community of faith—the Christian church universal. The tasks of the congregation include the making of Christians and the redemption of the world. New members come into the faith community by baptism. Baptism is not a private occasion; it is a public celebration. It is not a domestic event; it is an ecclesiastical service.

Every congregation needs to comprehend, accept, and exercise its God-given responsibilities, both to fellow members of the community of faith and to those who are still outside. As is made clear in the vows of the Baptismal Covenant, an important part of this responsibility is the overturning of structures and practices of discrimination and oppression, and the up-building of systems and actions of justice and peace. God's baptized people are to strive toward the inclusive community of reconciliation and love.

REVITALIZING THE SIGNIFICANCE OF BAPTISM

If God's baptized people are to live out these and other implications of their baptism, it is clear that the significance of the sacrament needs to be revitalized. This is the work of both church and home. Through published resources, The United Methodist Church has made available a range of excellent material to facilitate this work. (See the resources listed under "For Further Reading," on page 56.)

The necessity of nurture and teaching has already been stressed. Parents and/or sponsors of young children as well as people accountable for themselves should be given the benefits of conscientious preparation. Much can be accomplished in the very act of conducting baptismal rituals. Baptism should never be tacked on to the end of a worship service; it should occupy a position that expresses its importance. Much is lost by hasty abbreviation of the ritual. If time is an issue, there are other places to shorten the service.

Water was chosen by God as the material element of the sacrament of baptism. It should be used in ways and amounts that manifest its wealth of meaning. Worship leaders should guard against allowing infant baptisms to become "cute baby shows", what is central is the divine claim on the child's life. Neither is the focus the parents, proud and sincere though they be. Their dedication to raising the child as a Christian is secondary to the action of God's grace.

Equally crucial is what church and home do after baptism. A simple place to start is to recognize the baptismal anniversaries of all members, at least as often as their physical birthdays are noted. No matter the age, every baptized person should be incorporated into an appropriate process of nurture and formation in the faith. For youth and adults, this may be a Sunday school class, DISCIPLE Bible study group, or prayer cell. There are many possibilities. All these acts of nurture and formation should happen in addition to regular participation in corporate worship.

Diligence in practicing the spiritual disciplines should be expected and facilitated. For infants, the task of ongoing nurture is even more imperative. Baptized infants and children are members of the local congregation, of The United Methodist Church, and of the Christian church. They should be so regarded and so treated; therefore, they should partake of Holy Communion regularly. They should participate in structured programs and events in the church as their growing maturity allows, especially in corporate worship.[6] These activities are aspects of their preparation for profession of faith and confirmation.

Unfortunately, in the practice of the church, confirmation has often marked the end, or at least the sharp decline, of a young person's church involvement. Instead, this occasion of publicly accepting God's grace and committing oneself to the life of discipleship demands to be followed by ongoing work of nurture and formation as individuals are increasingly able to exercise the privileges and responsibilities of Christians.

Faithful nurture of baptized children at home is, especially during the early years, of even greater import than what goes on in the church. Parents are the chief religious teachers of their children, not just by what they teach intentionally, but perhaps even more through the example of

Baptism should never be tacked on to the end of a worship service; it should occupy a position that expresses its importance. Much is lost by hasty abbreviation of the ritual. If time is an issue, there are other places to shorten the service.

their attitudes and practices. At home, children should learn to pray, to value the reading and study of the Bible, and to begin modeling their lives in the image of Christ.

The significance of their baptism can be made very real to children if they hear stories about it, see pictures and videos, look often at their baptismal certificate, and celebrate the anniversary of their baptism as a joyful event. After all, none of us has any conscious memory of our physical birthday, but we have learned to observe it regularly. With a bit of effort by church and family, baptized people would quickly learn to appreciate the importance of their spiritual birthday as well.

CONCLUSION

Unfortunately, this discussion of baptism must end with some explanation of the confused and confusing situation in which The United Methodist Church still finds itself after a decade of dealing with baptism and related issues. This unhappy condition will, it is devoutly hoped and prayed, be remedied by action of our next General Conference in the year 2000. A recurring point of debate has been the relationship between baptism and church membership. In its adoption of *The United Methodist Hymnal* in 1988, and of *The United Methodist Book of Worship* in 1992, the denomination approved services of the Baptismal Covenant in which all baptized people, regardless of age, are recognized as members of the local congregations of The United Methodist Church, and of the universal church of Jesus Christ.

The 1996 General Conference approved "By Water and the Spirit: A United Methodist Understanding of Baptism" as the denomination's "official interpretive statement" on baptismal theology and practice. However, the Judicial Council ruled in 1997 that the categories of "baptized" and "professing" member, which had been placed in the 1996 *Book of Discipline,* were nullified because they are not in accord with a phrase in the Constitution of The United Methodist Church.

The result is that the church currently has rituals and an official statement that assert that all baptized people are members of the church, while the church's "law book" (*Book of Discipline*) defines membership differently. It is hoped and expected that upcoming General Conferences will act to remove this contradiction, so that the church can get on with its work of making Christians in ways that are clear, persuasive, and powerful.

FOR FURTHER READING

Baptism: Christ's Act in the Church, by Laurence Hull Stookey (Nashville, TN: Abingdon Press, 1982).

By Water and the Spirit: Making Connections for Identity and Ministry, by Gayle Carlton Felton (Nashville, TN: Discipleship Resources, 1997).

Hand in Hand: Growing Spiritually With Our Children, by Sue Downing (Nashville, TN: Discipleship Resources, 1998).

Remember Who You Are: Baptism, a Model for Christian Life, by William H. Willimon (Nashville, TN: Upper Room Books, 1980).

Sacraments as God's Self Giving, by James F. White (Nashville, TN: Abingdon Press, 1983).

This Gift of Water: The Practice and Theology of Baptism Among Methodists in America, by Gayle Carlton Felton (Nashville, TN: Abingdon Press, 1992).

ENDNOTES

1 From "Baptismal Covenant I," © 1976, 1980, 1985, 1989 by The United Methodist Publishing House; from *The United Methodist Hymnal,* p. 37. Used by permission.

2 From "Baptismal Covenant I," © 1976, 1980, 1985, 1989 by The United Methodist Publishing House; from *The United Methodist Hymnal,* p. 36. Used by permission.

3 "By Water and the Spirit" is also available with commentary and a study guide in *By Water and the Spirit: Making Connections for Identity and Ministry,* by Gayle Carlton Felton (Nashville, TN: Discipleship Resources, 1997).

4 From "By Water and the Spirit: A United Methodist Understanding of Baptism" in *The Book of Resolutions of The United Methodist Church—1996,* pp. 716–17. Copyright © 1996 by The United Methodist Publishing House. Used by permission.

5 See "Who Gets Communion?" on pp. 137–46 in this volume, for an in-depth analysis and critique of the connection between baptism and Holy Communion in United Methodism.

6 See "Who Gets Communion?" on pp. 137–46 in this volume. See also "How to Welcome Children in Worship," on pp. 119–25 in Volume II of *Worship Matters.*

A recurring point of debate has been the relationship between baptism and church membership.

7

Celebrating the Eucharist More Vitally and More Frequently

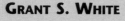

GRANT S. WHITE

Assistant Professor of Church History and History of Christian Worship, Saint Paul School of Theology, Kansas City, Missouri

CHRISTIANS TODAY LONG FOR AN UNDERSTANDING OF WHAT they do in church. They don't want to do things mechanically or simply by rote. They need and want to be able to employ both intellect and heart in the performance of all that they do as Christians. Unfortunately, one of the areas of Christian life in which this exercise of the intellect and heart is most lacking is worship, particularly the Eucharist.

As a church, we have not been in the habit of thinking about what the Eucharist is about, what its meaning is for the church and for daily life. This lack of disciplined reflection has cost the church dearly. We shouldn't be surprised, therefore, when attendance drops on Communion Sundays, or when our churches begin to practice theologically empty and positively harmful ways of celebrating the Eucharist, such as making Communion into a private devotion after the end of the Sunday service. Nor should we be surprised that many people fear that celebrating the Eucharist frequently risks making such celebrations mechanical or rote.

There are no simple answers to this dilemma. However, as the title of this article suggests, part of the answer has to do with the vitality of our celebrations of the Eucharist. But we must be careful to define *vitality* in this context. The word has nothing to do with the cult of energy so prevalent in North-American society today. It has nothing to do with the liturgical equivalent of being tanned, toned, and glowing with vigor! Nor does it have anything to do with making the Eucharist more folksy or turning preachers into roving talk-show hosts.

To celebrate the Eucharist more vitally means understanding who and what gives our celebrations life. (*Vital* comes from the Latin word *vita,* which means life.) It means to celebrate the Eucharist with understanding on the part of all those who are present. It means to celebrate the Eucharist in the context of ongoing reflection on the meaning of this sacrament for the holy struggle of life outside the Sunday service. If we can come to celebrate the Eucharist with these three elements in place, it might then be possible to celebrate the Eucharist with the frequency envisioned by the founders of the Methodist movement, and by *The United Methodist Hymnal* today: weekly, at the main congregational service. Let us look at each of these three elements.

Worship Matters: A United Methodist Guide to Ways to Worship (Volume I) © 1999 Discipleship Resources. Used by permission.

WHO AND WHAT GIVES OUR CELEBRATIONS LIFE?

God gives life to our celebrations of the Eucharist. God gives God's own life to us in the sacrament of the Eucharist. In turn, we respond to this unfathomable gift with the offering of our own lives, an offering made possible by Christ's own offering of himself on the cross. Finally, the pervasively thankful character of our response—Eucharist, after all, means thanksgiving—will determine the manner in which our celebrations express that thankfulness: with holy joy. That joy will be one of the most powerful expressions of the gospel we can offer to the world.

When the 1996 General Conference voted to accept the denominational statement on baptism, "By Water and the Spirit," the church made a momentous, potentially radical decision: to be a sacramental church. As news reports at the time correctly noted, that decision put United Methodists in the same camp as Roman Catholic, Orthodox, Lutheran, and Episcopal Christians. That is, United Methodists affirmed then and now that God is the primary actor in the sacraments. We also act: We respond in faith to God's giving Godself to us. But we believe, first and foremost, that God acts in these actions and elements, and that God acts first.

This can be a shocking belief to many United Methodists! As with other mainline Protestant denominations, United Methodism has passively accepted the non-sacramentalism, or a-sacramentalism, that was so much a part of the American-frontier liturgical tradition. For that tradition, the sacraments are pious exercises serving to remind us of what Christ has done for us. They may be important for that reason, but they are not occasions of God's *self-giving* to us. The emphasis and responsibility in the sacrament are all on us. The sacraments become *our* action rather than *God's* action. This theology fits well with the assumption so prevalent in North-American culture that the individual is self-sufficient.

Thus, for United Methodists to affirm that the Eucharist is a sacrament means that we believe that God gives Godself in it. More specifically, we encounter the living God in the Eucharist and receive the holy gift of God's very self in the body and blood of Christ. In addition, God gives us the very gift of ourselves: us, as the body of Christ. As Augustine reminded his congregation: "If, then, you are Christ's body and his members, it is your own mystery which you receive. It is to what you are that you reply, 'Amen,' and by replying subscribe. For you are told: 'The body of Christ,' and you reply, 'Amen.' Be a member of the body of Christ, and let your 'Amen' be true."[1]

In line with the Anglican theological tradition in which the Wesley brothers lived, taught, preached, and celebrated, Methodists have not attempted to define the precise means by which God gives the divine self in the Eucharist. As Charles Wesley astutely wrote, and as we continue to sing:

> O the depth of love divine, the unfathomable grace!
> Who shall say how bread and wine God into us conveys!
> How the bread his flesh imparts, how the wine transmits his blood,
> Fills his faithful people's hearts with all the life of God!...
> Sure and real is the grace, the manner be unknown;
> Only meet us in thy ways and perfect us in one.
> Let us taste the heavenly powers, Lord, we ask for nothing more.
> Thine to bless, 'tis only ours to wonder and adore.
>
> (*UMH*, 627)[2]

Thus the services of Word and Table in *The United Methodist Hymnal* (pp. 6–31) are content simply to affirm that God gives Godself, and that

God gives God's own life to us in the sacrament of the Eucharist. In turn, we respond to this unfathomable gift with the offering of our own lives.

believers receive God's self in the body and blood of Christ. To be sure, United Methodists are more likely to identify the presence of Christ in the Eucharist with the entire celebration rather than more narrowly with the elements of bread and wine. However, the important point to assert, whatever one's particular theological position on this issue, is the reality of God's self-gift. We really and truly are given and receive God's self in Christ's body and blood.

HOW DO WE CELEBRATE THE EUCHARIST WITH UNDERSTANDING?

Of course, nobody can claim to understand fully the Eucharist. But it would be wrong to conclude from that statement that it is not necessary to claim and own basic theological positions about the Eucharist. Why is this so? Because what we believe has profound outcomes for what we do.

If we celebrate the Eucharist believing that in it we truly encounter God, that we truly are given and truly receive God's self in the body and blood of Christ, and that the sacrament is a sacrifice of ourselves in response to Christ's self-offering on the cross, then these affirmations will affect how we celebrate the Eucharist itself, our attitudes toward it, and what we believe about how that celebration affects how we live.

For these things to happen, though, there must be a congregation that *knows* what it is they are doing when they celebrate the Eucharist. It is not enough for the pastor to have a clear grasp of Eucharistic theology. That theology must be part of the lives of congregation members. To put it another way: Congregation members need to know what they are doing in the celebration of the Eucharist so that what God does for them in it can bear fruit in their lives.

When we say that the Eucharist is a sacrament, we are voicing the expectation that God's gift will bear fruit in real, difficult, struggling, holy lives. Faith is certainly necessary for producing fruitfulness. Yet how is it possible for people to have faith if they do not have a basic grasp of what the church affirms about the sacrament in which they participate? That is, there must be a body of common meaning to which members can ascribe in order for the church's common celebrations of the Eucharist to have a coherent meaning.

It is that common, coherent meaning for which church members today hunger and thirst. They want to be able to participate in the sacraments with understanding of what they are doing, of what their participation in the sacraments implies for their daily lives. They earnestly desire to join the vitality of their piety with the vitality of their intellect. They hunger for the opportunity to make sense of their lives in terms of what they affirm as Christians.

Thus we United Methodists desperately need to find ways to nurture our people's reflection on the meaning of the Eucharist and of the implications of that meaning for their lives. The current situation in our churches requires more than the occasional church school or confirmation class to remedy. I suggest that we begin with the liturgical celebration itself as the primary, fundamental context for reflection. Experience of the service itself—through singing, prayer, and hearing the word of God in Scripture and sermon—is the raw material from which theological reflection flows.

HOW DO WE NURTURE ONGOING REFLECTION ON THE EUCHARIST?

Authentic reflection on the *common* faith of the church—the kind of reflection a person can truly own—is possible only if we are willing to use the liturgical texts the denomination has approved in its services of Word and Table. Pastors must renounce the arrogant notion that they can do a better job than what the church has struggled to live and articulate over the course of the past thirty years of liturgical revision—indeed, with the universal church, over the past nearly twenty centuries. The use of common liturgical texts provides a basis for common theological reflection; such reflection is impossible if the official texts and patterns are ignored or used piecemeal. (Even the most flexible of patterns, "A Service of Word and Table III" [*UMH,* pp. 15–16], requires that the presider know how to pray the Eucharistic prayer—its shape, intent, and theology.) It is quite striking to me that United Methodists today commonly voice a deep concern for United Methodist identity, yet refuse to worship according to the only norms and texts the denomination itself has approved.

A number of strategies for congregational reflection on the Eucharist are possible. (They will obviously vary according to the local situation of each congregation.) A good place to begin is the occasional, perhaps bimonthly, "teaching service" in which the pastor and others pause frequently to discuss the elements of the service in terms of their theology and history. This kind of celebration will help congregation members become familiar with the basic elements of the Service of Word and Table.

Teaching services alone are not enough. There must be at least two other strategies in place: a greater frequency of celebration of the Eucharist at the main congregational service, and a profusion of opportunities for congregation members to reflect on their liturgical experience in the context of their daily lives. Neither strategy will be easy to establish and nurture in local congregations.

There are many obstacles to more frequent celebration of Communion: the frontier approach to the sacraments (mentioned above); a sense of personal unworthiness to receive the Eucharist on the part of many worshipers; the length of the service, and, perhaps most potent of all, dreary, almost funeral-like celebrations of the Eucharist. While there are no easy answers to these issues, it is important to note that there exists a reciprocal relationship between *celebration* (using the liturgical texts) and *reflection*—a dynamic that can lead to more frequent celebration of the Eucharist. As people begin to discover the power and meaning of the Eucharist for their daily lives, they will want to celebrate it more frequently. At the same time, they will want to have celebrations that fully express the good news the Eucharist proclaims. Celebration leads to reflection, and reflection leads to the ongoing reform of the celebrations themselves. This basic dynamic is essential to the vitality of the Eucharist in the local congregation.[3]

How can a congregation have more frequent celebrations of the Eucharist? First, it is important that the celebrations happen in the main Sunday service. Otherwise, we risk making the Eucharist marginal to the life of the entire church. Second, if your congregation is celebrating the Eucharist quarterly at the moment, why don't you suggest moving to a monthly celebration? Third, if and when you are celebrating the Eucharist monthly, augment that pattern with celebration of the sacrament on the major feasts of the church (Easter, Pentecost, Christmas, Epiphany). From

When we say that the Eucharist is a sacrament, we are voicing the expectation that God's gift will bear fruit in real, difficult, struggling, holy lives.

this point, move to adding Eucharistic celebrations on the first and last Sundays of each of the liturgical seasons. The lectionary Gospel readings for late summer in Year B include readings from John 6. These texts provide opportunity in the "desert days" of late summer to preach and teach about the gift of the Bread of Life, as well as to celebrate it in the sharing of bread and cup. By that point, the congregation will be celebrating the Eucharist on a majority of Sundays in the year. After living with this pattern for some time (which may take years), your congregation may be ready to move to a weekly celebration.

Such radical change is possible only if it happens in the context of ongoing congregational reflection and discussion of the Eucharist and of the changes being made. The whole congregation must participate in this process if authentic ownership of change is to happen. The goal is to establish and nurture a deep-rooted Eucharistic practice that can withstand the occasional change of pastors that is a feature of the United Methodist system.

CONCLUSION

United Methodists are only at the beginning of a vast liturgical shift that, if it continues, will take years to accomplish in local congregations, and generations for the denomination as a whole. This shift must happen with pastoral wisdom and sensitivity. In other words, to quote the Latin epigram: "Make haste, slowly!" It is far better to move to a monthly celebration of the Eucharist with intentionality and understanding—with the goal, of course, of weekly celebration—than to move quickly and heavy-handedly to a more frequent celebration. Such a rapid move will doubtless alienate the congregation and set back the cause for which you are working: a more vital and frequent celebration of the Eucharist.

FOR FURTHER READING

Baptism, Eucharist and Ministry: Faith and Order Paper 111 (Geneva: World Council of Churches, 1982).

Eucharist: Christ's Feast With the Church, by Laurence Hull Stookey (Nashville, TN: Abingdon Press, 1993).

Eucharist: Symbol of Transformation, by William R. Crockett (Collegeville, MN: The Liturgical Press, 1992).

Sacraments as God's Self Giving, by James F. White (Nashville, TN: Abingdon Press, 1983).

ENDNOTES

1 From "Sermon 272 (PL 38.1247)," by Saint Augustine, in *Patrologiae Cursus Completus,* Series Latina, by J. P. Migne (Paris: Garnier, 1841), Volume 38. Translated by Grant S. White.

2 From "O the Depth of Love Divine," by Charles Wesley, in *The United Methodist Hymnal* (Nashville, TN: The United Methodist Publishing House, 1989), 627.

3 James F. White discusses the reciprocal dynamic between celebration and reflection in his book *Sacraments as God's Self Giving* (Nashville, TN: Abingdon Press, 1983), pp. 28–29.

Linking Liturgy and Life

E. Byron Anderson

Assistant Professor of Worship,
Christian Theological Seminary,
Indianapolis, Indiana

> Lord, whose love through humble service bore the weight of human need…we, your servants bring the worship not of voice alone, but heart, consecrating to your purpose every gift that you impart.
>
> (Albert F. Bayly, *UMH,* 581)[1]

IT IS 10:15 ON SUNDAY MORNING. IN THE PASTOR'S OFFICE A small group gathers for instruction and prayer. One will be preaching, one leading the congregation in prayer, one reading Scripture, several serving bread and cup. At the same time, two children are being robed and prepared as acolytes for the morning. A couple from the congregation has brought freshly made grape juice, which is now being prepared for flagon and chalice, another couple has brought freshly baked bread. The choir and its director are in the choir loft finishing last-minute rehearsal and warm-up. The rest of the congregation is moving from entrances and classrooms through the fellowship hall—some stopping for brief exchanges of news, some for a last sip of coffee—toward the stairs that lead to the sanctuary, where some people are already gathered in silence, while others are conversing with friends and visitors. In all of this, the work of worship—the liturgy—of this congregation has begun. It will continue as hymns, psalms, and anthems are sung, Scriptures read and interpreted, prayers prayed, and blessings given.

At 10:15 on Monday morning, a small group gathers in the pastor's office for instruction and prayer. In classrooms around the building, children are at play with teachers and caregivers. In other rooms, nurse practitioners and a handful of volunteers have begun receiving clients in this downtown "wellness center," providing care to the uninsured and underinsured. Other children, who are gathered with other adults in classrooms around the city, are busy with schoolwork. Some adults are gathered in office buildings; and some are in offices in their homes. Some are on the road to appointments; others traveling to care for dying parents. Still others, long retired, are busy in homes and workshops or are visiting and caring for longer-retired siblings. In all of *this* work, the work of worship—the liturgy—of this congregation has begun. And it will continue as meals are shared, homework and housework is completed, and prayers are said.

Unfortunately, our separation of the work of Sunday morning from that of Monday morning has become all too common. Sunday is for the work of *spiritual* things, Monday for the work of *earthly* things—as if Christian worship were not concerned with both. Perhaps this is because those in both pulpit and pew have permitted it to remain so.

Worship Matters: A United Methodist Guide to Ways to Worship (Volume I) © 1999 Discipleship Resources. Used by permission.

In a way, we are like the fourth-century hermit who upon hearing of the wisdom and gifts of the desert father Poemen went to visit Poemen. As the story goes, Poemen received the hermit with joy. They sat down to talk, the hermit speaking "of the Scriptures, of spiritual and of heavenly things. But Abba Poemen turned his face away and answered nothing." The hermit left in disappointment. When asked by another brother why Poemen would not speak to the hermit, Poemen replied, "He is great and speaks of heavenly things and I am lowly and speak of earthly things. If he had spoken of the passions of the soul, I should have replied, but he speaks to me of spiritual things and I know nothing about that."[2] In our separation of Sunday and Monday, we assume that the "passions of the soul" found in the joys and failures of daily life are earthly things inherently unrelated to the spiritual things of worship, and that the spiritual things of worship are inherently unrelated to daily life.

MISUNDERSTANDINGS ABOUT LITURGY AND VOCATION

The separation of the spiritual and earthly, of liturgy and life, occurs through several misunderstandings about our vocation as Christian people. In particular, three misunderstandings get in the way of our linking liturgy and life:

1. *Liturgy is someone else's work.* As we have developed in more detail in the introduction to Volume II of *Worship Matters,* liturgy is the public work of worship, engaged and enacted by the whole of God's people. Before its association with cultic actions (the work of worship enacted in the church building), liturgy referred to the representative work done by and on behalf of a community, much like the work intended by those we elect and send to school boards, city and county councils, and state and federal legislatures. Passivity in worship, as in the electoral process, assumes that those elected to representative ministries rightfully displace us from our work or can do a better job "because they know more than I do." Imagine a choir with only a director and no choir members, a librarian with no library patrons, a preacher with no listeners.

The work of worship is an interdependent process of readers/preachers and listeners; leaders of prayer and those who pray; hymn accompanists and hymn singers; makers of bread and wine and partakers of the same. Liturgy is not someone else's work; it is the work of a particular gathered community on a particular day and in a particular place. Whether formal or informal, "high" church or "low" church, urban or rural, liturgy is the work of the whole of a community gathered in Christ's name. Compared with other public gatherings (such as those in arenas and stadiums), social-service providers, and educational institutions, this work of worship is the most distinctive thing the church does week in and week out. Whether in pulpit or pew, we engage in our public work of worship as we gather, sing, pray, listen, affirm, intercede, confess, collect offerings, give thanks, share bread and cup, and are sent forth.

2. *Worship is the "setting aside" of the cares of the world.* As in the story of Poemen and the visiting hermit, our gathering for the work of worship tempts us to think that the place of worship permits us to step out of the world—to leave behind the cares of our other work from home, office, and school—to speak of spiritual things neglected by the competing demands of earthly things. We cannot and should not deny our need for a respite from the demands of daily life; we need a time and place of "sabbath rest."

There are several factors that conspire in the temptation to treat worship as the place of rest from our work. First is our strong Puritan inheritance that confuses the sabbath day (the seventh day of the week, on which even God rested) with the Lord's Day (the first day of the week, on which creation began, and the so-called eschatological "eighth day" of the week, on which God begins the new creation in the resurrection of Christ). The second factor is the way in which the visual and real structures of our calendars treat Sunday as the end of the weekend, and thus the last possible chance for rest before returning to the workplace. For early Christian communities, Sunday represented God's new workday as well as the reality of the beginning of another workweek. The beginning of that workweek is not in home, office, or school, but in the gathering of the Christian community for its public work of worship.

The task we face here is to claim our work of worship, not as a place in which we set aside the cares of the world, but as a place in which God transforms us, our cares, and our world. In this place of worship, we acquire eyes, ears, hearts, and minds that enable us to see, hear, feel, and understand the way of God's new creation, even in the midst of the very cares and burdens we bring with us to worship. Our prayer becomes, in the words Albert Bayly has us sing: "As we worship, grant us vision, till your love's revealing light in its height and depth and greatness dawns upon our quickened sight, making known the needs and burdens your compassion bids us bear" (*UMH*, 581).[3] Such is the work more commonly expressed in African American spirituals and gospel songs, such as "Nobody Knows the Trouble I See" (*UMH*, 520) or Thomas Dorsey's "Precious Lord, Take My Hand" (*UMH*, 474). It is also conveyed in Dietrich Bonhoeffer's hymn-prayer "By Gracious Powers" (*UMH*, 517). In the work of worship, we bring from the rest of our work what we have done, not done, or left unfinished in offering to God so that it and we may be transformed by God. We bring the passions of our souls because it is this that concerns God. I think this is at the heart of Paul's instruction and appeal to the Romans, and thereby to us, in Romans 12:1-2: We are "to present [our] bodies as a living sacrifice, holy and acceptable to God, which is [our] spiritual worship," not "conformed to this world, but... transformed by the renewing of [our] minds, so that [we] may discern what is the will of God—what is good and acceptable and perfect."

3 *Our vocation as Christians is what we do outside of worship.* In church buildings scattered across the country, door lintels are marked with words such as "You are now entering your place of ministry and service." On the one hand, this is an important reminder of the ministry that all Christians share in the world. It is also a reminder that our ministry should not and cannot be confined to what we do in church. On the other hand, it would be helpful to have these words marked on both sides of the door. The work of worship and life is not so easily separated. That is, when we enter our places of public worship, we do not leave our places of ministry and service. As noted in the preceding misunderstanding, we bring all of ourselves—the joys and sorrows of work, home, and school—to the work of worship. We can do no other.

Part of this separation of liturgy and life comes from misunderstanding our vocation as Christian people. We have confused Christian vocation with occupation. As Gary Badcock reminds us, God calls the human—and the Christian—"to love God with the whole self, involving all [our] human capabilities and energies." God calls us "to faith, to holiness, and to service." Our occupations, including the work of worship

Our separation of the work of Sunday morning from that of Monday morning has become all too common.... Perhaps this is because those in both pulpit and pew have permitted it to remain so.

and our work as parents, teachers, firefighters, friends, students, insurance managers, and even ordained pastors, become the means by which and the places in which we live out this calling by God.[4]

By understanding that our vocation as Christian people is all that we do to love God and neighbor, in liturgy and life, we discover that we cannot separate liturgy from life and work, perhaps even in spite of what happens in worship. In fulfilling our calling to faith, holiness, and service, we consecrate to God's service every gift that God imparts, offering to God the whole of our selves and presenting to the world the wholeness of a self transformed by God.

LINKING LITURGY AND LIFE

How, then, might those very things we treat as being *spiritual* rather than *earthly*—the practices of United Methodist worship—suggest, permit, and even enable the link between liturgy and life? How do we link "what we sing with our lips...believe in our hearts,...[and] practice in our lives" (*UMH,* 69)?[5] While there are many places throughout the public work of worship where we find these links, I want to draw attention to four such places: the baptismal renunciation and affirmation, corporate confession of sin, intercessory prayer, and the Great Thanksgiving or Eucharist prayer.

[1.] Renunciation of Sin and Profession of Faith

On behalf of the whole church, I ask you:
Do you renounce the spiritual forces of wickedness,
   reject the evil powers of this world,
   and repent of your sin?
I do.
Do you accept the freedom and power God gives you
   to resist evil, injustice, and oppression
   in whatever forms they present themselves?
I do.
Do you confess Jesus Christ as your Savior,
put your whole trust in his grace,
and promise to serve him as your Lord,
in union with the church which Christ has opened
   to people of all ages, nations, and races?
I do.   (*UMH,* p. 34)[6]

If there has been one place where pastors and congregations consistently stumble with the Baptismal Covenant service, it is in the renunciation of sin and profession of faith that provide the foundation of our response to God's gift of grace. Some wonder how we can ask these questions of parents, mistakenly believing that they respond on behalf of infant children instead of themselves. Others, seeing baptism only as a cleansing from sin or, inappropriately, as an act of dedication, wonder what these questions have to do with baptism in the first place. (See "Reclaiming the Centrality of Baptism," on pages 51–57 in this volume.) When I read the newspaper headlines each morning, with stories of children or parents killing children, the declining initial age of involvement in drug abuse, and the country's increasing disgust with, yet complacency about, the lack of moral character in our leaders, I wonder how we can *not* ask these questions.

These liturgical, and seemingly spiritual, questions ask about our relationship with very earthly things. The forces of wickedness; the evil powers of *this* world; our sinfulness; the forms of evil, injustice, and oppression: All these continue to present themselves to us. In the midst of a community "opened to people of all ages, nations, and races," we are asked to renounce these things by the power and freedom God gives us. Each day we are confronted by choices large and small: How will we respond to the trouble we see in our world?

As part of an adult class in one church, class members were asked to begin each day over the period of a week with the three questions quoted above. What they found was not the disconnection of liturgy and life, but the liturgy as a source for the transformation of that life. In work and home, each person found a seemingly new power to speak and act in fulfillment of his or her vocation to love God and neighbor in and through the places and things that "occupied" him or her. It also provided a new freedom to name experiences for what they were—patterns of wickedness, injustice, and evil as well as patterns of grace and love—and to name an alternative way of being in the world. These patterns of resistance, rejection, and trust are the ministries of the church to which we commit ourselves in the rites of baptism and church membership. They are a foundational link between liturgy and daily life, between the public work of worship and daily occupation.

2. *Corporate confession of sin.* As the baptismal questions bring us face to face with the reality of our world, so corporate confession confronts us with the disorder of our own lives. While the church must confess its complicity in shaping an unhealthy culture of shame and guilt, we are at risk of becoming a culture of guiltlessness and shamelessness. Singing Albert Bayly's hymn, we are brought up short by the second stanza: "Still your children wander homeless; still the hungry cry for bread; still the captives long for freedom; still in grief we mourn our dead" (*UMH*, 581).[7] At the heart of our corporate confession of sin is the reality of our failure to fulfill our vocation to love God and neighbor with the whole of our selves.

The temptation worship planners and leaders often fall prey to is the assumption that they can specify what and where in our daily lives we have failed. The result is moral exhortation cloaked in the language of prayer. The connection between our public work of worship—as represented by liturgical text and corporate prayer—and our daily work is better made when the prayer is less specific rather than more, and when opportunity is provided for silent, personal reflection on the ways in which we have failed in our own places to fulfill our vocation.

The prayer of confession and pardon in "A Service of Word and Table I" (*UMBOW*, p. 35; *UMH*, p. 8) provides a good model for us. At its heart, we are drawn to confess that we "have not loved [God] with our whole heart" and "have not loved our neighbors" or "heard the cry of the needy."[8] The silence that follows invites us to review the preceding week, the various places in which we live and work, and the people with whom we have been invited to love and service, and to honestly name our failure. The movement from the spoken corporate prayer to silent personal reflection to corporate forgiveness models our continual movement between Sunday and Monday in which each transforms the other—Monday filling out the details of our confession, Sunday transforming them in light of our vocation in the abiding grace and forgiveness of God.

3. *Interceding on behalf of the world.* If confession provides a means by which we name and transform our vocational failure, the practice of intercessory prayer provides a means by which we begin again the work of loving God and neighbor. As Gary Badcock notes: "Such service as Christ commands never makes entirely modest demands: it is to love the enemy, to pray for the persecutor, to be the salt of the earth and the light of the world."[9]

We bring all of ourselves—the joys and sorrows of work, home, and school— to the work of worship. We can do no other.

Among the liturgical practices in need of reform in our churches, intercessory prayer stands out among them. One of the difficulties with its reform is that intercessory prayer has been subsumed by the "pastoral prayer." In few cases does it seem, in Albert Bayly's words, to "[make] known the needs and burdens [God's] compassion bids us bear" (*UMH*, 581).[10] In some cases, the prayer becomes little more than the final point of the sermon. In others, it sounds like a child's wish list for Santa, repeatedly begging, "Give us, O Lord...". The public work of intercessory prayer, as the hinge between Word and Table in the basic pattern of United Methodist worship, is also the hinge between liturgy and life, worship and work. Don Saliers writes:

> To pray with the Church is to remember the world before God, to be in dialogue with God about the suffering and yearnings of all God's creatures. To pray such petitions and to intend them faithfully is to embody a way of life in solidarity with all for whom Christ bids us pray. In this way our spirituality is nourished in the truth of holding the world steadily before God.[11]

One way to recover this vital link between liturgy and life is to reclaim the prayer of intercession as the prayer of the people. The orders of daily praise and prayer (*UMH*, pp. 876–79; *UMBOW*, pp. 568–79) provide one model for this: A worship leader (appropriately a deacon or the lay leader of the congregation)[12] invites prayer for groups of people and concerns—those who suffer, the concerns of the local community—to which members of the congregation respond first by naming their prayer concerns and to which the whole congregation may respond: "Hear our prayer." A second model is "A Litany for the Church and for the World" (*UMBOW*, p. 495), in which the prayer leader guides the congregation more directly in its prayer. The importance of this prayer is the way in which it links petitions with the intent or aspiration of each petition. That is, for each thing we ask of God, the intent is our action in the world in God's name and power. This prayer can be expanded by inviting additional congregational participation in the naming of specific concerns.

Each of these models assumes that the liturgy is our work, not someone else's work. We are the ones who pray; it is our engagement with the world that shapes what we pray. In this, the cares of the world that we are tempted to leave at the door become the content of our public work of worship.

4. *The Great Thanksgiving*. Finally, we can ask how our prayer at the Lord's Table provides a link between liturgy and daily life. Although the whole of prayer requires attention, I want to focus on the closing petition: "By your Spirit make us one with Christ, one with each other, and one in ministry to all the world, until Christ comes...and we feast at his heavenly banquet" (*UMH*, p. 10).[13] The offering of ourselves that we receive back transformed in prayer and by the grace of God provides a model for fulfilling Paul's exhortation in Romans 12:1-2. It is the whole of our broken lives, the whole of our imperfect selves, that we offer to God for transformation, so that we may fulfill our vocation to love God and neighbor.

As God takes bread and wine from our hands to become the means for sustaining and transforming our lives, so God takes the offering of ourselves to become the means for sustaining and transforming the world. In the prayer, we learn to offer ourselves in thanksgiving rather than in regret, in joy rather than in sorrow, in hope rather than in despair. As in baptism, we accept the freedom and power God gives us, so in bread and wine received with thanksgiving, we receive and accept the sustaining power and presence of the Holy Spirit. This is the link between liturgy and life, for what we receive at this Table is but the model for the community gathered about each table at home and workplace, day in and day out—until the next Lord's Day and until the Lord comes.

> Called by worship to your service, forth in your dear name we go to the child, the youth, the aged, love in living deeds to show; hope and health, good will and comfort, counsel, aid, and peace we give, that your servants, Lord, in freedom may your mercy know, and live.
>
> (*UMH*, 581)[14]

FOR FURTHER READING

Liturgy and the Moral Self: Humanity at Full Stretch Before God, edited by E. Byron Anderson and Bruce T. Morrill, S.J. (Collegeville, MN: The Liturgical Press, 1998).

The Way of Life: A Theology of Christian Vocation, by Gary D. Badcock (Grand Rapids, MI: William B. Eerdmans Publishing Company, 1998).

Worship & Daily Life: A Resource for Worship Planners, introduction by Doris Rudy (Nashville, TN: Discipleship Resources, 1999).

Worship and Spirituality, Second Edition, by Don E. Saliers (Akron, OH: O.S.L. Publications, 1996).

ENDNOTES

1 From "Lord, Whose Love Through Humble Service," by Albert F. Bayly, in *The United Methodist Hymnal* (Nashville, TN: The United Methodist Publishing House, 1989), 581. Words copyright © 1988 Oxford University Press.

2 From the *Apophthegmata patrum, alphabetic series,* translated by Benedicta Ward SLG, *The Sayings of the Desert Fathers* (Kalamazoo, MI: Cistercian Publications, 1975), p. 140.

3 From "Lord, Whose Love Through Humble Service," by Albert F. Bayly, in *The United Methodist Hymnal* (Nashville, TN: The United Methodist Publishing House, 1989), 581. Words copyright © 1988 Oxford University Press.

4 From *The Way of Life: A Theology of Christian Vocation,* by Gary D. Badcock (Grand Rapids, MI: William B. Eerdmans Publishing Company, 1998), pp. 15, 16, and 106–7.

5 From "For True Singing" in *The United Methodist Hymnal,* 69. Copyright © 1989 by The United Methodist Publishing House. Used by permission.

6 From "Baptismal Covenant I," © 1976, 1980, 1985, 1989 by The United Methodist Publishing House; from *The United Methodist Hymnal,* p. 34. Used by permission. See also *UMBOW,* p. 88.

7 From "Lord, Whose Love Through Humble Service," by Albert F. Bayly, in *The United Methodist Hymnal* (Nashville, TN: The United Methodist Publishing House, 1989), 581. Words copyright © 1988 Oxford University Press.

8 From "A Service of Word and Table I," © 1972, 1980, 1985, 1989 by The United Methodist Publishing House; from *The United Methodist Hymnal,* p. 8. Used by permission. See also *UMBOW,* p. 35.

9 From *The Way of Life: A Theology of Christian Vocation,* by Gary D. Badcock (Grand Rapids, MI: William B. Eerdmans Publishing Company, 1998), p. 113.

10 From "Lord, Whose Love Through Humble Service," by Albert F. Bayly, in *The United Methodist Hymnal* (Nashville, TN: The United Methodist Publishing House, 1989), 581. Words copyright © 1988 Oxford University Press.

11 From *Worship and Spirituality* (Second Edition), by Don E. Saliers (Akron, OH: O.S.L. Publications, 1996), pp. 69–70.

12 See "The Role of the Presider" and "The Role of Deacons and Assisting Ministers," on pp. 123–29 and 130–36 in this volume.

13 From "A Service of Word and Table I," © 1972, 1980, 1985, 1989 by The United Methodist Publishing House; from *The United Methodist Hymnal,* p. 10. Used by permission. See also *UMBOW,* p. 38.

14 From "Lord, Whose Love Through Humble Service," by Albert F. Bayly, in *The United Methodist Hymnal* (Nashville, TN: The United Methodist Publishing House, 1989), 581. Words copyright © 1988 Oxford University Press.

This is the link between liturgy and life, for what we receive at this Table is but the model for the community gathered about each table at home and workplace, day in and day out—until the next Lord's Day and until the Lord comes.

Part Two

Perspectives on Theology, Culture, and Worship

Worship and Culture: Inculturating the Good News

**KAREN B.
WESTERFIELD TUCKER**

*Assistant Professor of
Liturgical Studies,
The Divinity School,
Duke University,
Durham, North Carolina*

I N ADDRESSING THE RELATIONSHIP BETWEEN WORSHIP AND culture, we first need to define our terms and lay out some general observations and principles. Then we will examine how local congregations already engage in multicultural, transcultural, and cross-cultural worship, and how they can come to participate in it more fully.

WORSHIP

The Scriptures make it clear that human beings, in obedience to the One in whose image they are made, are to "worship and bow down" before their Maker (Psalm 95:6), to "make a joyful noise to the rock of [their] salvation" (Psalm 95:1). Christians, however, specify further the focus of their worship: Praise is to be given to the triune God, revealed to humanity in various ways, but particularly by the second person of the Godhead, Christ the Son (Hebrews 1:1-2). And Jesus Christ, who revealed the uncompromising love of God and proclaimed that God's kingdom is near, is himself to be the object of Christian worship; for "at the name of Jesus every knee should bend, in heaven and on earth and under the earth, and every tongue should confess that Jesus Christ is Lord, to the glory of God the Father" (Philippians 2:10 11). It is by the continuous outpouring of the Holy Spirit that we are able to offer such praise, for the Spirit that knows the mind of God is able to intercede for us "with sighs too deep for words" (Romans 8:26). It is also by the power of the Spirit that Christians continually encounter God in Christ in the Word and sacraments.

Notice something present or implied in all of these statements. God first comes to us, offering us salvation and giving us the opportunity—and the gift—of worship. Having acknowledged or accepted these gifts, we worship God as a *response* to what God has already done for each one of us and for the world that God so loves. We are able to give to God only because of what God has already given to us. So we render praise and thanks to God, who created us, who first loved us, and who redeems us still.

In rightly offering God worship, we receive benefits. In other words, we receive twice from God in worship: first, from the encounter with God in Word and Sacrament, wherein God's promises are revealed; and second, as a consequence of our response of praise. By glorifying God,

Worship Matters: A United Methodist Guide to Ways to Worship (Volume I) © 1999 Discipleship Resources. Used by permission.

the worshiper is both edified and sanctified; a person learns about the gospel, is formed in the faith, grows in holiness, and is equipped for ministry and mission in the world. Therefore, in worship it is expected that we will both give *and* receive. We should never worship *solely* with an eye to obtaining the benefits God offers us.

CULTURE

Culture may be defined as "the means by which human beings of a particular time, place, and situation organize themselves with structures and rules for meeting the demands of life." Culture is created by human beings to articulate their view of the world, and includes both rational thought and practical behavior. In turn, culture influences and shapes both communities and individuals. Inclusive within culture are the values of a particular group, and the way those values are concretely expressed.

For those who claim the Lordship of Jesus Christ, there is what might be called an evangelical or ecclesial culture, a culture of the gospel and of the church. From the Christian point of view, this culture is not simply one culture among many cultures, but it is *the* culture par excellence that both embraces and judges all other cultures. At the heart of this culture there is not human work or human innovation but the gospel of Jesus Christ, which directs the Christian community's values as well as its symbolic and ritual expressions. The gospel speaks to a new way of life, a life formed by the constitutive elements of Word, sacrament, prayer, and praise in the midst of God's faithful people. From this flow other aspects of churchly culture such as teaching, fellowship, service, and witness, which press the faithful community toward the "culture" that awaits in the time to come: God's kingdom.

WORSHIP AND CULTURE

Worship as the manifestation of the church culture cannot be carried out in the abstract. Worship must take a specific, concrete form, and the form or forms it takes are related to cultures humanly constructed. Just as the incarnation of Christ of necessity took place within the confines of a particular culture, and the church itself is the body of Christ in the world, Christian worship is also related to time and place. We often say that we "go" to worship or that worship will "take place." Both of these verbs indicate that worship requires a location—not only a geographic location, but placement in a particular locale, a specific context. Worship must relate to the place and to the people where it occurs.

There are no "pure," cultureless origins of worship; Christian worship did not develop "out of nothing" (*ex nihilo*) and therefore has never existed without human cultural elements. Even the ritual forms of the sacraments, as described in the New Testament and as articulated in the theological treatises and liturgical texts of the early church, were laden with material incorporated from a cultural matrix. Ritual purificatory washings were common in the cultic environment of the New Testament; Roman imperial mausoleums provided architectural prototypes for early Christian baptistries; and the Eucharistic liturgy of the Constantinian centuries was replete with Roman court ceremonial.

But lest we think that cultural elements have been indiscriminately adopted for Christian worship from the beginning, we must also note that worship has sometimes reacted against the local culture, even from the earliest times. Sunday as the primary day of the week for Christian worship was selected in part because it distinguished Christians from their Jewish and pagan neighbors. Certain Christian festivals may have developed at particular times of the year as a means of counteracting, and sometimes reinterpreting, local pagan celebrations. So perhaps it was with Christmas and the midwinter feasts. Christian worship, because it must relate to the human situation, has always had to interface with human culture, positively or negatively.

From the very beginning of the church, Christian worship has shown a variety of forms; there has never been complete uniformity of practice throughout the church. Perhaps we might like to idealize and think that the worship of the New Testament church was the same in every place. But a good look at the letters of Paul surely paints a different picture. Christians have always worshiped according to their particular time and place. Because of this there has always been variety in the type or styles of worship's constituent elements, such as music and the language and content of prayer. Liturgical diversity has always existed. But the church has also distinguished between what is essential and what is not.

How are we to understand the relationship between culture and worship today? That Christian worship must be in dialogue with the surrounding cultures is clear, for the gospel message is to be proclaimed effectively and authentically to the ends of the earth.

What we are talking about here is the *inculturation* of Christian worship. Inculturation is a process whereby elements of a culture are integrated into the worship of a church, a process that may take place regionally or locally. The goal of inculturation is to create a form or style of worship that a local people can identify with and claim as their own—not that worship should be "relevant" for the sake of "relevance," but that by being authentic to a particular place and time, the worshipers are enabled to participate more fully and intelligently in their worship of God. This points us back to the definition of worship as a response to God's works of salvation with thanksgiving and praise.

Inculturation of worship allows a particular congregation to express themselves more authentically in rendering their sacrifice of praise by using their language, their art forms, their symbols, and stories from their heritage. The goal of inculturation is not human gratification or entertainment (which is an ever-present danger), but the full expression of a person's and a community's devotion to God that then leads to a deepening of the spiritual life of those gathered. By inculturation of worship, we are better equipped to appropriate the many gifts of God to us, because they are expressed in a language or manifested in a form that we understand.

For the sake of the mission and ministry of the church, Christian worship and human culture should be in dialogue. The challenge is to determine the extent, the boundaries, and the shape of that conversation.

One method of inculturation that has been suggested is what is called "dynamic equivalence," which begins not with the local culture but with the church and its worship. In dynamic equivalence, components of worship are re-expressed with something from the culture that is of an equivalent meaning and value. In other words, the content is not changed, only the form. An advantage of this style is that the unity of the tradition may be preserved, while at the same time allowing diversity of expression. A very obvious example would be the use of music in worship. Instead of a four-part hymn accompanied by piano or organ (a

Just as the incarnation of Christ of necessity took place within the confines of a particular culture, and the church itself is the body of Christ in the world, Christian worship is also related to time and place.

musical style familiar in the Western church from the eighteenth century onward), a community might include in its congregational song local styles of music accompanied with local instruments—as long as the content of that song is appropriate for Christian worship. This, in fact, is what the Wesleys did, for in their day the approved song in the Church of England's worship was the psalm. Methodist worship used hymns of "human composition," which were predominantly Scripture paraphrases or a catena of Scripture verses or Scripture images collected around one theme. These hymns were accompanied with popular tunes; some of these tunes, such as those provided by Methodism's first composer, Johann Lampe, can be traced directly to the music of the theater.

Inculturation of worship is a complex and serious issue, and decisions of what or what not to include in worship are very difficult. Several criteria can be used to determine which cultural forms are appropriate. Here three will be mentioned:

PRESERVATION OF THE ESSENTIALS

The proclamation of the Word, the celebration of the sacraments, and the offering of prayer and praise must remain central. Thus it would be appropriate to use local styles of the dramatic arts to interpret biblical stories or events in the history of the church, as long as the historical and biblical substance remains firm. On the other hand, addition of elements to the service that would stress, say, the individualism that is so much a part of popular Western culture—for example, the inclusion of music purely to elevate personal performance or to entertain—should be avoided, for such elements potentially could obscure the importance of the community in worship.

COMPATIBILITY WITH CHRISTIAN DOCTRINES

It must be determined whether a particular cultural element is compatible with basic Christian doctrines such as creation, sin, atonement, justification, and sanctification before it can be introduced into worship. If it is not compatible, it should be asked whether that element could perhaps be subverted—turned upside down and inside out—and *then* be used. To introduce a cultural element that runs counter to the basic doctrines of the faith would be to place the values of the culture above that of the gospel, thereby compromising the good news.

ILLUMINATION OF GOD'S SAVING GRACE

Cultural elements in worship must be able to convey the judgment and the graciousness of God, the hope of future glory promised by God, and the human duty of joyful obedience. They should serve to invite people—all people—into the fullness of the Christian life, and be vehicles of God's own hospitality in Jesus Christ.

We have spoken of the inculturation of local or contemporary elements into Christian worship. But it also must be made clear that sometimes worship should critique or reject components of the human culture; as Christians, we are called upon not to conform to the world, but to be transformed with it (Romans 12:2). Some elements of every culture are sinful, dehumanizing, and, indeed, counter to the gospel; and these should be challenged in worship. Worship, then, can be overtly counter-cultural. For example, cultural patterns of injustice or oppression should be actively countered by the prayers, praises, and actions of worship and thereby reflect the liberating word of the gospel.

While a local character of worship is to be encouraged, it must not be forgotten that congregations are not monocultural, and that the church is broader than a particular congregation. Christian worship should be multicultural, transcultural, and cross-cultural as a living reminder of the complexity and diversity of the body of Christ: a body that has many different members that form a whole (1 Corinthians 12:12-31); a body that recognizes distinctions but does not dwell on them, for among the baptized "there is no longer Jew or Greek, there is no longer slave or free, there is no longer male and female; for all...are one in Christ Jesus" (Galatians 3:28); a body that anticipates the society that will be created when "people will come from east and west, from north and south, and will eat in the kingdom of God" (Luke 13:29).

MULTICULTURAL WORSHIP

From what has been said, it should be clear that an individual does not exist in only one culture. A person may have a primary culture—the family culture into which one is born—but he or she also is a part of many secondary cultures. Each person is multicultural insofar as he or she participates in many cultures or subcultures, such as nationality, ethnic or racial background, place of birth, location of residence, age, gender, marital status, education, class, and economic status. Each individual brings to bear one or more of these cultures—these ways of viewing life and understanding the world—in interpreting every occasion and circumstance.

So when a person comes to Christian worship, that person brings a variety of cultural "eyes" by which to view the gospel. Add more people to the congregation, and there are many more human cultures represented, though obviously some of these cultures will overlap. Because the gospel must take material form, the question then becomes *which* forms from *which* cultures will be selected to mediate the gospel.

Christian worship, then, must always be multicultural because human beings themselves are multicultural. Even when people gather intentionally in groups that accentuate one particular culture, be it by gender, age, or ethnicity, worship must be—as the group itself still is—multicultural, because the people themselves are multicultural. Here we are using the term *multicultural* to refer to the many cultures that coincide not only in the individual but also in a particular gathered assembly. Every congregation consists of a cultural mix, though the degree and extent of that mix will vary from congregation to congregation.

But lest we despair about the difficulty of giving all these cultural voices expression, we must remember that in Christian worship the essentials of the faith are always to remain firmly normative; in the conversation between worship and culture, it is the gospel that must predominate. Therefore, not all cultural voices may be expressed or should be expressed. Two principles may be helpful in the creation of multicultural worship.

First, *a particular cultural element in Christian worship may, and perhaps should, be regarded as appropriate by the several cultures within a congregation, if not indeed by all of them.* Before a new cultural element is adapted or adopted for worship, it must be asked whether most people

In Christian worship the essentials of the faith are always to remain firmly normative; in the conversation between worship and culture, it is the gospel that must predominate.

will be able to recognize the gospel message as mediated by that cultural form, and whether over a period of time that element will facilitate faithful and authentic worship by the congregation or hinder it. Of course, when the element is first introduced, it may not be immediately accepted; but after several uses, the cultural element, transformed by the purposes of the gospel, should be regarded as appropriate for worship, and perhaps even embraced. An example might be the use of dance in worship.

Second, *the cultural element in Christian worship should be recognized by the various cultures as something different from, though related to, its original form.* A cultural element, when it is introduced into Christian worship, cannot simply be transplanted "as is"; the original meaning of the cultural element must be transformed by the gospel. An example of this process comes from the early church. Some communities took over the practice of using candles in worship, not only for illumination, but also to mark the observance of worship itself. Jews and participants in the pagan mystery religions used candles for their worship, but the Christian use of candles carried a different meaning: Jesus, the light of the world, was present in their midst as they gathered to give him praise. The act—the lighting of candles—was the same, but the meaning had been reinterpreted by the church. People in the church could recognize the continuity of the cultural form, but could also see that the custom had taken on a new significance.

So, by the transformation of a cultural element by the gospel, that cultural element is no longer associated with one culture alone, for it becomes a part of the broader, multicultural community. Although the roots of an element may be identified, it should also be seen as something new, recreated for the service of the church.

TRANSCULTURAL WORSHIP

While multicultural worship in a congregation gives attention to the many cultures that are represented in that congregation, transcultural worship begins not with human culture but with the church and its worship. The church as culture both exceeds and encompasses all human cultures—the church transcends all cultural boundaries. In this way the transcultural character of the church reflects the transcultural nature of our God, who knows no bounds: The God who created heaven and earth, the God who defeated death cannot be confined to any particular cultural form. We recognize this transcultural attribute when we speak of the universal church contrasted with the local church. When we are baptized, we are baptized not into membership in the local congregation alone, but into the wider communion that unites all Christians everywhere. The universal church takes in all God's faithful saints—past, present, and future—no matter where they may live, no matter how their styles of worship differ from our own. When a particular congregation gathers for worship, it joins in communion with all the churches of every time and place.

Transcultural worship, therefore, focuses on those universal elements of Christian worship, directly rooted in the gospel, that transcend cultural barriers and are therefore shared between and among cultures. Because the liturgical calendar unites Christians worldwide, its use will readily provide an opportunity for transcultural worship. Although some attention should be given to local custom and geographic variability, the underlying theological themes and central meanings of the liturgical year—such as the birth, death, and resurrection of Jesus, and the sending of the Spirit—should be kept paramount. For Christians of the Northern Hemisphere, who associate Easter with spring and Christmas with winter, a transcultural challenge may be to imagine appropriate metaphors for those holy days that are not dependent on a certain geography.

CROSS-CULTURAL WORSHIP

Because there is "one Lord, one faith, one baptism, one God and Father of all, who is above all and through all and in all" (Ephesians 4:5-6), we who have taken upon ourselves the name of "Christian" are called to be in union with him and with one another. One sign of our baptismal unity—our *koinonia,* our fellowship in Christ—is to share some of the cultural forms that have been used to celebrate the faith by our Christian brothers and sisters in other climes and in different strands of the broad Christian tradition. Cross-cultural worship, then, is worship that includes elements borrowed from other Christian communities, many of which are cultural elements that have already been "evangelized" and transformed for the sake of the gospel. These elements are not directly part of the original gospel, but they have been tried and found helpful in expressing it.

The sharing of worship elements cross-culturally is not to promote a faddish type of cultural pluralism, to encourage a "cafeteria" approach to ordering Christian worship, or to exploit the traditions of other Christian communities. Instead, the purpose of cross-cultural worship, whether it be sharing across confessional or geographical lines, is to express visibly and tangibly the oneness and the fullness of the body of Christ. For example, the "Las Posadas (Service of Shelter for the Holy Family)" in *The United Methodist Book of Worship* (pp. 266–68), though originally from Latin America, can even be a reminder to non-Hispanic congregations of the need to open doors (and hearts) to the One who knocks (Revelation 3:20).

CONCLUSION

The gospel is timeless, but its message embodied or inculturated in Christian worship must always take into account the languages and customs of those who are to hear and live out the good news. Christian worship should enable those gathered to offer authentic and heartfelt thanksgiving to the God of Jesus Christ, who comes to meet them at their particular time and in their particular place.

FOR FURTHER READING

Doxology: The Praise of God in Worship, Doctrine & Life: A Systematic Theology, by Geoffrey Wainwright (New York, NY: Oxford University Press, 1984). See especially Chapter 11.

Liturgical Inculturation: Sacramentals, Religiosity, and Catechesis, by Anscar J. Chupungco (Collegeville, MN: The Liturgical Press, 1992).

Worship: Culture and Theology, by David N. Power (Laurel, MD: The Pastoral Press, 1991).

The purpose of cross-cultural worship...is to express visibly and tangibly the oneness and the fullness of the body of Christ.

16

L. EDWARD PHILLIPS

*Associate Professor of
Historical Theology,
Garrett-Evangelical
Theological Seminary,
Evanston, Illinois*

Whose Worship Is It Anyway?

WHO DECIDES WHAT WE DO IN WORSHIP? ACCORDING TO ¶331.1a–b of the United Methodist *Book of Discipline,* the pastor has the primary responsibility for overseeing worship. Yet pastors also come with a variety of experiences and different kinds of expertise. They may be recent seminary graduates greatly influenced by the worship life and training of the seminary. They may have received training at a church-growth seminar in "seeker-oriented" worship, have a background in old-fashioned Southern revivalism, or have expertise in youth ministry. Pastors bring all of their experiences in worship leadership and training to their appointments, and their understanding of worship will inevitably shape how they contribute leadership to worship in their congregations.

Congregations, on the other hand, have their own distinctive worship practices that have developed over the years. Many of these practices arise organically out of the congregation. First Church in a large city with a big organ and auditioned choir will have a style of worship different from a small rural congregation with limited music resources, just as a congregation in a growing suburb with young professional couples and lots of children will differ from both of these. Some of the established practices come from their previous pastor; and these practices tend to accumulate over the years as clergy come and go.

United Methodist pastors and congregations, however, also are influenced by the official worship materials of the denomination: *The United Methodist Hymnal* is found in almost every pew, and most pastors and some lay leaders also use the *Book of Worship.* Furthermore, there are other worship resources that come from denominational agencies, such as *Interpreter* and *Circuit Rider,* which regularly have worship articles, suggestions, and occasionally complete orders of service.

With all of the voices contributing to and sometimes competing for the shape and content of a congregation's worship life, one may wonder, *Whose worship is it anyway? The pastor's? the congregation's? the denomination's?*

UNDERSTANDING THE QUESTION

Before we can answer this question, we must make sure that we understand what is being asked, because the question "Whose worship?" has a fundamental and important ambiguity about it. Do we mean "Who

Worship Matters: A United Methodist Guide to Ways to Worship (Volume 1) © 1999 Discipleship Resources. Used by permission.

is doing the worship?" Or do we mean "Who is receiving the worship?" Typically, the first meaning is the one we intend to be asking, but the second meaning is really more fundamental to Christian worship. From this perspective, the answer to the question "Whose worship?" must clearly be "It is God's worship."

The Christian philosopher Søren Kierkegaard illustrates this point by comparing worship to the theater.[1] A theatrical production has actors (those who perform the play), prompters (those who help the actors to do their job well), and an audience (those who watch and listen). Kierkegaard suggests that most Christians of his day assume that the actors are the clergy and musicians, who do the performance of worship; the prompter is the Holy Spirit, who inspires the preacher and musicians; and the audience is the congregation, who quietly listen and judge the words of the actors, joining in only when asked to respond.

But, according to Kierkegaard, this is not the way the comparison should work. Rather, in Christian worship, the actors are the whole congregation, who actively pray, praise, sing, and listen; the prompters are the clergy and musicians, who help the congregation do their performance well; and the audience is God, before whom the congregation performs their worship.

If God is the one to whom worship belongs, then it is important that our worship be the sort that God would want. Congregations who do surveys to find out what sort of worship people want, without asking the prior question, "What does God want from our worship?" are doing this backward. While we may not be able to ask God's opinion of our worship by using a questionnaire, we do have some clear indications in the Bible of what God expects.

When the people were quite satisfied with ritual sacrificial worship, Micah warned them: "With what shall I come before the LORD?... He has told you, O mortal, what is good; and what does the LORD require of you but to do justice, and to love kindness, and to walk humbly with your God?" (Micah 6:6, 8). When the Christians in Corinth were rather enthusiastic in their worship, Paul warned them: "All things should be done decently and in order" (1 Corinthians 14:40). Perhaps the most succinct statement of what God expects comes from Jesus: "True worshipers will worship the Father in spirit and truth" (John 4:23). Christian worship, moreover, means serving God with our whole lives, as Paul affirms in Romans 12:1: "Present your bodies as a living sacrifice, holy and acceptable to God, which is your spiritual worship." When we gather for public worship on Sunday morning, or at any other time, our worship serves God through prayer and praise, shaping our lives for prayerful and thankful service of God in the world.

DEFINING THE PARTICIPANTS IN WORSHIP

The first answer, then, to the question "Whose worship?" is "God's worship." The second response must be "Our worship." God is the recipient of worship, but we are the ones who offer worship. But who are the "we" that is implied in the response "Our worship"? This, too, is ambiguous and must be answered on a variety of levels.

The first level is "We, the members of this congregation." As noted at the beginning, each congregation has a distinctive practice of worship that develops over time out of the history of the congregation. Some members of congregations, pastors, lay leaders, choir directors, and so

> The first answer, then, to the question "Whose worship?" is "God's worship." The second response must be "Our worship." God is the recipient of worship, but we are the ones who offer worship.

forth, will have a large role in shaping worship. Over time, however, many people participate in the process by embracing, repeating, and occasionally rejecting the direction of the congregational leaders. On this local level, factors such as geographic locale, economic class, ethnicity, and median educational background all operate to make worship distinctive for each congregation.[2]

Worship must make sense on this local level if it is to be authentic to a particular congregation. This can be both a blessing and a curse. Positively, these factors work incarnationally, enfleshing the gospel in a particular group of real human beings who bring the best of their culture to the worship of God. Negatively, these factors can hinder congregational growth, since geography, class, ethnicity, and so forth, are factors the gospel will need to transcend. Without this transcendent dimension, "enculturated" worship of any kind can become stale, exclusive, and potentially idolatrous. Nevertheless, regardless of how faithful worship is to the transcending power of the gospel, it must make sense to the lives of those who are doing it, or it will not be authentic.

If "we" means the members of our congregation, "we" also refers to members of a particular tradition: United Methodism. At this level, congregations begin to transcend the local church setting. Among other things, our congregation shares with other United Methodists a commitment to John Wesley's understanding of the authentic Christian life: combining religion of the heart with social engagement of the good news in the world.

The United Methodist Church is a connectional church, which means that our shared commitments operate on an institutional level and under a common *Book of Discipline,* which we all follow. In relationship to our worship, we have *The United Methodist Hymnal* and *The United Methodist Book of Worship,* which contain the standard liturgical resources of our church. These two resources help to foster our denominational identity in congregations. We know we are United Methodists, at least in part, when we use our *Hymnal.* As we sing these hymns and pray these prayers, they become important factors that shape who we are as United Methodist Christians.

Our denominational identity can turn into a problem if we allow it to become either triumphalistic (we're the best!) or exclusive (we're the only one!). Indeed, to become either of these is counter to the character of Methodism and its Wesleyan heritage. Nevertheless, it is important that we claim our denominational identity. To use an illustration: In the great symphony of salvation, God has assigned many parts. We United Methodists dishonor God and ourselves if we do not play our own particular part in the symphony. The United Methodist tradition is our distinctive calling as we seek to identify the "our" in "our worship."

Furthermore, our United Methodist identity connects us to the next level of our religious identity: the universal church. Acknowledging the universal church is one of our most basic Christian affirmations, summarized in the Apostles' Creed: "[We] believe in...the holy catholic [universal] church" (*UMH,* 881). Among the marks of this universal church are the preaching of the word of God, as contained in the Scriptures, and the celebration of the sacraments of the Lord's Supper and baptism.

At this universal level, when we say "we," we mean all Christians everywhere, for the church is fundamentally one. Because the church is truly international, embracing all nations and races, our "we" can never exclude any nation or ethnic group. Furthermore, the church is eternal, embracing the faithful throughout all time.

There is an amazing passage in the Great Thanksgiving of our United Methodist ritual for Holy Communion that expresses this understanding of the universal, eternal church: "And so, with your people on earth and all the company of heaven we praise your name and join their unending hymn" (*UMBOW,* p. 36).[3] We don't make worship "happen" when we gather for public worship on Sunday morning; rather, we join in what is *already* taking place on earth and in heaven. Returning to our initial question, "Whose worship?" we respond, "Our worship of the God of Jesus Christ, as members of this congregation who are United Methodist Christians and part of God's universal church—which spans all people, all times, all places, in heaven and on earth!"

You may be thinking, *That is an overwhelming view of worship for those of us who plan services in local congregations!* It is overwhelming. Nevertheless, unless we grasp the fundamental divine and universal significance of our worship, we will forever miss the point. Worship, and even worship planning, can never belong to a few "professionals" who put services together for an audience.

Indeed, according to its Greek etymology, the word *liturgy* (one of the words we use for worship) means "the work (*ergos*) of the people (*leitos*)." Liturgy may be the work of the people, but it is not the work of people who are self-employed. Rather, our worship work is to serve God as the church of Jesus Christ.

ORDERING, PREPARING, AND LEADING WORSHIP

Let us now consider a few ways in which the understanding of worship outlined in this article can give direction to the worship life of a congregation. We'll look at the functions of ordering, preparing, and leading worship.

As I suggested above, we do not make worship happen on Sunday morning; rather, we join in what is already going on—the great universal liturgy of God's church. Still, we must give *order* to worship so that the congregation may participate in this universal prayer and praise. Here Paul's advice to the church at Corinth, mentioned above, would seem to apply. The Corinthians preferred a form of worship that they thought was "Spirit-led" and free. Paul, on the other hand, thought the Corinthians' worship bordered on chaos—hence his advice: "All things should be done decently and in order" (1 Corinthians 14:40).

Practically, the Apostle's advice means that worship needs stability for it to be truly communal. While few contemporary United Methodists will be drawn to the freewheeling worship of the Corinthians, many of us are very attracted to the idea of novelty in worship. Novelty has a place, but it is not the same thing as Spirit-led worship. Too much novelty can thwart true spontaneity because worshipers are not free to participate by memory—or, to put it another way, to participate by heart. If worshipers are forced to keep their noses buried in a bulletin to keep up with what's going on in worship, they will probably find it difficult to give themselves over to worship unselfconsciously.

Stability in the order of worship allows true creativity and spontaneity by giving worship a context. To use a musical metaphor: Jazz musicians are able to engage in creative, spontaneous improvisations because they know the overall structure and direction of what they are playing; and they trust that their fellow musicians know these structures as well. Likewise, the order of worship facilitates true creativity when the overall

> If we are worshiping God by the power of the Spirit of God, worship leaders must learn to stay out of the way.

structure and direction of worship are well-known by the congregation. If worship planners decide that the order of worship needs changing, they should introduce the changes gradually and explain the reasons for the changes.

Worship planners need to recognize that changes must be accepted by the congregation for worship to be the work of the people. Too much change introduced too quickly breeds apathy or outright resistance. Why should a congregation invest their hearts in worship if the order of worship changes arbitrarily with each new pastor or worship committee? Worship planners must be sensitive to a congregation's need for stability.

The order of worship includes music, readings, and prayers that change from week to week, and from season to season. Even with a stable order of worship, worship needs much *preparation*. In preparing worship, planners must be careful to choose music, readings, and prayers that are authentic to the congregation and congruent with Scripture and the Christian tradition. These choices should reflect the full range of who we are as Christians—as members of this congregation who are members of the universal church.

A predominantly middle-class, suburban congregation will likely prefer one style of religious music while an inner-city, Hispanic congregation will prefer another. There certainly is no one preferred Christian style of music. Nevertheless, the content of the hymns and prayers should always be grounded in Scripture and the Christian tradition; such grounding keeps us aware that we are members of the universal church as well as members of our local congregation or ethnic group.

Worship planners should strive to provide music and prayers that are appropriate for the God of Jesus Christ, the One whom we worship. Generally, it is best to try to avoid music and language that are trivial. While worship that is trivial or sentimental may be cute or entertaining, it distracts from focusing on the God who made heaven and earth. This does not mean that worship cannot express humor or that it must be somber. Laughter in worship can be a wonderful, holy experience when it makes us aware of the absurdities within our lives in the presence of the God who loves us. The difference is between going for the cheap laugh (such as telling jokes) and allowing humor to arise from situations (such as doing a good job of reading a humorous story from the Bible). Triviality in worship tempts us to hide from the presence of God, whose Spirit is a fiery wind. It tends to confirm us as we already are, rather than challenge us for what God wants us to be.

Worship must be ordered and prepared, but it must also be *led*. As we noted above in Kierkegaard's model, worship leaders are the prompters for the congregation. But leaders are more than prompters; they also model the action of worship. Worship leaders lead by drawing attention to themselves as *prompters and models;* they don't draw attention to themselves as individuals separated from the congregation's worship. As prompters and models, worship leaders *serve* the congregation in worship; they are servant leaders.

One way to acknowledge that worship involves the whole people of God is to use both clergy and lay worship leaders for the various liturgical ministries of singing, reading Scripture, announcing prayer concerns, and serving the Lord's Supper. Using leaders can become a problem, however, if this is done in a way that suggests that the worship leaders, rather than the entire congregation, are the ones who are really doing the worship. For example, I recently attended a church that listed the worship leaders as "the Participants." I wanted to say, "No, we, the congregation, are the participants." Leaders who are servant leaders will know that they are not the main attraction in worship.

Worship leaders will be able to "Let go and let God," to quote a statement we have all heard. One way to "let go" is to practice. Readers will rehearse readings; musicians will know their music; Communion servers will practice hospitable gestures in distributing the sacrament. Thoughtful rehearsal allows worship leaders to engage freely in worship without undue anxiety.

Also, worship leaders who are empowered by the Spirit will lead without being manipulative. Generally, simplicity of direction will be better than using many words. A simple hand gesture may be sufficient to have a congregation stand for a hymn. At the most, a song leader may say, "Let us stand and sing." However, it is manipulative when a leader tries to stir up enthusiasm by saying, "Let us all stand, take our hymnals, and turn to the page number listed in the bulletin. Now let us lift our joyful voices in song with this wonderful old hymn of the church that is the favorite of us all. And put your heart in it this time." When we "Let go and let God," we do not need to tell the congregation what they should feel. If we are worshiping God by the power of the Spirit of God, worship leaders must learn to stay out of the way.

CONCLUSION

Whose worship is it? God's worship. The church's worship. Our worship. And when we fully affirm all of these claims, we may finally say, "My worship," as we add our voices in the great universal song of praise to God. Only then will we know worship as the duty that pulls us beyond our personal likes and dislikes and as the delight that confirms in us God's gracious love.

FOR FURTHER READING

Blended Worship: Achieving Substance and Relevance in Worship, by Robert E. Webber (Peabody, MA: Hendrickson Publishers, 1996).

Participating in Worship: History, Theory, and Practice, by Craig D. Erickson (Louisville, KY: Westminster John Knox Press, 1989).

Worshiping With United Methodists: A Guide for Pastors and Church Leaders, by Hoyt L. Hickman (Nashville, TN: Abingdon Press, 1996).

ENDNOTES

1 See *Purity of Heart Is to Will One Thing: Spiritual Preparation for the Office of Confession,* by Søren Kierkegaard (New York, NY: Harper & Brothers Publishers, 1948), pp. 180–82. See also the discussion of the "work of worship" in the introduction to Volume II of *Worship Matters,* on pp. 6–9.

2 See the discussions of worship and culture ("Worship and Culture: Inculturating the Good News," pp. 73–79) and of congregational style ("Developing Congregational Style," pp. 86–92) in this volume.

3 From "A Service of Word and Table I," © 1972 by The Methodist Publishing House; © 1980, 1985, 1989, 1992 by The United Methodist Publishing House; from *The United Methodist Book of Worship,* p. 36. Used by permission.

Whose worship is it? God's worship. The church's worship. Our worship. And when we fully affirm all of these claims, we may finally say, "My worship," as we add our voices in the great universal song of praise to God.

11

Developing Congregational Style

MARK W. STAMM

Pastor,
Trinity United Methodist Church,
Roaring Spring, Pennsylvania
and
McKee United Methodist Church,
McKee, Pennsylvania

A SIGNIFICANT PROBLEM WITHIN THE MODERN DISCUSSION OF worship styles is the tendency to speak of the contextual issues—"relevance," "contemporary" versus "traditional"—without reference to historical cases, as if the challenge of contextualization were new. In fact, this challenge is as old as the first-century mission to the Gentiles, and the dynamics of the discussion remain much the same. At the Jerusalem Council, certain leaders insisted: "It is necessary for [the Gentile converts] to be circumcised and ordered to keep the law of Moses" (Acts 15:5). Others disagreed.

Participants in the Council were asking themselves, "Where is God at work in this new missionary situation? Given the demands of this new field, how do we remain accountable to the tradition as we have known and practiced it?" What are the essentials of the faith, and what parts can be adapted, changed, and even deleted? It is the question Saint Paul and other first-century Christians asked. It is the question John Wesley, Francis Asbury, and the early Methodists asked. It is the question every worship leader should ask as he or she works with a congregation. What are the essential aspects and acts of worship? What can be adapted, changed, and even deleted?

With that in mind, we move to our discussion of developing congregational style. Such work requires two essential commitments, each of them expressed in Jesus' summary of the law:

> "You shall love the Lord your God with all your heart, and with all your soul, and with all your mind." This is the greatest and first commandment. And a second is like it: "You shall love your neighbor as yourself." On these two commandments hang all the law and the prophets.
>
> (Matthew 22:37-40)

To develop congregational style with integrity, worship leaders must love God and the gospel, and they must love the people they are called to serve. These two commitments exist in creative tension.

THE FIRST COMMITMENT: ONE MUST LOVE THE GOSPEL

Our first commitment is to love Jesus Christ and the gospel. After listing various destructive behaviors and heretical tendencies, the author of 2 Timothy addressed the young pastor, saying: "But as for you, continue in what you have learned and firmly believed" (2 Timothy 3:14). Such an

Worship Matters: A United Methodist Guide to Ways to Worship (Volume I) © 1999 Discipleship Resources. Used by permission.

admonition is appropriate for all who plan and lead worship. It speaks to a problem facing all people in mission: We might adopt a people's style of dress, learn their language, and come to understand their music, *but then we may also begin to worship their idols.*

Every congregation presents us with this temptation; therefore, we must love the gospel and the God proclaimed in it. Practically speaking, this means the worship leader will insist on certain liturgical and sacramental norms that must be observed (and even defended) if the worship is to be *Christian* worship. Teaching and maintaining basic Christian norms has always been the work of bishops, pastors, and other leaders in the church, and keeping that duty has led to more than a little sacrifice.

What, then, should we defend? First, let there be no shedding of blood over the color and design of paraments, the number and size of candles, and whether one should kneel or stand for Communion! Taking our cue from the Jerusalem Council and its discussion of the mission to the Gentiles, it is best if we keep our list of norms rather short (Acts 15:19-20). Another text from Acts suggests three liturgical norms: "They devoted themselves to the apostles' teaching and fellowship, to the breaking of bread and the prayers" (Acts 2:42). Each of these is expressed in the Basic Pattern of Worship of The United Methodist Church (*UMH,* pp. 2–5) and in "The Articles of Religion" (*BOD,* ¶62, pp. 57–64. See Article V, "Of the Sufficiency of the Holy Scriptures for Salvation," as well as Articles VI, XIII, XV, XVI, XVII, XVIII, XIX, and XXII).

The first liturgical norm is the centrality of the Holy Scriptures: "[devotion] to the apostles' teaching." The people need to hear the Word of God; the orderly reading and preaching of the Holy Scriptures is the classical means for accomplishing that. The Revised Common Lectionary, or something like it, provides a means for this ordered reading.

The second liturgical norm is a clear emphasis on corporate sacramental practice: "[devotion] to fellowship" and "the breaking of bread." The church exists in communion (that is, *koinonia* or "fellowship") with Jesus Christ and *for* communion with Christ. As the writer of 1 John expressed it: "We declare to you what we have seen and heard so that you also may have *fellowship* with us; and truly our fellowship is with the Father and with his Son Jesus Christ" (1:3, emphasis added).

Those who "proclaim the faith of the church" insist that such communion begins in the Baptismal Covenant and is sustained at the Lord's Table. John Wesley understood these dynamics, teaching "the duty of constant communion"[1] and urging elders of the fledgling American church "to administer the Supper of the Lord on every Lord's Day."[2] While I look for the restoration of that practice, it is enough for our purposes simply to remind ourselves that even when the Eucharist is not celebrated, we anticipate the next such occasion. We continue to live in communion with Christ and one another, and we look forward to the great "marriage supper of the Lamb" (Revelation 19:9). Our worship should reflect that anticipation.

The third liturgical norm is that the prayer and praise of the church be expressed in forms that encourage and allow congregational participation: "[devotion to] the prayers." We believe that we are the body of Christ, and that each member has a contribution to make through "psalms and hymns and spiritual songs," through litanies and unison prayers, through the "Amen" (Ephesians 5:18-20; 1 Corinthians 12:27; 14:26-33). Therefore, a presentation designed to entertain a passive congregation is not adequate Christian worship. Nor will it suffice if the

To develop congregational style with integrity, worship leaders must love God and the gospel, and they must love the people they are called to serve. These two commitments exist in creative tension.

worship leaders—be they pastors, choirs, or praise ensembles—do all of the singing and praying. God's people need some sort of a liturgy, some recognizable means that enables corporate participation.

To worship with integrity, we must love these norms—biblical focus, sacramental foundations, and corporate participation—and we must hold them as bedrock principles. To speak of norms, however, is not to speak of a uniform liturgy. The same style and form of worship will not fit every circumstance, hence the second commitment: One must love the people.

THE SECOND COMMITMENT: ONE MUST LOVE THE PEOPLE

How does a worship leader love the people? Keeping the basic liturgical norms in mind, she or he engages a community and a congregation and works at the basic missional task. To use Wesley's phrase, one "offers Christ" to the people. All that I have discussed to this point is prologue to this work of developing congregational style.[3]

What do we mean by *style?* Indeed, a common use of the term betrays a critical misunderstanding. We speak of offering or developing various styles of worship; many times, *traditional* and *contemporary* are the terms of choice. One might hear about experiments with African American or Latino styles. We speak of choosing and developing styles, or even *abandoning* styles, as if one could simply pick a new style like one picks a new suit—as it were, giving up one's pinstripe-suit worship for a more casual look, say blue blazer with an overhead projector.

However, the reality expressed in the word *style* goes much deeper. One cannot learn a new style simply by mimicking techniques from other places and traditions. For example, it is unlikely that a predominantly white, suburban choir will sing "We Shall Overcome" in the same style manifested by an urban African American choir. The suburban choir could learn the tones, rhythms, and movements of their African American sisters and brothers, but they could not learn their style. Style expresses something deeper than technique. It is an expression of collective faith and experience, a corporate expression of a community's inner life and faith, a corporate expression of their value system.

Style is like the spring that proceeds from a powerful underground stream—it points to a complex and deep spiritual reality. According to this understanding of the term, style is less a matter of choice and development and more a matter of *spiritual discernment.* Style manifests a community's spiritual gifts and vocation. Therefore, one does not choose it; but rather, one discerns it, taking seriously what God has called into being. Only then does one consciously develop it.

Equipped with this understanding of style, we come back to the basic work of loving the churches and communities we serve. Such a specific loving of one's neighbor is the essential work of the missionary, whether he or she serves in Kenya or Kenosha. Such missional work is informed by the Wesleyan understanding of *prevenient grace,* which literally means "the grace that goes before us." Wherever we go to proclaim the gospel and worship the Lord, whatever good we try to do or evil we try to resist, we believe that God is preparing the way for us, making our work possible. Believing in prevenient grace can help relieve the pressure many of us feel to implement all the goals of the liturgical movement or achieve the next great church growth success. Understanding the prevenient workings of the Holy Spirit also encourages us to keep our eyes and ears open.

A good worship leader will seek to discern the movement of God's Spirit in a particular church and community. Like an observant parent, he or she will rejoice in the personality God is giving to a particular group of people and will seek to encourage and shape it, a work that is accomplished through persistent, committed listening and observation. The leader will ask where these people work and what this work is like. An observant worship leader will ask what sort of hymns these people sing with special fervor and why. Would Easter be complete if we omitted "Up From the Grave He Arose" (*UMH*, 322)? What does it mean when many of them can sing "Amazing Grace" (*UMH*, 378) without looking at their hymnals? Do they have any other hymns memorized? When my congregation in Roaring Spring has a hymn-sing, almost invariably someone picks "Here I Am, Lord" (*UMH*, 593). What does this say about the unique personality of the congregation?

The attentive worship leader will ask: What are the people concerned about? angry or happy about? What are their most important religious memories and experiences, and how have they expressed them? What happens when you as worship leader make an altar call? Are the people thrilled, embarrassed, indifferent? What does it mean when you sprinkle water on them during an Easter Vigil and they are still talking about it two months later? What does it mean when people can recount the details of a summer camp worship service thirty to fifty years after the fact? What are the key congregational stories? Why do they tell stories about certain people who were healed and others who died? Why is any particular story told over and over?

These questions and others like them point to meanings that one must discern with much patient listening and observation. Effective worship leaders will do this listening and observing and then will allow the concerns and corporate identity of the community to be expressed in their worship. When that happens, the liturgy becomes a catholic expression of the *community's faith*.

The same insight can be applied to the work of evangelism. Earlier I mentioned my conviction that one cannot learn a worship style by simply mimicking other worship styles or traditions. (Nor, for that matter, does one learn a worship style by attending a seminar, by reading a book, or by buying the right set of CDs.) In saying this I am not rejecting the church growth movement, but I am critiquing the way its insights are marketed. The most successful examples of ministry to the unchurched are built on the foundation of painstaking efforts to listen to the concerns and aspirations of a community: Where do they work? What do they worry about? What kinds of music do they listen to? What evokes wonder and awe? When worship leaders sit with a community and discern the answers to questions like these, they can develop a missional-liturgical style that has integrity. There is no quick fix, no add-water-and-stir method. One must sit with the people, listen, and discern how the Holy Spirit is at work in their midst.

DISCERNING CONGREGATIONAL STYLE

Let me relate a case from my pastoral experience that speaks to the issues of discerning and developing congregational style. I am the pastor of two United Methodist congregations in the Central Pennsylvania Conference. The first, Trinity Church in Roaring Spring, has about four hundred members and is my primary responsibility. The second, McKee

Style manifests a community's spiritual gifts and vocation. Therefore, one does not choose it; but rather, one discerns it, taking seriously what God has called into being.

Church in McKee, has a membership of about fifty. They are both fine churches, but they are not the same.

Trinity Church enthusiastically embraced the 1989 *Hymnal* along with its rites for the Baptismal Covenant and its services of Word and Table. I was sent there because they wanted to celebrate the Eucharist frequently and read the weekly lessons prescribed by the Lectionary. They are willing to sing a wide variety of hymns. When I asked them to buy a processional cross, a paschal candle, and a new pulpit Bible in the New Revised Standard Version, they did so with virtually no questions asked. It is a wonderful place for me to serve, and I am pleased that God and the bishop sent me there.

But, I am also glad to be the pastor at McKee, because they have taught me much. On my first day in this appointment, I found the following note on my desk: "McKee wants to go back to the old hymnal." Here I was, returning from four years of graduate school, having done doctoral work in liturgy, and one of my churches did not want to use *The United Methodist Hymnal!* They wanted to give up using the *Hymnal* and go back to their gospel songbook. Didn't they know that our *Hymnal* is the envy of churches far and wide? Didn't they know that it is an effective mixture of evangelical and catholic elements, with classical hymns and gospel hymns, and choruses from the charismatic movement? To this day, I don't know who sent the note, nor do I care, for it was one of the best things that ever happened to me, like a final exam on my graduate work. But, that's jumping ahead of the story.

Was I going to shelve the church's official *Hymnal?* Hardly! Did I need to stop and listen? Absolutely! I had spent the better part of two years working with Professor Linda Clark of Boston University, studying style and religious identity in churches, and here was a church trying to assert and defend *their style*. I had learned from Dr. Clark and from the mountains of field notes we compiled that the liturgical expression appropriate in one place is not necessarily appropriate in another.

So I responded like this: I asked the pianist at McKee Church, Eva Davis, to function as the director of music for the congregation and as the representative of the people and their musical style. I told her I would pick the hymns for the Trinity Church service, but that for the McKee service she could overrule me any time she wished on any or all the hymns. It was something of a risk, but it was better than giving up on *The United Methodist Hymnal;* and it was probably the only way to handle the problem.

At McKee, then, worship proceeds as follows: I read the lectionary lessons and preach, usually on the Gospel reading. We celebrate the Eucharist at least once a month. (Trinity Church, by the way, celebrates weekly during the Advent-Christmas and Lent-Easter cycles.) Eva has the final say on all the hymns. She is quite good at it, in both practical and insightful ways. For instance, one Sunday I had picked "Silence, Frenzied, Unclean Spirit" (*UMH*, 264) to accompany Mark 1:21-28, the pericope in which Jesus silences the unclean spirit and orders it to "come out of him." She substituted "There's Within My Heart a Melody" (*UMH*, 380). Fair enough! Only the most adventurous congregations sing "Silence, Frenzied, Unclean Spirit." Certainly, the musical style of "There's Within My Heart a Melody" made more sense for McKee; but the text was surprisingly appropriate. Read the second stanza:

All my life was wrecked by sin and strife,
discord filled my heart with pain;
Jesus swept across the broken strings,
stirred the slumbering chords again.
(*UMH,* 380; emphasis added)[4]

Eva had done her homework well, relating demon possession to a life filled with strife, discord, and pain. The image of Jesus sweeping across "broken strings" to heal the pain of a troubled soul reminds me of David playing his lyre to ease King Saul's troubled mind (1 Samuel 16:14-23).

My favorite surprise from Eva, however, came on Transfiguration Sunday in 1997. I had chosen "O Wondrous Sight! O Vision Fair" (*UMH,* 258) to accompany that day's Gospel lesson, Mark 9:2-9, an account of Jesus and the disciples on the Mount of Transfiguration. "O Wondrous Sight! O Vision Fair" is a very strong theological text. Read the first stanza:

O wondrous sight! O vision fair
of glory that the church shall share,
which Christ upon the mountain shows,
where brighter than the sun he glows!
(*UMH,* 258)[5]

Eva substituted "Fairest Lord Jesus" (*UMH,* 189), which did not make sense to me *until we sang the third stanza.* Read it:

Fair is the sunshine, fairer still the moonlight,
and all the twinkling starry host:
Jesus shines brighter, Jesus shines purer
than all the angels heaven can boast.
(*UMH,* 189; emphasis added)[6]

This stanza provides an excellent commentary on the Transfiguration. Indeed, I looked to see if the editors of *The United Methodist Hymnal* and *The United Methodist Book of Worship* had made that connection. They had not. As you can see, McKee Church's pianist did not simply pick the "old favorites" every Sunday.

CONCLUSION

Our system at Trinity Church and at McKee Church works far better than I would have imagined. But why should I be surprised? When worship leaders take the happy risk of loving both the gospel and the people, they give the unique style of congregations and communities an opportunity to emerge. When that style is discerned and affirmed, worship leaders can develop it to the glory of God, in service of the one holy, catholic, and apostolic church.

FOR FURTHER READING

Food for Pilgrims: A Journey With Saint Luke, by Dwight W. Vogel (Akron, OH: O.S.L. Publications, 1996).

Liturgical Inculturation: Sacramentals, Religiosity, and Catechesis, by Anscar J. Chupungco (Collegeville, MN: The Liturgical Press, 1992).

Music in Churches: Nourishing Your Congregation's Musical Life, by Linda J. Clark (Bethesda, MD: The Alban Institute, 1994).

Trouble at the Table: Gathering the Tribes for Worship, by Carol Doran and Thomas H. Troeger (Nashville, TN: Abingdon Press, 1992).

When worship leaders take the happy risk of loving both the gospel and the people, they give the unique style of congregations and communities an opportunity to emerge.

ENDNOTES

1 See "The Duty of Constant Communion," by John Wesley, in *The Works of John Wesley,* Volume VII (Grand Rapids, MI: Zondervan Publishing House, n.d.), pp.147–57.

2 See "Bristol, September 10, 1784," by John Wesley, in *The Letters of the Rev. John Wesley, A.M.: Sometime Fellow of Lincoln College, Oxford,* edited by John Telford, B.A. (London: The Epworth Press, 1931), p. 239.

3 My thinking about style has been deeply influenced by the work I have done with my colleagues Linda Clark, Joanne Swenson, and Gregory Allen on the Boston University Worship, Music, and Religious Identity Project.

4 From Stanza 2 of "There's Within My Heart a Melody" in *The United Methodist Hymnal* (Nashville, TN: The United Methodist Publishing House, 1989), 380.

5 From Stanza 1 of "O Wondrous Sight! O Vision Fair" in *The United Methodist Hymnal* (Nashville, TN: The United Methodist Publishing House, 1989), 258.

6 From Stanza 3 of "Fairest Lord Jesus" in *The United Methodist Hymnal* (Nashville, TN: The United Methodist Publishing House, 1989), 189.

The Future of African American Worship

MARION A. JACKSON

Southwest District Superintendent, Southern New Jersey Conference, Cherry Hill, New Jersey

AFRICAN AMERICANS HAVE BEEN A PART OF METHODISM IN the New World since the days of John Wesley. From the time John Wesley baptized two black Methodists in 1758, setting an example of evangelism among slaves, African Americans have been co-partners in the evolution of the Methodist church in America. Grant Shockley, in the introduction to his book *Heritage and Hope,* states: "Since [Methodism's] inception in this country in the 1760's, a black presence has influenced every decade and development of its more than two-hundred-year history."[1] Blacks were attracted to early Methodist worship. It was revivalistic, with fervent preaching and lively singing. Methodism was an experiential faith that appealed to the African sense of the sacredness of everyday life.

It is important at this point to distinguish the difference between worship and liturgy, because this article is about both. To worship is to ascribe glory to God; it is those acts done before God to glorify God. Liturgy is a part of worship; it has to do with the rites, symbols, and form that worship takes. The African American experience in worship continues to reshape Christian liturgy.

WORSHIP AND LITURGY IN AFRICAN AMERICAN HISTORY

Blacks are a spiritual people for whom religion and faith are the central locus of life. During the days of slavery, despite the threat of severe punishment, slaves would often "steal away" to the brush for secret prayer meetings.[2] During the years of slavery, blacks outnumbered whites where there was mixed worship. Early African American worship was enthusiastic, participatory, and filled with the spontaneity of the Spirit. Virtually every aspect of worship was related to everyday life and living and was filled with testimony and witnessing.

With the passing of time, worship in the black church began to change and diversify. Today, African American worship includes a range of styles. As Lawrence Murphy states: "In the general populace there are worship styles and behaviors that correlate to differing socio-economic identifications, and black religious life reflects this as well.... Similar factors of location seem to figure in how one expresses public religious devotion."[3] Within any community of people, regardless of color, there is a variety of preferences and personalities. Some people are by nature more contemplative and introspective. Others are more demonstrative and exuberant in expressing themselves. To suggest that either African or African American worship is nonstop sound and movement is to be misinformed. Within African American spirituality the commonality between the two extremes is the depth of feeling and the willingness to give freedom of expression to others. But, in some instances, whole congregations began to insist on worship that was "reverent" and therefore silent. Passion gave way to propriety and order. The more educated and suburban the congregation became, the less it wanted to "shout." To some degree, vigorous outward expression became associated with the poor, uneducated underclass.

Black Methodists were and are generally upwardly mobile. The Methodist Church founded many educational institutions for African Americans, beginning with the many elementary schools established by the Freedman's Aid Society, which was begun in 1866. One hundred years later there were ten colleges, a school of medicine, and a theological school. The effect of education on the worship life of black Americans across denominational lines was sometimes manifested as a desire for more liturgical and staid worship. Certainly, not all black churches, not even all black Methodist churches, responded in this manner; but until recent years, a congregation's self-image (which determines worship style) was based on economics, geography, lifestyle, or education.

Although worship remained restrained even through the Civil Rights Movement, the pendulum began to swing back to a more exuberant style in the 1970's. This is reflected especially in the music in the black church. Through music we can see a movement that corresponds to world events and the impact the world has on the African American community. The thread winds from Negro spirituals seeking God's deliverance to the early twentieth-century struggle with Jim Crow to the freedom songs of the Civil Rights Movement to the present threshold of the new millennium.[4] The music produced by young black Christians has an insistent, heavy rhythm section. The lyrics are simple and repetitive. Short phrases are sung over and over to an ever-increasing crescendo. It is almost as if young people are crying out for some new thing that has not come yet to the church.

Until just after the middle of the twentieth century, the church was the center of life for African Americans. It was the foundation of their social life, the source of information about and interpreter of the world and society, as well as a place of worship. John E. Brandon describes black worship as "Christian worship informed by an African heritage, the Bible, and a Western understanding of Christianity under the conditions of slavery."[5] One hundred years ago it was sufficient to the need, but as time has passed the need has changed.

WORSHIP, LITURGY, AND THEOLOGY IN THE AFRICAN AMERICAN EXPERIENCE

The African American church is at a threshold. Crossing this threshold will require a new liturgy. It is not a matter of returning to our roots but of moving forward to the mission to which God has called us. The Christianity that we have been exposed to in white churches is a Western liturgy that suits Western needs. During slavery, even those blacks who were participating members of white churches sought refuge in the hidden places of worship at night. It was there that the liturgy reflected the spirit, psyche, and needs of the African American people. It was there that the Negro spirituals were born. The call to worship began in the fields as workers sang "Steal Away to Jesus." That liturgy was vastly different. Now the black church must write its own liturgy again. A new liturgy will not necessarily be different in style but rather in psyche. White Western worship is designed to describe what people think about God. John Brandon writes: "The [black] worship experience shows what black people 'feel' about God."[6]

How do African Americans feel about God? And how do we hear the message? The second chapter of the Book of Acts describes how the Holy Spirit gave birth to the church in a way that allowed the message to be heard and understood by all. What God had done, was doing, and would do was communicated so that people were converted and transformed: "We hear, each of us, in our own native language" (Acts 2:8). Hearing in one's own language refers to more than just words; it includes hearing within a framework of understanding.

That framework of understanding is what helps people make the connection between the gospel and the needs in their lives. Christ meets us where we are and speaks our language. He goes to the tax collector's table and home. He visits the well to talk to a woman about water. He speaks to fishermen about catching fish. The promised Holy Spirit comes and is revealed in a way that can be heard and understood by all. People find or return to Christ through the mediation of those who speak a language that they can comprehend. How can the church speak the language of the African American?

James Cone, one of the leading figures in black theology, articulates how African Americans feel about God, giving words to the reality of the gospel message in ways that can be heard by black ears. How do we hear? First of all, Cone posits a theology that describes a God who is in a positive relationship with blacks, and who is the God for blacks here and now rather than only in heaven. Cone continues: "This is the key to Black Theology. It refuses to embrace any concept of God which makes black suffering the will of God.... To be the God of black people, he must be against the oppression of black people."[7]

These were radical thoughts in 1969 when Cone's book was printed. This "God of the oppressed" was revolutionary. For according to the gospel, God is present among human beings right now, actively opposing the forces that seek to hold us in bondage. And, concludes Cone, theology and the church have the duty to discern the places where God is at work in our world, so that Christians can join forces with God in the struggle against evil.[8]

As more black theologians and historians began to investigate the place and role of people of African descent in the history of the Bible, the church, and the world, the concept of God shifted. God was no longer a passive bystander who would reward in heaven, but rather an avenger and advocate who sought justice now. This was the crux of the Civil Rights Movement. With it the language of society and the church began to change. Unfortunately, society changed faster than the church.

The black cultural revolution brought about a change in symbols, rituals, and words. Slogans such as "Black Is Beautiful" were revolutionary. *Black* had been considered an unacceptable term for describing people of color. *Afrocentrality* was born before the word was coined as people began to reappropriate all that was considered African. The church was left behind.

The African American church is at a threshold. Crossing this threshold will require a new liturgy. It is not a matter of returning to our roots but of moving forward to the mission to which God has called us.

In the midst of the Civil Rights Movement, despite the leadership of clergy like Dr. Martin Luther King, Jr., and others, the black church did not immediately make the connection between the social gospel message and the worship life of the people. The unchurched heard and responded to both Christian and non-Christian "street liturgies." George Garrelts describes these street liturgies as liturgical acts and symbols that are done out in the world and not behind the pulpit: "[These] street liturgies are oriented to seeking political, social, and economic change for black people.... [Martin Luther] King's activity in the streets of Montgomery and Birmingham demonstrated that the power is present in the black church to produce a public worship oriented to social change."[9] He goes on to say that even though the powerful leaders who did street liturgies are gone, it is still possible to "begin to fashion Sunday liturgies capable of doing more about changing social structures."[10]

THE LANGUAGE OF THE LITURGY AND SONG

Liturgy means "the work of the people." Teresita Weind defines liturgical ministry as "the ritualized expression of the hopes and aspirations residing in those who constitute the local church."[11] There are those who sometimes say they are not liturgical or they do not want to be liturgical. These people reject "being liturgical" because for them liturgy has become synonymous with that which is stilted, mechanical, lacking in spirit—and, most of all, not black.

But it is difficult to be totally non-liturgical. To be so is to have chaos and disorder. African Americans are people of ritual; as such, they can embrace the concept of liturgy if not the word itself. What better example of liturgy as work of the people than in the old-time singing and lining out of hymns? Congregational response to black preaching is liturgy as the exchange between preacher and congregation is necessary for the preaching to be effective. Participatory worship in a Spirit-filled church can be liturgy at its best. It is the work of the people as they express their hopes and aspirations.

The parts of the standard liturgy in The United Methodist Church (*UMH*, pp. 6–31) have meaning and purpose. They can become more powerful when understood and used in a context that gives expression to the black experience. For example, the Great Thanksgiving recounts biblical history and the acts of God in Jesus Christ. It speaks of who Jesus is and what he has done. This Eucharistic prayer can include what God has done for and through black people. We may include in the Great Thanksgiving how Jesus delivered us from the captivity of slave labor in southern cotton fields and the oppression of overseers. The escape on the underground railroad is much like the experience the Israelites had going to the Promised Land. Consider also how through Christ we may sit in any seat on a bus and are no longer required to pay a poll tax. God broke the bonds of segregated facilities, Jim Crow laws, and inequality in many forms.

It has been said that without this remembering, blacks lose their history and their reason for giving thanks. When statements about black history are included as acts of God within the Communion liturgy, the language of the people is spoken. So, too, with the thanksgiving over the water in the baptismal liturgy, as we recount the many rivers African Americans have crossed.

LITANIES, PRAYERS, AND THE PSALTER

Many African American pastors have begun to write their own litanies, calls to worship, and responsive readings. This provides an opportunity for the congregation to express their hopes, pains, joys, and sorrows in a language that can be heard by black ears.

Some of the sung responses for the Psalter in *The United Methodist Hymnal* can be intimidating for any congregation lacking trained voices and musicians. It becomes a foreign language, providing an excuse to be "non-liturgical." A creative way to use the existing Psalter is to create different sung responses that build upon the imagery and language of the psalm. Consider "Psalm 40:1-11" (*UMH*, 774) with the refrain from the hymn "My Hope Is Built" (*UMH*, 368). "On Christ the solid rock I stand, all other ground is sinking sand"[12] is fitting and is the language of the people. With creativity it is possible to find many musical responses.

SYMBOLS AND VESTMENTS

Symbols and vestments are changing throughout the African American church. Stoles have become multicolored, often reflecting a theological or sociological position rather than the liturgical calendar. This is manifested by Afrocentric vestments: Altar hangings, banners, stoles, and robes made of Kinte cloth and designs have become commonplace. The cut of many vestments resembles the clothing in Africa.

Symbols, too, are being reexamined and revised. In some instances the picture of Christ reflects the face of the congregation. Pictures of a Scandinavian Jesus with blond hair and blue eyes are noticeably absent. Jesus has woolly hair and olive to chestnut skin. Sunday school rooms are adorned with pictures of African and African American heroes. George Garrelts even suggests using the iron pot as a symbol of the secret liturgical life of the slaves.[13]

OUR SPECIAL TIMES

Women's Day and Men's Day are not the same as United Methodist Women's Day and United Methodist Men's Day. (Some United Methodist congregations have both.) These special days as well as family celebrations have been common in the black church for generations.

New additions that celebrate African American history have emerged. Three in particular come to mind: the celebration of the birthday of the Reverend Dr. Martin Luther King, Jr.; the celebration of Black History Month; and Kwanzaa.

These three distinctly African American celebrations are not intrinsically Christian but are part of the heritage of people of African descent. These celebrations blur the distinction between the sacred and the profane. The founder of Kwanzaa designed this holiday as a cultural expression. Indeed, Dr. Maulana Ron Karenga did not consider himself a Christian; but almost thirty years later, this celebration held in community centers and churches often begins with prayer and incorporates religious elements.

AFRICAN AMERICAN WORSHIP AND CONTEMPORARY WORSHIP

One of the gifts African Americans bring to the larger church is passionate spirituality and worship. The words *emotional* and *emotionalism*

> One of the gifts African Americans bring to the larger church is passionate spirituality and worship.

are not accurate descriptions of the black experience in worship. African American worship does not connote out-of-control, nonsensical actions, but rhythmic and deeply felt sensations that are expressed outwardly. Much of what is characterized as "contemporary" in worship incorporates this freedom in worship.

African Americans have appropriated some of the elements of Euro-American contemporary worship, but they have given these elements new names so that they can be expressed in a language that can be heard. For example, liturgical dancers are often called praise dancers, which is an accurate description of what the dancers are doing.

Praise bands and praise singing are little more than opening devotions in the black church. The praise time of contemporary worship is much like what the black church calls devotions. The major difference is that people of African descent are generally oral people rather than people of the written page. Songs of praise are generally spontaneous, with a leader either lining out a hymn or singing the verses while the congregation acts as audience. (I doubt if overhead projectors will ever catch on.)

Many congregations are experiencing a change in music style as more churches are introducing a new kind of gospel music. This, too, is an indication of returning to the language of the people. The emphasis in the new gospel music is on rhythm rather than on melody. This is a reclaiming of the drum as central to the ritual and spiritual life of African American people. One concern with the advent of new gospel music is the tendency for it to be a "spectator" activity that takes up a significant part of worship. While the music itself is Afrocentric, its use becomes non-participatory. Congregational singing is an important part of worship in the black experience. It is a testimony to God and a reflection of the people. I suspect that at some point the rhythm will cease being directed at the people but will be an expression of the people. It is the language of the people. Another concern over the new gospel music is that it may lead to a neglect of the rich heritage of hymnody—especially the Negro spirituals—bequeathed to us by both black and white composers. While such neglect is a real danger, it need not happen if congregations will intentionally incorporate hymns into worship.

The influence of African Americans on United Methodist worship continues. At the general church level, African Americans have a part in the shaping of United Methodist worship and liturgy by virtue of serving on committees, boards, and agencies. Blacks have contributed to the music ministry of the church. *The United Methodist Hymnal* includes music arranged or composed by blacks. The supplement, *Songs of Zion,* has added richly to the music repertoire in our churches.

As the black church begins to speak in its own language, it will be able to add even more to the universal church, the body of Christ. The full expression of the wholeness of life is manifested when all are able to hear in their own language the gospel message of Jesus Christ.

FOR FURTHER READING

African American Christian Worship, by Melva W. Costen (Nashville, TN: Abingdon Press, 1993).

Lead Me Guide Me: The African American Catholic Hymnal (Chicago, IL: G.I.A. Publications, 1987).

O Freedom!: Afro-American Emancipation Celebrations, by William H. Wiggins, Jr. (Knoxville, TN: University of Tennessee Press, 1987).

Praise the Lord: Litanies, Prayers and Occasional Services, by Gennifer B. Brooks (Lima, OH: CSS Publishing, 1996).

Praising in Black and White: Unity & Diversity in Christian Worship, by Brenda E. Aghahowa (Cleveland, OH: Pilgrim Press, 1996).

Songs of Zion, edited by J. Jefferson Cleveland (Nashville, TN: Abingdon Press, 1981).

The African American Holiday of Kwanzaa: A Celebration of Family, Community and Culture, by Maulana Karenga (Los Angeles, CA: The University of Sankore Press, 1989).

The Ministry of Music in the Black Church, by J. Wendell Mapson, Jr. (Valley Forge, PA: Judson Press, 1984).

Worship Across Cultures: A Handbook, by Kathy Black (Nashville, TN: Abingdon Press, 1998).

ENDNOTES

1 From *Heritage and Hope: The African-American Presence in United Methodism,* edited by Grant S. Shockley (Nashville, TN: Abingdon Press, 1991), p. 11.

2 See *Slave Religion: The "Invisible Institution" in the Antebellum South,* by Albert J. Raboteau (New York, NY: Oxford University Press, 1980), pp. 212–19.

3 From "African American Worship and the Interpretation of Scripture," by Lawrence Murphy, in *Ex Auditu: An International Journal of Theological Interpretation of Scripture,* Volume 8 (Allison Park, PA: Pickwick Publications, 1992), p. 95.

4 Jon Michael Spencer does an excellent job of tracing black religious musical history and the relationship of music to world events in his book, *Protest & Praise: Sacred Music of Black Religion* (Minneapolis, MN: Augsburg Fortress Publishers, 1990).

5 Printed with permission from "Worship in the Black Experience," by John E. Brandon, in *The Journal of the Interdenominational Theological Center,* Vol. XIV, Numbers 1 and 2, Fall 1986–Spring 1987 (Atlanta, GA: The ITC Press, 1986), pp. 109–10. This article—now with slight editorial changes—originally appeared in *Nexus* (Boston, MA: Boston University School of Theology, 1979).

6 Printed with permission from "Worship in the Black Experience," by John E. Brandon, in *The Journal of the Interdenominational Theological Center,* Vol. XIV, Numbers 1 and 2, Fall 1986–Spring 1987 (Atlanta, GA: The ITC Press, 1986), p. 112. This article—now with slight editorial changes—originally appeared in *Nexus* (Boston, MA: Boston University School of Theology, 1979).

7 From *Black Theology and Black Power,* by James H. Cone (Maryknoll, NY: Orbis Books, 1997), pp. 124–25. Copyright © 1997 by James H. Cone. Original edition © 1969 by Harper & Row.

8 See *Black Theology and Black Power,* by James H. Cone (Maryknoll, NY: Orbis Books, 1997), p. 39.

9 From "Black Power and Black Liturgy," by George Garrelts, in *The Journal of Religious Thought,* Volume 39, Number 1, Spring–Summer 1982 (Washington, DC: Howard University Divinity School, 1982), p. 34.

10 From "Black Power and Black Liturgy," by George Garrelts, in *The Journal of Religious Thought,* Volume 39, Number 1, Spring–Summer 1982 (Washington, DC: Howard University Divinity School, 1982), p. 35.

11 From "Woman Clothed in Black," by Teresita Weind, SND deN, in *Liturgical Ministry,* Volume 1 (Fall 1992), p. 134.

12 From "My Hope Is Built," by Edward Mote, in *The United Methodist Hymnal* (Nashville, TN: The United Methodist Publishing House, 1989), 368.

13 See "Black Power and Black Liturgy," by George Garrelts, in *The Journal of Religious Thought,* Volume 39, Number 1, Spring–Summer 1982 (Washington, DC: Howard University Divinity School, 1982), p. 42. Slave folklore tells of turning the iron pot upside down near prayer meeting places to keep the slave master from hearing what was happening.

As the black church begins to speak in its own language, it will be able to add even more to the universal church, the body of Christ.

13

The Future of Asian American Worship

YOUNG HO CHUN

*Professor of Theology,
Saint Paul School of Theology,
Kansas City, Missouri*

SINCE WE ARE ALL LIMITED BY TIME AND SPACE, IT IS IMPOSSIBLE to foresee what the future of Asian American United Methodist congregations may be with regard to their worship patterns and life. Thus, this article is not an attempt to foretell the future of Asian American United Methodist worship; rather, it outlines what may be a *desirable* future direction for such worship. This calls for careful diagnosis and evaluation of the current liturgical patterns and worship life of Asian American United Methodists.

THE BOUNDARY OF CULTURE

First of all, what do we mean by *Asian American?* The term often refers to those "naturalized" Americans who came from the Asian Pacific Rim, and their direct descendants and relatives. Hence Asian American United Methodists are people who belong to these groups and who participate in spiritual activities offered by The United Methodist Church. Even though I have worshiped in Thailand, Taiwan, and China, I will limit the discussion in this article to my observations and worship experiences among Japanese, Chinese, and Korean congregations in the United States of America.

I do not presume that these visits and worship experiences give me a full understanding of the cultural and spiritual richness of Japanese American, Chinese American, or Korean American worship. My sense is that these worshipers share a much deeper and richer meaning among themselves, imperceptible to the outsider. All of us worship and live at a level much deeper than we perceive and consciously acknowledge. German philosopher Martin Heidegger once observed that language is the "house of Being."[1] This suggests that, unless one can enter the "house" of another person's language and culture, one can never experience and attain the depth of that person's world of meaning. I am a Korean American; what I say in these pages is unavoidably shaped by my social and cultural location.

THE TRANSCULTURAL STRUCTURE OF WORSHIP

When I came to the United States of America in 1967 to study in Rochester, New York, I was assigned for field education to Asbury

Methodist Church. The fall semester began during the first week in September. It had been a month since I had left my home and family, and already I was feeling the pain of being alone and away from home.

I am a preacher's kid, which meant that I went to church every Sunday. It also meant that I knew the church's hymns and liturgy, so much so that one could say what the church "does" in worship was ingrained in my bones. All this was to stand me in good stead in my new assignment. On the second Sunday in September, I was introduced to the congregation at Asbury Methodist Church. The church sanctuary was huge; in fact, it was the largest church building I had ever seen. I was so overwhelmed by the size of the congregation and of the space that I felt diminished and lost. But when the people started singing the opening hymn, I instantly knew that I was "home." Though the language was different, all the melodies, Scripture readings, symbols, and prayers were familiar. There were many aspects of the worship experience that I did not cognitively grasp; nevertheless, I was able to participate in the deeper dimension to which the hymns, prayers, symbols, and worship pattern pointed. I knew the hymns, prayers, and symbols by heart; so my heart was connected! I was no longer alone. I belonged. Because of—or despite—the cognitive dissonance, the familiar hymns, prayers, and symbols became more intimate to me; through them I was able to enter deeper into the mystery of God.

I feel to this day that God is truly transcultural and transhistorical. God can be experienced beyond a particular linguistic form or cognitive apparatus. God is transcendent, and to that extent God is very close to me. God is transcendent-immanent. Perhaps the reason I was able to experience God as simultaneously transcendent and immanent in that first worship service at Asbury Methodist Church has to do with the *particular structure of worship* that had formed me since my earliest days— a structure shared by Methodists around the world.

We are taught that the purpose of worship is to glorify God. This is the "official" view of what worship is. This is a view generally embraced by many Asian Americans. The structure of worship, therefore, should be designed to be solemn, dignified, serene, holy, and respectful; and one should be properly attired for the occasion. Purity of heart is demanded. Such purity should manifest itself in behavior and commitment. Piety and truthfulness are important spiritual virtues. A worshiper is to direct his or her attention to God, and God alone. Christians are called to be holy as God is holy, and they should endeavor to become holy. Being determines doing.

Such a view of worship provides a point of contact between the new religion (Christianity) and the old religious traditions for many Asians and Asian Americans. Especially when seen from the perspective of communities with religious roots in Buddhism and Confucianism (as well as in Shamanism), ritual is something that is made in heaven. It carries an objective power that participants often experience as an entity over which they have no power to make substantive changes. The ritual is sacred and inviolable. The faithful must adapt themselves to the ritual rather than adjust the ritual to fit their tastes. This attitude gets transferred when these people become Christians. Many Asians who are pragmatic in their approach to spirituality yet hold this view. Consequently, one finds in Asian American worship more Western Christian traditions than Asian traditions.

> **God is truly transcultural and transhistorical. God can be experienced beyond a particular linguistic form or cognitive apparatus.**

THEOLOGY AND WORSHIP

All clergy know that there is a connection between theology and worship. In other words, the knowledge of God is inseparable from the adoration of God. Perhaps the highest knowledge of God comes in silent communion with God. The dictum *lex orandi lex credendi* (the rule of prayer shapes the rule of belief) contains a profound truth: Genuine theology is shaped by the living knowledge of God in prayer and worship. Such theology transcends the subjective-objective disjunction, and draws strengths from both sides.

Yet we must also think of the relation between theology and worship as a reciprocal one, for if worship shapes theology, worship must also be subjected to the reflective criticism that theological thinking engenders. Such a reciprocal relationship allows a view that the way one worships reveals one's theological character and orientation.

Asian churches were children of the nineteenth-century American missionary movement. This movement was fired by the zeal for the Word preached. The Asian Protestant churches have been deeply shaped by Reformation divines such as Calvin and Luther, and also by Wesley. In an earlier generation of the twentieth century, many theological schools were further influenced by the theological commitments of Barth, Bultmann, and Bonhoeffer. These theologians have one thing in common: They think of God's presence and approach to humanity almost exclusively in terms of the *preached* Word. The stress has been on preaching, instruction, hearing, and understanding. Even today many worship services are centered around the sermon. The congregation expects "good preaching."

The emphasis on preaching correlates with an emphasis on *knowing*. It elevates the "reasonable" character of the gospel. This leads to a kind of docetism, as if we were almost disembodied, spiritual beings. Many Asian American churches still suffer from this early intellectualist and subjectivist tendency. Such subjectivism issues in a view of religious practice as private. It lacks the public character of Christian living. Perhaps this is a weakness found throughout Protestantism. This accounts for the lack of social involvement and active social outreach. Many are politically inactive and indifferent to policy issues. Theology is not integrated with ethical decision-making. Worship becomes one-sided, focused on "words." This inevitably leads to a disembodied presence in the world.

The future of Asian American churches calls for a more wholesome, more holistic approach to worship, stressing the sacraments in addition to the Word. The sacraments may lead these churches to appeal to the senses rather than to the mind only. Many Asian American churches seldom celebrate the Lord's Supper (the Eucharist). When some congregations do administer the Eucharist, many members opt to stay at home on those Sundays. Church members have a limited (if any) understanding of the sacrament; some vaguely associate it with cannibalism. With education and instruction, this can be changed.

Change is not only desirable; it is imperative. Openness to the senses and to feeling through sacramental spirituality may help Asian American churches to loosen up their age-old patriarchal leanings toward male-dominated propriety and religious bureaucratic exclusivism. Men and women are embodied creatures of flesh and blood. Christianity is the religion of incarnation. We learn through our senses as well as through our minds. The whole aim of the sacramental liturgy and life is not so much instruction as *incorporation*. A sacramental liturgy may help in our fight against individualism, subjectivism, and privatism.

A liturgy rooted in the sacraments may also teach us to appreciate the objective substance of the faith. This new stress on the sacraments is needed, particularly given its attendant emphasis on the *physical* aspects of sacramental action and devotion. Word and Sacrament are to be embraced as essentially complementary. Worship that incorporates these two essential elements asserts the real objective presence of God in our midst.

The complementarity of Word and Sacrament may help the Asian American churches create and shape more prophetic, more just, more inclusive, and more liberative worship and theology. And Asian American churches can retrieve this complementarity of Word and Sacrament by reclaiming the Wesleyan heritage, which is well represented in *The United Methodist Book of Worship*. Such churches will become better in serving their communities with *shalom;* that is, with harmonious cooperation aimed at the welfare of all.

THE BABYLONIAN (WESTERN) CAPTIVITY OF ASIAN AMERICAN WORSHIP

Walk into any Chinese, Japanese, Korean, or Filipino congregation on a given Sunday and the faces of the people you encounter are definitely "Asian" in character. But the worship settings, liturgy, hymns, prayers, vestments, symbols, musical instruments, and gestures are identical to those in First United Methodist Church or Central United Presbyterian Church in Houston or Boston, or anywhere else. With minor variations, this sense is replicated in any major Christian church in Tokyo, Seoul, Manila, Taipei, and Hong Kong. Some thoughtful Asians characterize this situation as the "Babylonian Captivity" of Asian Christian worship to the Western church. Consequently, many Asian Christians became outsiders to their own culture.

This is the other side of the transcultural structural dimension of the worship life of those who are at the receiving end of the missionaries' work. Most of these congregations, consisting of diverse cultural, national, and ethnic identities, are the fruit of the American missionary movement of the previous century. This movement brought to these people a rich spiritual legacy. It helped plant the seeds of the gospel in these Asian nations, offering Christ through education, medical services, and a new sense of dignity and self-esteem to those who were on the fringes of their societies. Many people took advantage of these gifts of life. They had been offered similar religious enlightenment before, but this time it was something new and different. What was once good, many felt, should not be dismissed. Rather, what is good only needs to be repeated. Truth and goodness are in repetition! Hence they kept what they had received. No one forced them to be such; they did it "that way."

While appropriating these new truths was good, what happened over time is that people began appreciating less and less what they had in their own culture, preferring and adopting Western ideas and practices over their own. Many people erroneously identified what is Christian with what is Western. To some, becoming Christian meant becoming Western. Many turned "West." Many Asian Americans came to the United States of America for an opportunity to fulfill their lives. Instead, once they arrived they experienced a rapid loss of their identity and cultural "soul." Many Asian Americans realized that they were being drowned and lost in the homogenizing force of American culture. Therefore, many joined churches where they could worship in their native languages,

Many people erroneously identified what is Christian with what is Western. To some, becoming Christian meant becoming Western.

could hear familiar sounds that awaken their souls, and could express their thoughts in their own languages. In *hearing* the elements of worship and thoughts expressed in their linguistic tools, many Asian American Christians found life renewed; indeed, one could go so far as to say that these Christians "came into being" through hearing themselves worship, think, and sing in their own languages.

The United Methodist Church revealed its God-inspired wisdom in that it allowed "linguistic space" for these various Asian American groups and supported their births into ministry in their native tongues. This helped the groups to maintain significant relationships with churches in their countries of origin and to establish spiritual exchange programs. In addition, a continuous influx of new immigrants added a pressure to adopt whatever was being developed in a group's native land.

WORSHIP AS CELEBRATION

Influenced by the rapidly growing evangelical-church movement and its popular music programs, as well as by creative contributions from indigenous composers, the younger generation now pressures congregations fixated on old habits to adapt. A growing number of people from older generations are joining them. Successful worship now means not just sitting in the pew listening to sermons for thirty to forty-five minutes; rather, it means putting an emphasis on experience and self-expression in worship. Perhaps it should not be either that or this.

Worship is no longer viewed as centered only around the Word and words; rather, worship has to do with celebration of life as a whole. This includes celebrating the systems of one's native culture: language, music (with its indigenous percussive beats and rhythms as well as melodies), architectural designs, and spiritual *ethos* (character). It calls for a more active, participatory presence of all people in worship—men, women, children, the elderly, and people with disabilities. In older forms of worship, worshipers were not encouraged to be active participants because male clericalism prohibited it. Worshipers were passive recipients of divine grace. All they needed to do was wait patiently; hence they prayed, mostly asking for what they were waiting to receive. (Some clergy members are still obstinate in holding on to this old pattern of worship.)

This kind of passiveness in worship is quite unlike the receptiveness that characterizes the contemplative spirituality of new forms of worship. In these worship services, there is hardly a moment of silence. All worship space is filled with sound. The newer trends move away from a passive and word-centered approach to worship. Many congregations now use their own music, rhythms, percussive beats, and musical instruments in celebrating their faith and spiritual experiences. In so doing, they form their particular identity as *people of God*. This new mood indicates that worship and liturgy exist for the sake of the worshipers. The task of worship is to help the worshipers be fully alive and to wholly glorify God.

The old pattern of worship induced people to bury their indigenous spiritual tastes and thereby to become forgetful of their true spiritual destiny. They unknowingly imitated Westerners in worship. Of course, there is a dimension in the human spirit that can grasp what are transhistorical, transcultural, and transnational elements in truth and goodness. But this is possible only through concrete manifestations in concrete symbols that emerge out of the collective life of a people. In the past, one had to abstract oneself from one's social, cultural, and religious location to be in touch with a God who is transcultural. Now people embrace the view that all truth is mediated through the particularities of social and cultural location. We meet God where we are; God comes to where we are. God is truly global, because God is truly local.

EMERGING PERSPECTIVES

God is the Creator of all the universe. God created the Chinese, the Japanese, the Korean, the Filipino, and the Vietnamese. This forces one to reflect on why God would create each of these people with their own taste for food, own sense of beauty, and ability to express themselves through their own languages and symbols, and then replace these with something "better"—something Western. Did God create these people with the distinct ability to create cultures of their own, only to refuse to accept worship offered through these cultures? God truly created these people with distinctive gifts, and declared it good. Why should these people ignore their spiritual impulses that can best be expressed through their own words, music, dance, incense, gesture, and instruments? What and who prohibits them from doing so?

I am not suggesting that Asian American Christians reject everything that is foreign to "Asian-ness" in order to rediscover their being within the total scheme of God's creation and plan of salvation. We are connected globally today. That means we cannot gain our identity either through isolating ourselves from others or through allowing ourselves to be absorbed into a "melting pot." Instead, we must let God truly pitch God's tent among us, weaving the tent from our cultural materials, so that we may encounter God in our "household" in the way that God wishes to meet us, and right where God has placed us in creation.

The United Methodist Hymnal in large measure embraces such a spirit of diversity, affirming the distinct cultural forms and dispositions inherent in the songs and prayers in it. Various traditions of rhythm and percussive sensitivities are also represented in the *Hymnal*. Many Asian Americans enthusiastically embrace this new perspective on worship. People desire for their voices to be heard and to experience redemption as they are included and affirmed by the church, the body of Christ. They become active agents of their destiny in response to God's gift of freedom. This signals that worship and liturgy are no longer viewed as entities efficacious in and of themselves. However, this should not be interpreted as ignoring the importance of the objective mystery of God's saving work in Christ by preferring a subjectivist stance. On the contrary, this new perspective is concerned with securing a more wholesome and relational—and, hence, more participative—dynamic in worship.

The new perspective on worship is not yet fully realized among Asian American United Methodists. Indeed, at present it is more of an "appetite" than a full-blown reality. Most of the leadership in Asian American congregations resist this perspective on worship. Most members were taught to be passive and stationary in worship; therefore, they have a basic aversion to gesture and movement in worship. Their religious cultural upbringing shaped them to prefer serenity and tranquility over the "boisterous" expressions of their faith. Truth is to be attained in meditation and contemplation; this better fosters their being, or so they are told. Worship has to do with being—being in God, being in Christ, being in the worshiping community. For many of these people, then,

> We must let God truly pitch God's tent among us, weaving the tent from our cultural materials, so that we may encounter God in our "household" in the way that God wishes to meet us, and right where God has placed us in creation.

being precedes *action*. Their tacit conviction is that religion is for the sake of being. This perspective is deeply ingrained in many Asian approaches to meaning, truth, and life—hence the vigorous resistance to a perspective that encourages more participation in worship.

POURING NEW WINE INTO AN OLD WINESKIN

The tension between the old and the new patterns of worship among Asian American United Methodists is not easily resolved. It will require intentional education. Perhaps the educational effort should start with a curriculum in theological schools that takes seriously knowledge of religious music as integral to liturgy and worship leadership. Such education may include an orientation to contemporary music, various ethnic musicology, and the depth of knowledge of the ritual and worship in the history of religions. Courses in drama, musicals, and aesthetics may broaden the theological and liturgical horizon of the future leaders of the church. Insights gained from such disciplines may help the leaders of the church as well as the laity to design worship services that reflect the order of salvation in critical correlation with the life situation of the immigrant communities.

Recently, a new committee was formed to redesign the Korean American hymnal and the attendant worship and liturgical materials. Many are of the opinion that this worship material should reflect something of the Christian spiritual ethos that Korean American Christians have in common with other Christian brothers and sisters; at the same time, the material should also reflect something of the indigenous spiritual heritage of Korean Americans. This effort will surely mark a new chapter in liberating Asian American Christians from their "captivity" to the predominantly Western flavor of their worship life. The strategies in our movement toward freedom include the following:

- remembering ancestors at the points of their births or deaths;
- celebrating milestones of people's lives;
- singing songs of children in the past;
- adapting indigenous funeral rites to the Christian service of the celebration of death and resurrection;
- adopting elements of native wedding customs in services of the marriage covenant;
- using traditional musical instruments, perhaps initially as accompaniment to the choir;
- wearing traditional garments or vestments as modified to a modern taste;
- using songs composed by musicians of one's own country. A particular congregation may even commission these musicians to compose such songs.

CONCLUSION

There are many encouraging signs to indicate that the new mood and spirit regarding worship is catching the imagination of many young Asian American laypeople. Through their positive experiences in retreats, workshops, and seminars where new songs are tried and celebrated, new attitudes are being formed. I saw many elderly people stand up and join in rhythmic dances and sing along with the guitar, drums, and percussive instruments.

May God hear in Asian American United Methodist worship voices that are no longer muffled through somebody else's musical instruments but rather sung gloriously through our own instruments. And may God be glorified by us all in all our diversity!

FOR FURTHER READING

Hymns From the Four Winds: A Collection of Asian American Hymns (Nashville, TN: Abingdon Press, 1983).

Third-Eye Theology: Theology in Formation in Asian Settings, Revised Edition, edited by Choan-Seng Song (Mayknoll, NY: Orbis Books, 1991).

Sung-Sil-Mun-Hwa, a journal edited by Jung-Hoan Lee (Seoul, Korea: The Center for Sung-Sil Worship Resource Research, Sung-Sil Methodist Church).

ENDNOTES

1 See *On the Way to Language,* by Martin Heidegger, translated by Peter D. Hertz (New York, NY: Harper & Row Publishers, 1971), p. 63.

There are many encouraging signs to indicate that the new mood and spirit regarding worship is catching the imagination of many young Asian American laypeople.

**MARIA LUISA
SANTILLÁN BAERT**

*Pastor, El Divino Salvador
United Methodist Church,
Sherman, Texas*

14

Worship in the Hispanic United Methodist Church[1]

Cantemos al Señor un himno de alegría....
¡Aleluya! ¡Aleluya! Cantemos al Señor. ¡Aleluya!
(Let's sing unto the Lord a hymn of glad rejoicing....
Alleluia! Alleluia! Let's sing unto the Lord. Alleluia!)
(*UMH*, 149)[2]

THUS READS IN PART THE FIRST STANZA OF ONE OF THE eighteen Spanish language hymns composed by Hispanics and included in *The United Methodist Hymnal.* An English translation is given below the Spanish words to enable non-Spanish speakers to participate in the faith expression of thought and rhythm of Hispanics. For the first time *The United Methodist Hymnal* (1989 edition) includes worship resources from its multicultural and pluralistic constituency. The more recent publication of *Mil Voces Para Celebrar: Himnario Metodista* provides a complete Spanish-language hymnal for United Methodists.

The United Methodist Church has struggled to understand the uniqueness of a people that can give expression to their faith powerfully through their gifts and graces, and through their culture. In the last few years the Church has begun to accept the validity and richness of the Hispanic culture as a bona fide, genuine, authentic, basic form of Christian expression that can enrich the life of the whole church.

The adopting and adapting of certain Hispanic celebrations such as *la quinceañera* (a ceremony for fifteen-year-old girls) and *las posadas* is a sign of a committed effort to celebrate "God with us" as the family of God.

The United Methodist Church has always been a connectional church. Missionaries who went out to Latin America took with them the customs, traditions, and worship styles of the sending church. The younger churches, excited by the "good news," followed the worship patterns introduced and established by the missionaries. Their cultural traditions were dismissed because they were considered stumbling blocks for spiritual growth and thus deemed unacceptable to God. And so the separation of faith and life, religion and culture began.

Hispanics were attracted to the Methodist Church through the inspiring hymns, the dynamic preaching, the moving prayers, the powerful witnessing, and meaningful worship.

Hymns were translated from English into Spanish as were the orders of worship. Anything resembling Roman Catholic practices, such as Ash Wednesday services, candles, acolytes, *quinceañeras,* and *posadas,* was

Worship Matters: A United Methodist Guide to Ways to Worship (Volume I) © 1999 Discipleship Resources. Used by permission.

discarded and labeled non-Christian. Today, many Hispanic United Methodist churches in the United States are slowly incorporating these very elements into their worship experiences.

Methodists were known for their enthusiasm and fervor. Some were even called "Shouting Methodists." One of the characteristics of Hispanic Methodist worship is the religious fervor that is manifested by believers. They sing with overflowing joy and seem never to tire even after a long period of singing or even if hymns have five or more stanzas. Enthusiasm seems to be the natural climate in worship, especially in the more charismatic congregations where more *estribillos* (choruses) rather than hymns are sung. People are often moved to clap as they sing, raise their arms in praise, and play tambourines. Such lively participation is spontaneous, unavoidable, and contagious. It indeed becomes a celebration.

Hispanics have different types of worship services. There are the praise and prayer services in which the congregation feels moved to sing wholeheartedly, recite favorite Bible verses, share blessings received during the week, meditate, and pray. Testimony services are those in which participants stand up one at a time voluntarily and publicly testify in word and song about their Christian experience and their faith journey. Agape services or love feasts occur in which Christians gather to sing, fellowship, and share a meal or simple refreshments, such as bread and water.

Growing up in a Methodist church in a Spanish-speaking community in Dallas, Texas, I remember that on the first Sunday of the month the pastor would invite four boys and girls to help him (there were no women pastors then) with the serving of bread and water. The children wore short white robes similar to those worn by acolytes, and they would walk down the middle of the aisle, two on each side. In each pair, one carried the small pieces of bread and one the glasses of water. They walked slowly down the aisle, pew by pew, offering to all the gifts of bread and water. I do not remember, but I am sure the pastor must have explained the symbolism of the agape meal before it was served. This happened during the morning worship service. In the evening, bread and wine (grape juice) were used for the celebration of Holy Communion. The bread and the water were served in the pews; the bread and the wine were served at the altar rail. It has been many years since I have seen the celebration of the agape meal in any Hispanic United Methodist church.

Holy Communion is one of two sacraments observed faithfully by Hispanic United Methodists, usually on the first Sunday of the month. Dr. Roberto L. Gómez, in an article in *Apuntes,* compares Holy Communion in the Roman Catholic and in the Protestant traditions. He indicates that for the Roman Catholic, the Mass is the "center of religious life." Those who belong to that branch of Christianity participate in the Mass at least once a week and some do so on a daily basis. He goes on to say that because of the way we were evangelized and became Protestants, "the Sacrament of Holy Communion is de-emphasized." He continues that the preaching from Scripture and the spontaneity of worship became more important than Holy Communion to Protestants, but that "the de-emphasis on Holy Communion is a high price to pay to become a Protestant."[3]

Hispanic United Methodist churches observe the ritual for Communion found in the *Himnario Metodista* or similar rituals in Spanish, printed in worship resources published by the General Board of Discipleship. These are translations from the rituals in English. Because there is flexibility

> **In the last few years the Church has begun to accept the validity and richness of the Hispanic culture as a bona fide, genuine, authentic, basic form of Christian expression that can enrich the life of the whole church.**

within The United Methodist Church, Hispanics are beginning to develop their own liturgy for Holy Communion as well as for other celebrations. They have discovered that they need not depend always on translated resources or they will lose the opportunity to gift the church with their faith experience and will rob the church from seeing with new eyes.

We are awed by the sense of mystery and the plenitude of Holy Communion. We remember how deeply God loved us in Jesus Christ, and we celebrate the opportunity to experience the living presence of Christ that we may be and live and taste the goodness of God's grace now.

Hispanics generally go as a family to the altar. Even when the congregation numbers more than a hundred, Hispanics prefer going to the altar rail rather than just walking by, taking the elements, and going back to their pews without ever kneeling and praying.

More and more churches are beginning to use the common cup and the intinction method rather than the small glasses. An offering for the poor and the needy is often left at the rail.

The other sacrament, baptism, takes on special meaning for Hispanics, for it becomes more than a family affair or a customary religious practice.

Roberto L. Gómez also talks about baptism in his article "Mestizo Spirituality." He quotes from Father Virgilio Elizondo's book *Christianity and Culture* in regard to baptism in the Hispanic context:

> One of these moments which is most important in a Latin American family is Baptism, for the people value the family highly. Baptism is the sign through which the person becomes incorporated into the Christian community. The Spanish speaking have a profound sense of *compadrazgo*, the spiritual relationship that is established between the godparents and the parents of the baptized child. This bond is deeper than blood relationships because it is freely chosen and freely accepted.[4]

The majority of Hispanic parents baptize their children as infants. Each child is regarded as a gift from God not only to the parents but also to the community. Through baptism the church is declaring that the child is not an orphan and never will be because each baptized child will always be a part of the family of God.

Baptism enables the congregation to become the welcoming committee that brings the child into the faith community. Godparents are not chosen at random or haphazardly, but very carefully. The chosen godparents become part of the extended family. A bond of intimacy is affirmed between families. It is a sacred moment when godparents understand the responsibility they assume.

Guitars, other instruments, and *mariachi* bands are becoming more and more a part of Hispanic worship. In early 1994, a beloved church member of one of the Hispanic United Methodist churches in Dallas died. He was the music director of a Dallas high school. He had been instrumental in building pride in his Hispanic students for their culture. The mariachi band he organized played at his funeral and interment services. Mariachi bands would not have been acceptable in worship, much less funeral services, a few years ago.

Among his many gifts and legacy this brother left behind was the formation of a children's choir in his church. One year the children sang at an annual conference banquet. At first the children had no interest in singing in anything but English, but he won them over. They sing enthusiastically, joyously, blending their voices beautifully in English and Spanish. So, bilingual children's choirs are a rich resource of blessing in some of our Hispanic churches.

Does the passing of the peace during the worship service, especially a Communion service, have a new or deeper meaning for Hispanics? The question arises because from the time Hispanics enter the church building the passing of the peace begins with the embracing, the handshakes, and the holy kiss. And people will do it again after the service with the same people. They do not wait until the appropriate time in the worship service, even though they will participate again in the ritual of friendship if the order of worship or the liturgy so prescribes it. It is a vital part of the faith experience of Hispanics.

The sharing of joys and concerns is part of the worship service. People usually stand up and share what is in their hearts. Others come forward and speak and remain standing until it is time to kneel and pray. Then the pastor invites whoever wishes to come forward and kneel before the pastoral prayer is offered. Some pastors place their hands on the head or shoulders of those who have come forward to the Communion rail for prayer, as he or she prays individually for each one.

Hispanic Methodists have also produced their own hymnologists and composers such as Vicente Mendoza ("Jesús es mi Rey soberano"), Federico Pagura, Mortimer Arias, Raquel Mora Martínez, Raquel Achón, Pablo Sosa, Justo L. González, Manuel V. Flores, and many others.

For many years Hispanic United Methodists in the United States used different hymnals because there was no Methodist hymnal in Spanish. Congregations were free to choose from the available Spanish hymnals. This became problematic when visiting other Methodist churches. Church members carried their Bibles and their hymnals to church with them every time they attended services. In visiting other churches or in going to meetings outside the local church, one soon discovered the confusion when everyone had a different hymnal.[5]

Because of the rising interest in *estribillos* (choruses), two books have already been published. Dr. Roberto Escamilla was the editor of *Celebremos* (1979)[6] and *Celebremos II* (1983). The *Celebremos II* Task Force responded to MARCHA's (Methodist Associates Representing the Cause of Hispanic Americans) recommendation that more indigenous music be used in Hispanic worship. The *estribillos* and other songs chosen had to meet the following criteria:
1. a good theological basis
2. good poetic and musical qualities
3. inclusive language
4. an awareness of spiritual and secular values
5. wholeness of thought.[7]

The compositions are presented in both English and Spanish so that non-Spanish-speaking congregations may be enriched by the message and rhythm. This effort was also intended to help the church at large to understand the contributions that Hispanic United Methodists can make to their worship experience. This second book contains forty-six songs and most now bear names of poets and composers. These books, too, were well received.

In 1992 the General Conference of The United Methodist Church authorized the publication of another hymnal, which was presented to the 1996 General Conference. Hispanic United Methodists have eagerly awaited the publication of this hymnal, edited by Raquel Mora Martínez. This hymnal, *Mil Voces Para Celebrar: Himnario Metodista,* is named as one of the official United Methodist worship resources in the *Book of*

How can we sing in a foreign land when all we hear is "Speak English only"?

Discipline (¶1112.3). It includes ritual texts for baptism, Communion, marriage, funeral, healing and other services, a liturgical Psalter and other acts of worship, service introductions, and a full range of hymnody and *choritos*.

Spontaneous prayer continues to be a vital part of Hispanic worship. Written prayers are used, but the pastor or liturgist often calls upon a church member to lead the congregation in prayer. I have not yet heard anyone say, "No, I can't."

In many churches the congregation stands when any portion of Scripture is read, not just the Gospels. Hispanics accept both Testaments as the inspired Word of God. Many people, especially adults, still carry their Bibles with them to church even when there are Bibles in the pews.

A special celebration in a worship context is "la quinceañera," the time when a young girl celebrates her fifteenth birthday. It is a way of presenting her to the community and declaring that she is now ready for responsibility. Earlier in the century it was a way for parents to present their daughter to society and say, "She is available for marriage and motherhood." There is no such celebration for a male youth. The quinceañera dresses in white and is escorted toward the altar by a young man, generally of her own choosing. They are followed by fifteen young men and fifteen young women who accompany them in this special occasion. The worship service includes congregational singing, prayers, Scripture readings, music, a sermon, and an allusive liturgy. *Padrinos* and *madrinas* ("sponsors") present the quinceañera with special gifts, such as a Bible, jewelry, and coins. The community joins the parents in thanking God for their daughter and praying that God may grant her life, joy, and health. After the worship service, there is a party or reception.

Most Hispanic United Methodist churches have not followed the pattern of the majority church in canceling the Sunday evening services and midweek Bible studies. These services are generally more informal. There is more singing; people usually choose their favorite hymns, and explain why they like them. Singing may go on for thirty to sixty minutes. Also, this is the time when many congregations sing *estribillos* or learn new hymns. It is also a time for quoting favorite Bible verses, offering prayers, listening to God's Word, and from time to time dialoguing with the pastor on a Scripture passage.

A book of the Bible is usually chosen for careful examination and reflection during the midweek Bible study. There are also prayers and hymn singing.

A service that is becoming more and more a part of Hispanic United Methodist worship is the one observed on Ash Wednesday. Until recently it had not been part of Hispanic Methodist tradition. It still is not a part of Methodist tradition in most Latin American churches. Because it was a Roman Catholic religious practice, it did not become a part of the liturgy of the Hispanic United Methodist churches at first.

Most Hispanic United Methodists observe Ash Wednesday as the beginning of the Lenten season. It serves to remind Hispanics of their mortality and calls them to reflect on their relationship to God and to their neighbors. The ashes are either bought or made from the palms used on Palm Sunday the year before. They are blessed and placed on the foreheads of the faithful during a worship service. A cross is traced with the ashes as words are pronounced by the pastor, who also invites the congregation to enter into a season of prayer, reflection, Bible study, and good works, and to choose a spiritual discipline during Lent. To receive ashes implies one is willing to humble oneself before God, that one is willing to participate in the suffering of Jesus. Most Hispanic United Methodists do not make vows to fast or abstain from eating certain foods or from participating in certain activities. Submitting to a disciplined life during this period is difficult for many. Some churches offer Lenten studies dividing the congregation into cluster groups, each with a lay leader.

Hispanic United Methodists generally have the same worship services and activities that other churches do during Holy Week: Holy Communion and/or foot washing service on Maundy Thursday; a service on the seven last words, or a dramatic presentation and the stripping of the sanctuary on Good Friday; and a sunrise service on Easter Sunday. A breakfast usually follows the early morning or sunrise Easter service. Special music by church choirs highlights the resurrection message at the regular worship service on Easter morning.

Hispanic United Methodists have been researching the tradition of *las posadas,* because it has not been a part of our religious experience. It is an attempt to reenact Mary's and Joseph's search for an inn in Bethlehem. Children learn about this tradition in school, but there has been little written to help The United Methodist Church celebrate this tradition.

When I arrived in Mexico the Methodist Church of Mexico was having *noches invernales* (winter nights) during the nine nights the secular world was having *posadas* (that is, parties with much drinking). What The Methodist Church of Mexico did was to provide religious services and a celebration for nine consecutive nights. Each church organization was assigned one night. Each organization was responsible for the worship service, the refreshments, the *piñatas,* and the fruit and candy bags, and each group was encouraged to be as creative as possible. Some organizations, especially the youth, presented dramas or pageants, some rather spectacular. It was a time for worship and fellowship. These activities were always well attended.

Worship services are not restricted to one hour. It is not that time is not important to Hispanics, but rather that when the Spirit of God is given control of the worship experience, God cannot be bound by time and space. Hispanics stay around until they have greeted all their friends after the service, even though many greeted one another before the service. There is no rush to beat the Baptists to the cafeteria line.

More Hispanic pastors are becoming lectionary preachers. For many Hispanics, the sermon is the heart of the worship service. Congregations expect powerful and inspiring messages. The preacher is free to be genuinely expressive. There need not be a revival or an evangelistic service for the preacher to have an altar call. In many congregations it is essential that the pastor be bilingual, for both preaching and ministry. A bilingual liturgy is used in such churches.

The captors of the Hebrew exiles in Babylonia taunted them by saying, "Sing us a song from your country" (Psalm 137:3, author's translation). And the exiles cried out, "How can we sing if we are so far from our homes and our land?" The large number of immigrants from Latin America in the United States could easily raise the same question, "How can we sing in a foreign land when all we hear is 'Speak English only'?" The saying *Tan lejos de Dios y tan cerca de los Estados Unidos* (So far from God and so close to the United States) becomes a living nightmare.

The Hispanic United Methodist churches are here to say to the stranger and alien that God is here and that there are resources in their own language that can assure them they are *en su casa con la familia de*

> **The Hispanic United Methodist churches are here to say to the stranger and alien that God is here and that there are resources in their own language that can assure them they are *en su casa con la familia de Dios* (at home with the family of God).**

Dios (at home with the family of God). Thus they can sing and worship in a foreign land where there is freedom to do so in one's own language.

A saying in Spanish goes *muchos amenes al cielo llegan* (literally "many amens get up to heaven" or, "the one who perseveres goes far"). As Hispanics we have persevered and will continue to do so because of our desire to worship in spirit and in truth in our own tongue and tradition, experiencing the oneness of faith and life, religion and culture.

FOR FURTHER READING

¡Alabadle!: Hispanic Christian Worship, by Justo L. Gonzáles (Nashville, TN: Abingdon Press, 1996).

Gente Nueva: Casetes para Comunidades de Fe (Nashville, TN: Discipleship Resources). Two cassette tapes of vocal and instrumental music for communities of faith; includes a booklet with the words of the songs (in Spanish only).

Meztizo Worship: A Pastoral Approach, by Virgilio P. Elizondo and Timothy M. Matovina (Collegeville, MN: The Liturgical Press, 1998).

ENDNOTES

1 This article is used by permission of the author, Maria Luisa Santillán Baert.

2 From "Cantemos al Señor (Let's Sing Unto the Lord)," by Carlos Rosas, translated by Roberto Escamilla, Elise S. Eslinger, and George Lockwood, in *The United Methodist Hymnal* (Nashville, TN: The United Methodist Publishing House, 1989), 149. Copyright © 1976 by Resource Publications, Inc. Translation © 1989 by The United Methodist Publishing House. (Administered by The Copyright Company c/o The Copyright Company, Nashville, Tennessee.) All rights reserved. International copyright secured. Used by permission.

3 From "Mestizo Spirituality: Motifs of Sacrifice, Transformation, Thanksgiving, and Family in Four Mexican American Rituals," by Roberto L. Gómez, in *Apuntes,* Year 11, Number 4 (Winter 1991), p. 89.

4 From *Christianity and Culture: An Introduction to Pastoral Theology and Ministry for the Bicultural Community,* by Rev. Virgilio P. Elizondo (Huntingdon, IN: Our Sunday Visitor, Inc., 1975), p. 190.

5 During my childhood and teen years our church used *Himnos de alabanza pureza y poder, Himnos de gloria, Cantos de triunfo, Himnos de la vida cristiana, El nuevo himnario evangélico, Himnos selectos,* as well as a few more.

6 The Division of Evangelism, Worship, and Stewardship of the General Board of Discipleship in Nashville, Tennessee, published a book with twenty-three *estribillos* arranged by Esther Frances. Many of these *estribillos* were orally transmitted, so there was no known written music for many of them. Most of them are by unknown composers.

7 From *Celebremos II,* edited by Roberto Escamilla (Nashville, TN: Discipleship Resources, 1983), p. iv.

Feminist United Methodist Worship in the Twenty-First Century

MARY B. POPE

*Adjunct Professor,
Simpson College,
Indianola, Iowa*

F EMINIST WORSHIP IN THE TWENTIETH CENTURY OFFERS MANY
contributions to the formation of worship praxis in the twenty-first
century. The creative tension between *comfort* and *challenge,*
always present in worship experiences, is informed by groups who worship in ways that critique traditional norms. For example, if we sang only
familiar congregational songs, most of us would sing "Jesus Loves Me."
Somewhere, somehow, we were forced (or coerced) to move beyond the
familiar and comfortable to learn a larger repertoire of congregational
song. Those additional songs are now part of our dearly loved music.
But it was not always so!

THE SCOPE OF UNITED METHODIST FEMINIST WORSHIP

Wide variations exist within women's worship of the late twentieth
century.[1] On the one hand, conservative or fundamentalist women question the need to offer any critique of traditional worship patterns and
resources. This position sees no need to change the language of hymn
texts to reflect all of humanity. For example, women at this end of the
spectrum would never expect, or even desire, the alternative text of "Rise
Up, O Men of God" (*UMH*, 576), which is "Rise Up, Ye Saints of God." In
other words, the original text is quite acceptable.

On the other end of women's worship experience stand those who
have virtually rejected Christianity as a male patriarchal religion with little
or no relevance to women's spirituality. While these women critique
Christianity in ways that must be heard in order to understand the
emerging culture of the twenty-first century, their critiques tend to be
less helpful in shaping United Methodist worship that seeks to be
grounded in Scripture and tradition as well as experience and reason.

Feminist theologians and liturgists who stand somewhere between the
two extremes challenge United Methodists to expand the boundaries of
worship praxis, yet also recognize the need to preserve the best of tradition. The feminist challenge critiques all areas of worship—the use of
Scripture and other texts, textile arts and visual arts, music and congregational song, symbols of the faith, spatial concerns, and leadership roles.

Worship Matters: A United Methodist Guide to Ways to Worship (Volume 1) © 1999 Discipleship Resources. Used by permission.

THE FEMINIST CRITIQUE OF
UNITED METHODIST WORSHIP

The basic questions feminists use to critique United Methodist worship patterns are the same as those used by other liberation theologies: What or who is included? What or who is left out? The questions asked next grow from these two: Why is the item included or excluded? What difference does that make in worship? All of these levels of questioning lead to the most important questions: Who feels less than welcome in worship? What attributes of God are being ignored when we fail to broaden our perspectives? As with many other facets of life, those who stand at the edges of tradition are those who can most clearly see the unexamined assumptions upon which we base ordinary thought.

The use of Scripture and other texts is perhaps the first area to be critiqued. Janet Tanaka clearly shows the effect of misused texts on domestic violence. Glib sermons based on "wives, be submissive to your husbands..." appear to condone domestic violence against women. This is especially apparent when the second half of the passage, "husbands, love your wives as Christ loves the church," is muted. Since both perpetrators and victims of domestic violence worship on a Sunday morning, the Word of God may be seriously distorted by frequent use of the "wives, be submissive" passage.[2]

Also, women have held leadership roles in the church since its earliest days. Philippians 4:2-3 mentions two women, Euodia and Syntyche, who worked beside Paul to spread the gospel. Yet this particular passage from Philippians is never read within the lectionary cycle, while the remainder of Philippians 4 is read three times in each three-year cycle. This omission of Scripture passages, which speak of women in leadership roles, creates the impression that women clergy are something new and radical in the modern world.

In addition, the ways of determining the canon, both formal and informal, of Scripture is an important critique of today's worship. Liturgy as the work of the people intimately connects worship with all of life. Connections between Christian education and worship are especially clear. The informal canon used in church school and vacation Bible school curricula is forming the next generation of worshipers. At the present time, that curricula appear weighted toward male models of leadership. The informal canon that is forming future generations of worshipers will expand and diversify when feminist critiques of the informal canon are heeded.

Language used in congregational song is an issue that has been most widely discussed during the past twenty years. Tension exists between those who feel that inclusive language changes too much of a traditional faith stance and those who desire changes more radical than the broad mainstream can support. A few years ago, the compilation of *The United Methodist Hymnal* became a focus of this struggle between divergent views on language usage. In some ways, this struggle with language of congregational song is the prototype of all the tensions produced when feminist critique is taken seriously by the denomination.

A central issue in the discussion of inclusive language is the effect that language has on the self-perception of women and men. How important is the language we use in worship? One simple exercise is simply to ask all the "men" in a gathered group to stand. The group leader may then observe that few, if any, women stood. The general population no longer understand the word *men* as gender-inclusive. A feminist critique, based on this exercise, argues the need for gender-inclusive terms. This argument is similar to recognizing the difficulty in comprehending King James' English in today's culture, while still enjoying the beauty of the King James Version of the Bible.

Sermon illustrations, stories for children's time, and biblical allusions are often oriented toward males; yet equitable use of imagery is rarely requested by either women or men. Deborah and other strong women of the Old Testament (Hebrew Bible) are rarely mentioned. Nor are we given the opportunity in worship to learn of and to grieve the fate of women who were abused and threatened. For example, Lot, rather than break the oriental laws of hospitality, offered his two virgin daughters to the men of Sodom to do with as they pleased (Genesis 19:8).

When we listen to a sermon, we often accept without question certain cultural assumptions that are gender based. Listen carefully to the next sermon you hear. How many illustrations are male oriented, based for example on football and basketball? How many are from the life of a stay-at-home mother, such as cooking and cleaning and childcare? How many relate to the life of a single person of either gender, and how many presuppose living in a nuclear family? How many illustrations are gender neutral that could be related to almost anyone? Critiquing unexamined assumptions and cultural norms is a significant facet of feminist contribution to worship praxis.

Additional critique of United Methodist worship patterns comes through current psychological research, which suggests that women and men stereotypically bring to worship differing patterns of perceiving their world. It has often been stated that if a man's greatest sin is pride, a woman's greatest sin is low self-esteem.

When the Lent-Easter cycle of the church year is examined from this vantage point, the current heavy emphasis on the forty days of Lent, with its attendant themes of self-examination and self-denial, may be seen as helpful in addressing a neglected portion of male spirituality. However, when viewed from a female perspective, the empowerment of the Great Fifty Days of Easter speak to a neglected portion of a woman's spirituality. Late twentieth-century worship praxis in most congregations celebrates Lent with much fanfare and emphasis; however, the Easter season is often an afterthought.

Feminist critique offers a useful corrective even in areas of church life, such as the need to balance the introspective emphasis of Lenten activities with the acts of empowerment, which Easter celebrates.

THE INFLUENCE OF FEMINISM ON UNITED METHODIST WORSHIP SYMBOLS

Feminist worship also reinvests traditional worship symbols with new vitality. Cultural symbols such as the circle, biblical symbols such as milk and honey, and traditional women's crafts such as quiltmaking enrich Christian worship leading into the twenty-first century.

The circle is common to many Native American cultures as well as to feminist experience. An illustration of the difference between traditional Christian experience and women's experience is found in recently added stanzas of the spiritual "We Are Climbing Jacob's Ladder" (*UMH,* 418). The original stanzas focused on climbing a ladder, thus moving closer to God through vertical motion. More recently, in the style of folk music, stanzas have been added around the theme "We are dancing Sarah's

The basic questions feminists use to critique United Methodist worship patterns are the same as those used by other liberation theologies: What or who is included? What or who is left out?

circle." Theological implications of these additions focus on the theme of God-with-us, God in our midst. The horizontal plane also helps worshipers connect with one another as "brother and sister" rather than in the hierarchical mode of "parent and child."

Some of the earliest documents of the baptismal liturgy suggest that "baby" Christians of all ages be fed with milk and honey. The Old Testament names the Promised Land as the land of "milk and honey" (Jeremiah 32:22), while New Testament passages refer to milk as food for new Christians (Hebrews 5:12-13). It is unfortunate, then, that lack of biblical literacy has caused some people to accuse feminist worshipers, such as those at Re-Imagining Conferences, of creating new worship symbols when these worshipers used such traditional Christian symbols as milk and honey. In reality, feminist liturgists help the church reclaim some of these ancient traditional symbols of the Christian faith.

Quilts and tapestries come from women's traditional crafts. These art forms create new possibilities for expressions of faith in God and each other. Both quilts and tapestries are created by ordinary people from a variety of materials in a variety of colors. Quilts are folk art, created by groups of people rather than by one highly acclaimed artist. For many generations, women have created quilts for warmth and practicality. Yet quilts are now recognized as a rich traditional art form that takes available materials, even discards, and creates something new and vibrant. As a new creation, a quilt may symbolize many things. For example, it could stand for a new way of being together in community, with unifying features as well as rich diversity.

Architectural and spatial considerations also change as feminist perspectives become more pronounced. Worship in the round, with worshipers either standing or sitting in a circle, fits well with mainstream feminist worship praxis. The hierarchical imagery of high pulpits with the preacher speaking from above the assembly gives way to preaching within the assembly, within the circle. Such an arrangement invites dialogue rather than the monologue implied by the elevated pulpit.

Women's leadership in worship is evolving as the millennium approaches. Women clergy are a relatively recent phenomenon. Few baby boomers have had a woman pastor during their early years. This means that in the 1990's most United Methodists associated the male voice with the authority of preaching. Consequently, for many people, including some women clergy and feminists, a woman's preaching voice simply does not carry as much authority as a man's. This unconscious assumption about authority invades other areas of church life and pastoral responsibility as well. For example, anecdotal evidence suggests that a woman's quieter voice may be ignored in an administrative council meeting while a male voice commands the attention of all present. The old folk saying that men are "assertive" and women "aggressive" unfortunately still seems believable in the context of church business meetings. By the time a congregation has received its third or fourth woman pastor, these unconscious assumptions have often receded. However, these are very real issues for "our first lady pastor."

Women bring more diversity into preaching styles. Many women have brought a gentle serenity to preaching that makes sermons easy to listen to. Unfortunately, those who use a gentle style may be perceived as having less authority because many people still expect important points to be announced with a strong, deep voice. A very important issue for women preaching is the need to develop a preaching style that is not only authentic to the person but also able to be heard with authority by the listeners.

Preaching styles and issues of authority among women and men become a rich ground for learning within congregations. This is especially true of congregations that are large enough to support a team of clergy, provided the team exhibits an adequate mix of male and female clergy who work in an atmosphere of mutual respect. A church with a proper balance of male and female staff has a diversity that equips it to minister to many different people; it also enables them to lead worship creatively.[3]

CONCLUSION

Liturgy is the "work of the people." What happens within a congregation's worship is intimately connected with the rest of the congregation's life. Feminist critique of United Methodist worship praxis is positioned at the forefront of the mainline tradition, asking serious questions about the openness of "mainstream" denominations to accept new ways of worshiping, of coloring outside the accepted liturgical lines. As United Methodism enters the twenty-first century and seeks to share the good news with all God's people, feminist critique helps this denomination hear the voice of some who are outsiders and who seek to be given their rightful place at God's own banquet table.

FOR FURTHER READING

In Her Own Rite: Constructing Feminist Liturgical Tradition, by Marjorie Procter-Smith (Nashville, TN: Abingdon Press, 1990).

Praying With Our Eyes Open: Engendering Feminist Liturgical Prayer, by Marjorie Procter-Smith (Nashville, TN: Abingdon Press, 1995).

ENDNOTES

1 A variety of feminist perspectives may be found in *Weaving the Visions: New Patterns in Feminist Spirituality,* edited by Judith Plaskow and Carol P. Christ (San Francisco, CA: Harper San Francisco, 1989).

2 See "The Role of Religious Education in Preventing Sexual and Domestic Violence," by Janet Tanaka, in *Women's Issues in Religious Education,* edited by Fern M. Giltner (Birmingham, AL: Religious Education Press, 1985), pp. 91-114.

3 For more information, see *The Male-Female Church Staff: Celebrating the Gifts: Confronting the Challenges,* by Anne Marie Nuechterlein and Celia Allison Hahn (Bethesda, MD: The Alban Institute, 1990).

As United Methodism enters the twenty-first century and seeks to share the good news with all God's people, feminist critique helps this denomination hear the voice of some who are outsiders and who seek to be given their rightful place at God's own banquet table.

Part Three

PERSPECTIVES ON DOING THE WORK OF WORSHIP

The Role of the Presider

E. Byron Anderson

*Assistant Professor of Worship,
Christian Theological Seminary,
Indianapolis, Indiana*

THE LANGUAGE OF *PRESIDING* IS NOT UNFAMILIAR TO UNITED
Methodists, although it is not often used in worship. Our tradition
gives us presiding bishops, responsible for particular annual conferences, and presiding elders, appointed to facilitate the work of charge
conferences. In both cases, the designation *presiding* indicates a particular
kind of authority. A presider (president!) occupies the chair of authority,
ruling over business meetings, governmental operations, and community
life. The presider determines when particular actions are in or out of
order, who has permission to speak, and when a meeting will begin or
end. These are familiar roles, enacted throughout the life of the church.

What might it mean for us to think about a presider in worship? We
are comfortable with *pastor* and *preacher,* and increasingly so with *liturgist. Presider* may seem foreign to many United Methodists when we
think about worship, particularly as we think about the presider as one
who occupies the chair of authority. Rather than begin with the question
of authority, let us consider the general work of a presider in worship.

It may bring some discomfort in saying, but a presider in worship
does carry some of the same responsibility we find in a business meeting. Someone must determine when the meeting will begin and end, if
particular actions are in or out of order, and when particular voices will
be heard. In another place, we might fruitfully elaborate the parallels
between the role of the presider in the business meeting and in worship.
For now, it is sufficient to note the difference: In place of old and new
business, committee reports, motions to be discussed and voted on, the
presider is involved with a community engaged in its work of worship. It
is this involvement in a community and its work of worship that gives
the presider in worship particular responsibilities.

THE FUNCTION OF THE PRESIDER

Although I will return to the particular tasks of the presider below,
some general comments provide a foundation for thinking about this
work. First, the presider participates in a *representative ministry* rooted in
the baptismal vocation of all Christians. All Christian people are called
(*vocaré,* "called out") to the work of worshiping the triune God by virtue
of their baptism into the life, death, and resurrection of Jesus Christ and
by the animating power of the Holy Spirit. Our vocation as a Christian

people is to praise, worship, and glorify God. This vocation is not reserved to the ordained, the consecrated, or the licensed. It is the common work of all Christian people.

As a participant in a representative ministry, the presider discovers quickly that one does not choose or appoint oneself to this ministry. The presider is called forth from a community of faith by that community (in the United Methodist traditions, both the local and general church). The authority of the presider is bestowed upon her or him by the church in ordination and appointment. This is particularly true of the ordained elder: "Take authority as an elder in the Church to preach the Word of God, and to administer the Holy Sacraments" (*UMBOW,* p. 678).[1]

Second, the presider's work in worship is not to invite a community to his or her personal work but to *animate* and *prompt* the whole community in its work of worship. There is something of the stage manager, master of ceremonies, even the cheerleader, involved in this work. Although the presider is one who comes with a particular kind of authority on behalf of the whole church, the task assigned is to assist, direct, invite, and enable the community in its own work of worshiping God.

Third, as a participant in a representative ministry, the presider, particularly the ordained elder, *draws together* Service, Word, Sacrament, and Order in the context of Christian worship. Although the elder is not the only one who may preside in worship (some exceptions are discussed below), the ordering of ministry found in The United Methodist Church understands presiding in worship to be a basic function of the order of elders. The *Book of Discipline* describes the work of the elder, and in many ways the work of the presider in worship, as one who "exemplifies and leads the Church in service to God in the world, in remembering and celebrating the gifts of God and living faithfully in response to God's grace" (¶310).[2] Such representative ministry flows in two ways: from the local church to the general and from the general church to the local. In this the presider, even as she or he is not the whole life of the church, becomes a "visible sign" of the life of the local church in connection with the general church.

Fourth, the presider, as the one charged with care for the worship life of a community, *gathers and leads* the worship team in its preparation and planning for service in worship. In some congregations, this team is no more, and no less, than the preacher and musician. It need not, perhaps should not be so, even in small congregations. A frequent, and incorrect, assumption is that small congregations do not have a worship team. Even the smallest church often has a pianist or song leader, trained lay speakers, and people skilled in leading prayer or in reading Scripture. Also, in multiple-point charges, the lay leader of the congregation often serves as the one who gathers the community for worship as the preacher/pastor travels between charges. Each of these people is part of the worship team and should be involved in the planning and preparation of each service.

Nevertheless, it is the presider's responsibility to know what will happen, when, by whom, how, and for what purpose in each service of worship. It is also the presider's responsibility to have a clear sense of the interrelationship of the parts and a sense of the whole of the liturgy. By gathering and leading the worship team, the presider makes such coordination and relationship possible.[3]

As a representative minister responsible for planning, preparing, and coordinating worship, the presider enables the gathered community's prayer and its sacrifice of praise and thanksgiving. By means of such care-filled preparation, the presider and the congregation as a whole are freed for worship and life in the Spirit. That is, when we are freed from worry about who is going to do what next—"Is Susan prepared to read the Scripture lesson?" "Did Mr. White bake bread for Communion this morning?"—we become more receptive to the "unplanned" possibilities of God's transforming work in worship. Where the careless presider may get in the way of such transformation, the care-filled and careful presider enables such transformation to happen.

THE CHARACTER AND STYLE REQUIRED OF A PRESIDER

The work of the elder as described in the *Book of Discipline* suggests particular actions that characterize a form of ministry: The elder exemplifies, leads, remembers, celebrates, and lives faithfully. These actions describe the character and style required of any presider in worship. Perhaps Robert Hovda best summarized this character when he wrote: "Presiding is a service of leadership in a common and participatory action called 'liturgy,' therefore an action that with full intent and purpose is done in the presence of God."[4]

Because the work of worship is a common, participatory action, the presider must understand her or himself as serving with and in a community of faith. It is this understanding that often finds conflict with the image of the presider as the one who occupies a position of authority. Presiding in this sense is "servant leadership." The presider summons, invites, and encourages a community to participate in God's saving work in Christ. Worship is God's work undertaken by and with the community of faith. The work of the presider, as noted earlier, is not to invite the community of faith into the presider's work as if it were his or her own, but to participate in God's saving work. A presider must understand that this work of worship is our work together.

With this understanding in place, it becomes possible for the presider, with the community, to create an *ethos* (character) of hospitality. The work of creating an ethos of hospitality requires that we set aside the image of the presider as "one with authority" and claim a different biblical understanding. Those passages that speak of presiding (especially Romans 12:8; 1 Thessalonians 5:12; 1 Timothy 5:17) use the word *proistemi*, which is translated often as "rule over." But this word also carries with it the alternate understanding "to protect" or "care for." While the translations often emphasize the first definition, the intent is to call leaders in the church to a particular kind of care for people and community, rather than to emphasize a rank or authority.[5] This understanding is found in a number of early-church writings, such as those of Justin (circa 150 C.E. [Common Era]) and Tertullian (circa 200 C.E.).[6] The one who would preside in Christian worship must be one who is ready to care for the community and its work of worship. The hospitality of worship does not mean a feigned friendliness, nor does it mean "put your feet up and make yourself at home." Rather, it is the feeling—sometimes even when the facts may be to the contrary—that everything needed for worship has been carefully prepared and is ready to receive guests. The hospitality of worship is when guests, whether invited or uninvited, are actually received by the worshiping community.

Such readiness to receive guests suggests four important characteristics required of the presider in worship today. First, to create an ethos of

The work of the presider...is not to invite the community of faith into the presider's work as if it were his or her own, but to participate in God's saving work.

hospitality, the presider must evidence a disposition to prayer, praise, and thanksgiving. It is hard to create, much less to express, a feeling of care, preparedness, invitation, and hospitality when one is not inclined toward a life of prayer and worship. Pastoral leaders, as presiders in worship, must know within themselves the importance of the work of worship in individual and communal Christian life. While called upon to be teachers, managers, counselors, pastors and preachers, presiders must also be worshipers.

Second, the presider must be able to receive the liturgy of the church as a gift rather than as a burden. This is a task placed on the elder in the ordination service itself, when, on behalf of the church, the bishop asks: "Will you be loyal to The United Methodist Church, accepting its order, liturgy, doctrine, and discipline…?" (*UMBOW,* p. 676).[7] This question reminds us, on the one hand, that the presider is a member of a community and tradition of worship, and therefore is accountable to that community and tradition. Liturgy and worship are "of the church" and are not ours, individually, to set aside. On the other hand, the question reminds us that worship begins as God's gift; it is God's gracious saving work that evokes our response in gratitude, praise, and thanksgiving.

Third, the presider who receives the liturgy as a gift must convey an enthusiasm and conviction about the importance of liturgical action, words, and gestures. When we treat particular words and actions as unimportant or as burden rather than as a gift, those with whom we preside learn to treat these as unimportant and a burden as well. We might ask ourselves why we are doing or saying particular things. If we believe that worship and the things of worship matter to our life together in Christian community, we as presiders need to treat them as such. This has less to do with formality or informality than with the care and attention the presider gives to how she or he acts in worship. Is it important to the presider that a community offer its sacrifice of praise and thanksgiving to the holy God? Is this communicated in the tone of the presider's voice, the posture of the presider's body, and the genuineness of the presider's gestures?

Fourth, even as he or she conveys enthusiasm and conviction about worship, the presider must be informed about, interested in, and attentive to the work of worship as it happens. As a leader of worship, the presider must know what and why the community is doing what it does in worship. Although *how* Christians worship is increasingly disputed, the *fact* of worship is not. Week in and week out, Christian communities have gathered to proclaim and hear God's Word, pray on behalf of the world, offer thanksgiving with bread and cup, and be sent in mission to the world.

Attention to the work of worship is two-fold. One kind of attention requires the presider to attend to the working details of worship. This attention, however, should happen primarily in planning. The presider's attention in worship will be fragmented unnecessarily if she or he is still preparing as the liturgy gets under way. The presider who has been careful in preparing for worship will find it easier to attend to the work of worship, that is, to be a worshiper. This attention as a worshiper is the other kind of attention required of the presider. A presider might ask her or himself: *Do I attend to worship as a worshiper? Do I participate in worship with the congregation? Do I sing the hymns and psalms? Do I listen as the Scriptures are read and anthems sung? Do I pray as a deacon leads in prayer? Do I worship?*

All of these comments about the character and style of the presider point us away from an emphasis on technique and skill (although not unimportant) and toward the worshipful care required of those who preside in Christian worship. There is much to be said for the presider who, with simplicity and prayer, "[acts] consciously and humanly and with grace in every living moment."[8] In this, the presider will serve the community of faith in its work of worship and, with the community, create a place of hospitality in which people may praise and glorify God.

THE PRESIDER IN WORSHIP

Because the presider participates in a representative ministry rooted in the baptismal vocation of all Christians, the presider shares a number of tasks with other members of the worshiping community. First, as a member of the worshiping community (as mentioned earlier), the presider prays, listens, and sings with the community. The presider standing with closed hymnal and closed mouth during a congregational hymn has removed him or herself from the community. The presider checking signals with the organist during the Scripture reading not only betrays a lack preparation but also effectively says to the congregation, "This isn't important."

Second, the presider not only enables the community's prayer and praise but also leads the gathered community in praise, prayer, and confession, as well as in the reading of Scripture. These tasks, however, are not the sole responsibility of the presider. They are and should be shared with assisting ministers of all ages and abilities. The reading of Scripture, while a role for trained lay speakers, can be shared with children. Again, the presider's care for worship and preparation of the worship team require working with readers and speakers to facilitate their comfort with their work.[9]

Third, the presider enables the community's intercessory prayers with and for the world. This task is shared particularly with deacons, whose responsibility it is to embody "the interrelationship between worship in the gathered community and service to God in the world" (*BOD*, ¶310).[10] However, models of intercessory prayer other than the "pastoral prayer," such as the litany and bidding prayer, encourage and provide for the congregation's active participation in shaping these prayers as well.[11]

With each of these tasks, it is assumed that within the pattern of Word and Table the presider is an ordained elder. Other patterns, such the orders for morning and evening praise and prayer (*UMBOW*, pp. 568–76; *UMH*, pp. 876–79), do not require an ordained elder to preside. While it is appropriate that deacons preside in these services, laypeople may also be called on to preside. This does not negate, however, the necessary work of planning and preparation of a worship team.

Although sharing many tasks in the work of worship, the presider (here understood as an ordained elder), as the one who draws together Service, Word, Sacrament, and Order in the context of Christian worship, also has four distinctive tasks. These tasks parallel the basic pattern of United Methodist worship. First, the presider gathers the community in the name of Jesus Christ. There are many voices on any given Sunday morning that will announce, "Good morning." It is the presider's task to announce the evangelical greeting that distinguishes this community and this gathering from all others. This greeting may take an apostolic form, such as Paul's: "Grace to you and peace from God our Father and the Lord Jesus Christ" (1 Corinthians 1:3), or Peter's: "May grace and peace be yours in abundance in the knowledge of God and of Jesus our Lord" (2 Peter 1:2). It may be as simple as: "The peace of Christ be with you."

If we believe that worship and the things of worship matter to our life together in Christian community, we as presiders need to treat them as such.

Second, the presider interprets and proclaims the Word. Just as the presider as a preparer and planner of worship must enable printed liturgical text and rubric to become prayer and prayerful action,[12] so, too, the presider must enable printed and proclaimed Word to become the Word in our day and place. In Word proclaimed and preached, the presider leads the worshiping community to remember, celebrate, and live faithfully in response to God's gifts and grace.

Third, the presider, called to the distinctive ministry of Word and Sacrament, offers thankful praise with and on behalf of the community at the Lord's Table. Unfortunately, it often has been at the Lord's Table where presiders most reveal their discomfort with prayer and gesture, text, and rubric, as well as the lack of conviction about the importance of liturgical action. It is precisely at the Lord's Table that presiders must evidence most clearly a disposition to prayer and praise, hospitality and graciousness.

Significantly, this prayer and action, while distinctively that of the presider, depends on the participation of the whole worshiping community as it answers and authorizes the presider's prayer through the opening dialogue: "Let us give thanks to the Lord our God. **It is right to give our thanks and praise**" (*UMBOW,* p. 36).[13] With these words, the congregation gives the presider permission to continue with the prayer. At the Table and with the community, the presider stands both in front of and in the midst of the community in the church's greatest act of prayer. Here, too, the presider enables the community to remember, celebrate, and live faithfully.

Finally, the presider sends the community to continue its worship in witness and ministry to the world. This sending is two-fold: It is both blessing (or benediction) and dismissal. As the work of worship began, so it ends with the word of grace and peace in Jesus Christ. With this word the presider makes clear that this work, while the work of the gathered community, is first and last God's saving work in Christ through the power of the Spirit. No other word has the power to sustain the community until it gathers again the next Lord's Day. The last word, the dismissal, sends us from this work of worship, connecting it to the worshipful work of the now-scattered community.

CONCLUSION

What is a presider and what does a presider do? Presiders invite, enable, animate, and prompt; they prepare, plan, and coordinate worship. Presiders exemplify, celebrate, and live faithfully; they gather, proclaim, give thanks, break bread, and send forth. In all of this, the presider's existence depends on the Christian community fulfilling its vocation of praise and worship. Only in the midst of this community at work are the ministries of Service, Word, Sacrament, and Order fulfilled.

FOR FURTHER READING

Strong, Loving and Wise: Presiding in Liturgy, Robert W. Hovda (Collegeville, MN: The Liturgical Press, 1981).

The Lord Be With You: A Visual Handbook for Presiding in Christian Worship, by Charles D. Hackett and Don E. Saliers (Akron, OH: O.S.L. Publications, 1990).

ENDNOTES

1 From "The Order for the Ordination of Elders," © 1979 by the Board of Discipleship, The United Methodist Church; © 1992 by The United Methodist Publishing House; from *The United Methodist Book of Worship*, p. 678. Used by permission. See also *Revised Services for the Ordering of Ministry in the United Methodist Church* (Nashville, TN: The General Board of Discipleship, 1998), p. 44.

2 From *The Book of Discipline of The United Methodist Church—1996*, ¶310. Copyright © 1996 by The United Methodist Publishing House. Used by permission.

3 See the articles under "Part One: People in Worship," on pp. 13–82 in Volume II of *Worship Matters*, and especially "The Work of the Worship Planning Team," on pp. 15–22.

4 From *Strong, Loving and Wise: Presiding in Liturgy*, by Robert W. Hovda, p. 7. Copyright © 1980 by The Order of St. Benedict. Published by The Liturgical Press, Collegeville, Minnesota. Used with permission.

5 See Bo Reicke, *"proistemi"* in *Theological Dictionary of the New Testament*, Volume VI, edited by Gerhard Friedrich, translated and edited by Geoffrey W. Bromiley, D. LITT., D.D. (Grand Rapids, MI: William B. Eerdmans Publishing Company, 1968), pp. 701–2.

6 See "The Presidency of the Eucharist According to the Ancient Tradition," by Hervé-Marie Legrand, in *Worship*, Volume 53, Number 5 (September 1979), pp. 413–38.

7 From "The Order for the Ordination of Elders," © 1979 by the Board of Discipleship, The United Methodist Church; © 1992 by The United Methodist Publishing House; from *The United Methodist Book of Worship*, p. 676. Used by permission.

8 From *Strong, Loving and Wise: Presiding in Liturgy*, by Robert W. Hovda, p. 63. Copyright © 1980 by The Order of St. Benedict. Published by The Liturgical Press, Collegeville, Minnesota. Used with permission.

9 See "The Work of Reading the Word in Public Worship," on pp. 23–28 in Volume II of *Worship Matters*.

10 From *The Book of Discipline of The United Methodist Church—1996*, ¶310. Copyright © 1996 by The United Methodist Publishing House. Used by permission. For more information on the role of deacons in worship, see "The Role of Deacons and Assisting Ministers," on pp. 130–36 in this volume.

11 See "A Litany for the Church and for the World" (p. 495), as well as the "Prayers of the People" sections in the services for "Daily Praise and Prayer" (pp. 568–76) in *The United Methodist Book of Worship* (Nashville, TN: The United Methodist Publishing House, 1992).

12 See *The Lord Be With You: A Visual Handbook for Presiding in Christian Worship*, by Charles D. Hackett and Don E. Saliers (Akron, OH: O.S.L. Publications, 1990), p. 3.

13 From "A Service of Word and Table I," © 1972 by The Methodist Publishing House; © 1980, 1985, 1989, 1992 by The United Methodist Publishing House; from *The United Methodist Book of Worship*, p. 36. Used by permission.

The presider's existence depends on the Christian community fulfilling its vocation of praise and worship. Only in the midst of this community at work are the ministries of Service, Word, Sacrament, and Order fulfilled.

DANIEL T. BENEDICT, JR.

Worship Resources Director,
The General Board of Discipleship,
Nashville, Tennessee

M. ANNE BURNETTE HOOK

Music Resources Director,
The General Board of Discipleship,
Nashville, Tennessee

The Role of Deacons and Assisting Ministers

A DEACON IN THE EPISCOPAL CHURCH ADDRESSED A GROUP OF would-be United Methodist deacons at an event held in Nashville, Tennessee. The purpose of the event was to allow diaconal ministers to explore the new United Methodist Order of Deacons and to discern God's call into this servant order. Part of that process included hearing from deacons in other denominations about their understanding of the role and work of a deacon. The Episcopal deacon described for those gathered the role of deacons in worship leadership in his denomination. In addition to reading the Gospel lesson and leading the prayers of intercession, the Episcopal deacon's role in celebrating the Eucharist is that of the table server. This includes setting the table for Communion, clearing the table after serving—even holding the worship book for the presider as she or he leads the Great Thanksgiving.

As one of many considering ordination as deacon in The United Methodist Church, I (Anne) was comfortable until my Episcopal friend mentioned holding the worship book for the presider. My reaction was swift (and a little embarrassing): I am *not* going to hold a worship book! Yes, I felt called by God to be a deacon, one who serves and leads others to serve God's people in the world. I was ready to connect the congregation's worship to service in the community and to participate in acts of servant ministry myself. Or so I thought.

Just as swiftly I realized that if I were to become a deacon, if I answered what I believed was God's call for me to be a servant leader, then I needed to model that servanthood in *all* that I did—including, and perhaps especially, providing leadership in worship. No one placed that vocational yoke on me; I chose to embrace that role as an act of obedience to God.

So, what exactly is the appropriate role for a deacon in worship? The answer is simple: *The role of the deacon in the liturgy is to mirror his or her vocation in the world.* And what is the nature of the deacon's vocation in the world? The verb form of the word *deacon* (*diakoneo*) provides a clue. It means to wait on someone (at table), to serve, to care for, to help. The early church drew upon these functions of serving, caring, and helping to formulate its understanding of the vocation of the deacon.

As United Methodists continue to live into what the two distinct orders of ordained ministry (elder and deacon) will mean for the future of our denomination, we need to understand the equal and unique roles

Worship Matters: A United Methodist Guide to Ways to Worship (Volume I) © 1999 Discipleship Resources. Used by permission.

each order plays in all aspects of the church, including worship leadership. While neither elders nor deacons depend on the other for their call or identity, they share both a common history and a call to be in partnership for the purpose of equipping the baptized for ministry in the world.

To understand the role of deacons in worship, we start with a broad focus on the historical roots and theological structures of ministry.

THE ROLE OF DEACON AND THE STRUCTURES OF MINISTRY

By structures of ministry we mean the richly textured sources and values of the ministry of all the baptized, which include the ministry of the ordained. These structures of ministry are grounded in God's mission of redeeming and reconciling the whole creation in Jesus Christ.

The vocation of the ministry of all the baptized is set forth in *The United Methodist Book of Discipline* under the heading "The Ministry of All Christians" (¶¶101–20). This vocation given to all believers at baptism expresses itself in servant ministry in daily life and shared servant leadership. The primary focus of such servanthood is on the transformation of the world and the making of disciples who share fully in the service (*diakonia*) of the church. From within the context of the vocation of all the baptized, the Holy Spirit orders the life of the church by ordaining some people to a lifetime of servant leadership. The task of these ordained ministers is to support, equip, and lead the baptized in fulfilling their corporate and personal vocation of living the gospel of Jesus Christ.

Any attempt at stating faithfully the liturgical role of deacons in relationship to elders must be grounded in the underlying commitment to ministry that both *builds up and unifies* the church in Jesus Christ and *links and extends* its life in service to the poor and marginalized.

LITURGICAL PRACTICE: PAST AND PRESENT

Even a cursory look at liturgical history reveals an evolving collage of images and impressions. The challenge is to see whether from among the many pictures a pattern emerges that informs the ways elders and deacons lead the church in its worship and work, in its liturgy and life. Let us briefly survey the history of liturgical practice.

The terms *deacon* and *elder* come to us from the New Testament, though the New Testament offers no single pattern of the ministry of leadership that may be normative for all future ministry in the church. Deacons served with the bishops (Philippians 1:1; 1 Timothy 3:8) and in the Pastoral Epistles seemed to be charged with the stewardship of material goods. The office of elder (*presbyteros*) derived from the model of the governing board of elders found in the Jewish synagogue. In the emerging Christian church, the term *elder* was used interchangeably with *overseer (episkopos)*. Note: As used in this article, *presbyter* and *elder* are equivalent terms. In United Methodist practice, we generally use *elder* for what the Scriptures designate as *presbyter (presbyteros)*.

The church during the New Testament period did not define the roles of deacons and elders in worship. This may be due to two reasons: First, the meaning of the terms *deacon* and *elder* at this stage had more to do with governance and management. Second, worship was clearly focused on the priestly work of Christ's singular sacrifice and the continuing "priestly" ministry of the assembly of the baptized, collectively. Nowhere

> Any attempt at stating faithfully the liturgical role of deacons in relationship to elders must be grounded in the underlying commitment to ministry that both *builds up and unifies* the church in Jesus Christ and *links and extends* its life in service to the poor and marginalized.

in the New Testament is the sacerdotal term *priest (hierus)* used for Christian ministers individually. Through baptism the whole church continued to proclaim and celebrate the all-sufficient sacrifice of Christ in the Eucharist—the weekly constitutive act of the collective priesthood.

By the second century, elders came to have a sacerdotal role in worship. At first, the term *priest* was associated with bishops (overseers), not with the presbyters (elders) who served as an advisory body to the bishop. Nevertheless, as urban faith communities grew to include multiple worshiping communities, bishops called upon elders to preside in the bishop's name in the several congregations of an area. The liturgical role of presbyters (elders) developed as the presidential work of the bishop was transferred to them and they became extensions of the bishop in each episcopal area.

In the early centuries, the worship leadership of the deacon commonly included reading or chanting the lessons—especially the Gospel—at the Eucharist; directing the prayers of the people during the service; receiving the offerings of the faithful (the gifts for the poor and the widows and the elements of bread and wine); assisting the bishop in the distribution of Holy Communion; and giving the signal for the penitents and catechumens to leave the worship before the beginning of the Eucharist.

In time, the power of the deacons began to threaten that of the presbyters. The outcome of the power struggle resulted in the hierarchical inferiority of deacons and their relegation to lesser roles. By the Middle Ages the diaconate was a mere step in preparation for the priesthood. At the discretion of the priest, deacons continued in some of the liturgical roles they had in earlier times; however, due to the short time normally spent in the diaconate and the scarcity of deacons, priests increasingly performed the liturgical functions proper to deacons.

For many centuries deacons had few specific functions in worship. Only with special permission was the deacon allowed to preach or administer baptism, to present the offerings to the presider, to invite the congregation to pray, to chant the *"Ite, missa est"* ("Go, you are dismissed") at Mass, and to sing the *Exsultet* at the Easter Vigil. Apparently, the deacon retained the right to read or chant the Gospel, even when other functions required permission.

The point is that the roles of elders and deacons in the liturgy evolved and were influenced by circumstances and needs of the church expanding in its pastoral care and missionary thrust. In a sense, the relationship between deacons and elders has been a dance: At times, they have moved and developed in harmony with each other; at other times, each has moved and developed in ways independent of the other. The evidence seems to be that the liturgical role of the deacon evolved very early in the life of the church and persisted despite setbacks due to periods of presbyters seeking hierarchical superiority over deacons, and the church as a whole neglecting its servant character.

The structures of the ministry of deacons and elders (presbyters), as well as of bishops, are clearly articulated in the consensus document, *Baptism, Eucharist and Ministry (BEM),*[1] which describes the functions of presbyters and deacons as follows:

> Presbyters serve as pastoral ministers of Word and sacraments in the local Eucharistic community.... Deacons represent to the Church its calling as servant in the world. By struggling in Christ's name with the myriad needs of societies and persons, deacons exemplify the interdependence of worship and service in the Church's life.[2]

BEM summarizes the deacon's worship roles as that of reading the Scriptures, preaching, and leading the people in prayer.

According to the *Book of Discipline* (¶415.6), ordination is an act of the whole church. This is confirmed in our practice: We United Methodists do not "reordain" persons previously ordained in another denomination; we recognize their orders (*BOD*, ¶¶337–39). Our recognition of orders rather than "reordaining" persons manifests a basic self-understanding: We see ourselves at once as part of the whole church while seeking to be a distinctive expression within the whole. We United Methodists see ourselves as recipients of the "common heritage" of Christians of every age and nation. Within this ecumenical partnership, we continue to practice a "practical divinity, the implementation of genuine Christianity in the lives of believers" (*BOD*, ¶60; especially pages 39–46).[3]

For this reason, United Methodists will be wise to steer a course that is simultaneously attentive to our unique vocation within the whole church and to the liturgical practice of the larger church as we learn our way into the partnership of elders and deacons in the liturgy. The time may have come for United Methodists to see these practices as a gift to us as we seek to discern the role of deacons in worship leadership.

In other churches with ordained deacons, such as the Roman Catholic and Episcopal churches, the deacon's distinctive liturgical role is to serve as the primary assistant to the presider, proclaim the Gospel reading, lead the intercessions, set the table in order before and after Communion, and dismiss the people. Deacons fulfill an "iconic" role, linking liturgy to life. Ormonde Plater sees the deacon's role in the drama of worship as "angel/messenger," "master of ceremonies" (as distinct from the presider), and "table waiter" so that the presbyter (priest) may preside as "pray-er" and represent Christ as host at the feast.[4]

THE ORDINAL AS SOURCE FOR REFLECTION

While there is much more work to do in exploring the office and work of the deacon, the ordinal (reflecting ¶¶310–14, 319–20 in the *Book of Discipline)* is explicit that the Order of Deacons is made up of people whose vocation is to lead the baptized in linking liturgy to life. In the service for the ordination of deacons (*UMBOW*, pp. 663–69), the examination of the candidates makes clear that the assisting role of the deacon is not that of *subordination* to the elder. Deacons are ordained to the distinctive work of service and servant leadership for the sake of a wounded and needy world.

Again, the underlying structure and values of our new understanding of the orders of elders and deacons guide us in outlining the shape of the deacon's liturgical leadership and ensure that deacons and elders avoid turf conflict. We believe that to ignore the distinctiveness of each order impoverishes the church's worship life and diminishes the fullness of Christ's ministry as both priest and servant in liturgy and life.

IMPLICATIONS FOR LEADING WORSHIP

There is evidence that the practice of leading worship in most United Methodist congregations in the latter part of the twentieth century has not changed much, even if the order of worship has. Many congregations are now using the Basic Pattern for Sunday worship (*UMH*, pp. 2–5); however, the *practice* of leadership is still similar to the "frontier"

> The relationship between deacons and elders has been a dance: At times, they have moved and developed in harmony with each other; at other times, each has moved and developed in ways independent of the other.

pattern of worship. In this pattern, the sermon is the focal point, with the assisting minister (sometimes called "the liturgist") leading all of the preliminary acts: the greeting, the opening prayers, the offering. The preacher reads the Scripture text, preaches, issues the invitation to discipleship and church membership, and blesses and dismisses the people. This approach amounts to a pragmatic division of labor based on both a principle of "equal" or "fair" distribution of leadership and the desire to avoid breaking the flow of worship by changing leaders too often.

We propose a contrasting principle for leading worship in United Methodist churches: *Those who lead worship—elders, deacons, and other leaders—should reflect in the liturgy their call and vocation in the church and the world.* This means that the liturgical function of the deacon and other assisting ministers (lay or clergy) is to link and extend the assembly's celebration of Word and Sacrament to its service *(diakonia)* in daily life. Deacons live, look, and listen on the margins of human life and human need. They interpret the tension between the good news celebrated in liturgy and the tragic news of the poor and oppressed. They lead the baptized in Christ's servanthood.

Instead of presiding at the "preliminaries" of worship, deacons lead those acts of worship that reflect their unique call to servant ministry. They act as partners with elders in leading worship, with each order reflecting its unique and distinct call to ministry in the church and in the world.

SPECIFIC SUGGESTIONS FOR LEADING WORSHIP

As you think about the unique ministry roles of elder, deacon, and baptized members and how these roles are reflected and conveyed in worship, consider the following guidelines. We offer these not as prescribed rules to follow but as helpful suggestions. The guidelines assume the Basic Pattern and Word and Table order as outlined in *The United Methodist Hymnal* (pp. 2–5) and in *The United Methodist Book of Worship* (pp. 13–32).

- The liturgical leadership roles of deacons and elders serve the church best when the distinctives of each order are not glossed but are enacted with clarity and charity. Mutual respect for the office and work of each order within the ministry of all Christians enables each to sacramentalize (mirror) the nature and mystery of the church: Christ as priest and Christ as servant.
- Deacons most appropriately lead in linking the community's worship to Christ's service and in extending the Lord's service by reading the Scriptures, particularly the Gospel reading; preaching to interpret the hurts and hopes of the world; leading the people in prayers for the world and the church; receiving the offerings of gifts for ministry in the community; receiving the elements and preparing the table for the Eucharist; assisting in serving Communion and setting the table in order after all have been served; and sending the people forth to serve, following the blessing of the elder. The deacon may train and guide others to do these tasks or to assist in doing them.
- Elders most appropriately preside at the community's worship by greeting the assembly in the name of God; proclaiming and interpreting the Word of God in preaching; announcing God's forgiveness to the people (and receiving God's forgiveness from the people); presiding at the Eucharist; and blessing the people as they go forth in the world.

- Deacons should, according to their gifts, preach from time to time in the regular weekly worship service.
- Deacons should assist or lead in weddings, funerals, morning and evening praise and prayer, healing services, and other pastoral liturgies. In some cases, because of the close servant relationship of the deacon to the people involved, it may be more appropriate for the deacon to preside in particular services.
- In circumstances where there is not an ordained elder, the deacon may serve the assembly by presiding in a worship service where the Lord's Supper is not celebrated. Presiding at the Table is not appropriate unless authorized under the provisions of the *Book of Discipline* (¶¶319, 320, 323, and especially 341).
- Because elders are ordained to Service, as well as Word, Sacrament and Order (*BOD*, ¶303.2), they are not exempt from linking liturgy and life in their presiding and proclaiming. Especially in circumstances where there is not an ordained deacon, the elder may appropriately serve the assembly by linking the assembly's worship to its work in daily life.
- A deacon may assist an elder with the baptism ritual. Based on historical and theological grounds, it is currently unclear what the limitations on such assistance should be. We may gain some insight into this from our understanding and practice of celebrating the Eucharist, as well as from studying the roles of deacons in other denominations. Further conversations are needed and are being instigated in order to clarify the appropriate role of deacons in the baptism ritual.

THE ROLE OF ASSISTING MINISTERS (LITURGISTS)

The presence of a deacon in worship should not eliminate the leadership of other members of the assembly. The task of the deacon is not only to model servant ministry for the assembly but also to equip the baptized for this ministry. It is therefore appropriate for the deacon to train one or more members of the assembly to serve as assisting ministers. Such ministers may read the Scriptures; lead the people in prayer for the world and for the church; prepare the table for Holy Communion, assist with serving; and send the people forth in service.

Using trained assisting ministers is especially appropriate in situations where the service and professional duties of a deacon are needed at a particular time in worship (for example, when the deacon who is also music minister is busy leading congregational singing while Holy Communion is being served). We strongly encourage elders in congregations where there is no deacon to provide for this important leadership opportunity for those in the assembly gifted and motivated to lead in worship.

DEACONS AS PARTNERS WITH ELDERS IN WORSHIP AND MINISTRY

Because the guidelines above focus on the liturgical roles of deacons in partnership with elders, they do not define or describe the distinctive work of deacons in the larger picture of the church's ministry. As more and more people heed the call of God to servant ministry and join the Order of Deacons, the church will continue to grow in its understanding of this unique and important calling.

Those who lead worship—elders, deacons, and other leaders—should reflect in the liturgy their call and vocation in the church and the world.

When deacons act out their calling in intentional acts of servant ministry within the context of worship, they contribute to both the church's understanding of this order and, more importantly, the call of all the baptized to be engaged in intentional acts of servanthood in the world. Our theological and missional logic prompts us to affirm that those who are ordained to specific and distinctive tasks of ministry reflect those tasks in worship.

In the end, deacons with elders will have to forge a partnership, in worship and in other aspects of ministry, that suits their context and styles of relating with grace, mutual respect, and joy in leading the faith community into the fullness of Christian faith and service.

FOR FURTHER READING

Deacons in the Liturgy, by Ormonde Plater (Harrisburg, PA: Morehouse Publishing, 1992).

Documents of Christian Worship: Descriptive and Interpretive Sources, by James F. White (Louisville, KY: Westminster John Knox Press, 1992).

Many Servants: An Introduction to Deacons, by Ormonde Plater (Boston, MA: Cowley Publications, 1991).

Strong, Loving and Wise: Presiding in Liturgy, by Robert W. Hovda (Collegeville, MN: The Liturgical Press, 1981).

The New Westminster Dictionary of Liturgy and Worship, edited by J. G. Davies (Louisville, KY: Westminster John Knox Press, 1986).

The Oxford Dictionary of the Christian Church (Third Edition), edited by F. L. Cross and E. A. Livingstone (New York, NY: Oxford University Press, 1997).

ENDNOTES

1 See *Baptism, Eucharist and Ministry: Faith and Order Paper No. 111* (Geneva: World Council of Churches, 1982), pp. 24–27.

2 From *Baptism, Eucharist and Ministry: Faith and Order Paper No. 111* (p. 27), 1982 © World Council of Churches, Geneva, Switzerland. Used with permission.

3 From *The Book of Discipline of The United Methodist Church—1996,* ¶60, p. 43. Copyright © 1996 by The United Methodist Publishing House. Used by permission.

4 See *Many Servants: An Introduction to Deacons,* by Ormonde Plater (Cambridge, MA: Cowley Publications, 1991), pp. 131–33.

5 It seems there may be a strong argument for deacons baptizing candidates if the roles of elders and deacons in the service of Holy Communion are considered. In the Eucharist, the elder presides in the whole service and specifically leads the Great Thanksgiving. At the giving, the deacon assists the elder by serving the elements. By analogy, it may be reasoned that the elder should pray the "Thanksgiving Over the Water," and either the elder or the deacon administer the water to the candidates. If this approach is taken, the deacon might baptize those persons that he or she has led in baptismal instruction.

Who Gets Communion?

SUSAN J. WHITE

Lunger Professor of Worship and Spirituality, Brite Divinity School, Texas Christian University, Fort Worth, Texas

I T SEEMS A SIMPLE ENOUGH QUESTION ON THE SURFACE: "WHO gets Communion?" But to ask it rigorously and seriously is to place ourselves at the center of a theological discussion almost as old as the Christian church itself. It is a question that calls us to consider carefully not only the meaning of the Lord's Supper but also of baptism, evangelism, pastoral care, and Christian nurture. All of these must be taken into account as we consider what qualifications, if any, are to be expected of those who are invited to the Lord's Table. The answers we arrive at as we wrestle with this question have wide-ranging consequences, not only for individual believers and congregations but also for relationships among different Christian traditions within the one body of Christ.

In most congregations, the discussion about qualifications for admission to Communion is precipitated by certain very practical situations. The first of these is a request by Christian parents that their baptized children be received at the Lord's Table at a very young age. The second usually arises when a congregation, which is growing quickly, begins to see significant numbers of people who have been baptized in other Christian denominations (or who have never been baptized at all) coming forward for Communion. In still other cases, questions of "worthiness" or "readiness" are raised when particular people wish to receive Holy Communion.

Of course, common sense and pastoral sensitivity dictate that no one who presents him or herself at the Lord's Table to receive Communion be turned away or refused the bread and wine. At the same time, many pastors and congregations are concerned with making general policy decisions in these critical areas of sacramental practice, so that people can know in advance whether it is appropriate to request the sacrament. It soon becomes clear that before such policies can be established, a number of questions about the relationship between the Lord's Supper and baptism must be addressed.

"SUFFER THE LITTLE CHILDREN": THE ISSUE OF INFANT COMMUNION

Few of us today are accustomed to seeing very young children given the elements of bread and wine at the Lord's Supper. In the Orthodox churches, however, it is a regular occurrence; indeed, infants are given Communion immediately after their baptism, using a mixture of bread and wine delivered by a special spoon. Orthodox Christians believe that in receiving children at the Lord's Table they are keeping alive the tradition of the early church and making a clear statement about the permanent Eucharistic center of the Christian life initiated in baptism. But for Western Christians (including United Methodists) things have not been so straightforward. Theological and biblical controversies, and even simple accidents of history, have conspired to fuel uncertainty about the admission of very young children to the Lord's Supper.

LANDMARKS IN THE HISTORY OF INFANT COMMUNION

Evidence for the admission of young children to the Lord's Table in the earliest centuries of Christianity is far from abundant. In the first unambiguous reference to infant baptism (from the early third century), the Communion service for the newly baptized is described in detail, but no specific provision for young children is mentioned. The service simply implies that all who have just been baptized join together to receive the Eucharist for the first time. There are also one or two references from this early period to children who are baptized just before their death and who are given Communion at the same time. But it is hard to build a strong case for infant Communion as the normal practice of the church from these slight indications.

Just a few decades later, the practice of infant Communion seems to be well-established. Cyprian (d. 258), for example, makes it clear that, along with baptism, participation in the Lord's Supper establishes a newly baptized child's identity as a Christian. At the end of the fourth century, Augustine (354–430) insists that what is given to adults in the sacrament of Communion is also needed by children. Indeed, for Augustine, children are the model for the way all Christians must come to the Supper, helpless and dependent on God alone.

If the Communion of infants was the norm for early Christianity, certainly by the Middle Ages this had changed radically, and a person's "first Communion" was delayed for several years after birth. The reasons for the disappearance of children from the Communion rail are varied and complex. Certainly it is true that regular Communion for adults had also diminished precipitously, to the point that church legislation in the twelfth century had to insist that everyone receive the sacrament at least once a year or be liable to penalty. At the same time, confirmation established itself as a separate rite of initiation, signifying the receiving of the Holy Spirit, which itself came to be associated with an activating grace necessary for worthy reception of Holy Communion.

With the Protestant Reformation and the Enlightenment came an increasing "intellectualization" of both baptism and the Lord's Supper. In the Reformation churches, there was an emphasis on the knowledge of the essential doctrines of the faith as a prerequisite for partaking in Communion, as well as a strong conviction that without it people would "eat and drink judgment against themselves" (1 Corinthians 11:29). In churches of the Anabaptist and Baptist traditions, the capacity to understand and assent was also necessary for baptism.

As a part of the Evangelical Revival, the early Methodists were clear that infant baptism was a profound statement of the gospel message—namely, that the grace of God comes before everything else, even our own ability to respond. To this day this has been the consistent theological position of Methodism with regard to baptism. There is less clarity on the qualifications necessary for receiving Communion. Because Methodism began as a "society" for spiritual discipline and pastoral oversight within the Church of England, it was expected that most members would receive the sacrament of the Lord's Supper in the parish church under the existing regulations governing admission. The Methodist Societies were then free to impose more rigorous qualifications for the life of the Society, including for inclusion in Love Feasts, Holy Communion, and Covenant Renewal Services.

As Methodism gradually began to take on the characteristics of a church in its own right, it became more difficult to negotiate the relationship between qualifications for full participation in a closed Society and those for participation in an open church. For most Methodists a "double standard" prevailed: Baptism was open to all as a sign of God's prevenient grace, but the Lord's Supper was restricted to those who could actively assent to the doctrines of the faith and were earnestly seeking repentance.

In order to bridge the gap between these two sacramental events (and, indeed, two theologies), American Methodists adopted the language of probationary and full membership. This terminology allowed Methodists to retain the sense of a "closed Society" even while striving to be a church. Although John Wesley deliberately removed the rite of confirmation in the *Sunday Service* (his revision of the 1662 *Book of Common Prayer* for the Methodist Societies in America), the sense of some further qualification for full initiation was strong and put Methodists in an ambiguous position when it came to admission to the Lord's Supper. On the one hand, Wesleyan theology was clear that all Christians, from the time of their baptism, were on a journey toward salvation and that Holy Communion was both nourishment and assurance for that journey. On the other hand, a profession of evangelical faith was seen to be the prerequisite for full membership in the Methodist family of churches, the principal sign of which was the invitation to gather with the church at the Lord's Table.

THE "CIRCUMCISED HEART":
BAPTISMAL THEOLOGY AND COMMUNION

More recently, however, this "double standard" has begun to be questioned on serious theological grounds. It has seemed to many people that if baptism is full initiation into the body of Christ, visible as the local community of faith, then all aspects of community life should be available to all the baptized, including very young children. This argument rests on a number of theological foundations.

Many note that throughout our history Christians have sought to relate baptism theologically to the ancient Jewish practice of circumcision. Just as circumcision was the sign of a man's inclusion in the covenant community, so baptism is the sign of a Christian's inclusion in the community of the new covenant. Just as circumcision was an emblem of God's willingness to accept repentance, so too is Christian baptism. Peter is reported to have said on the Day of Pentecost: "The promise is for you [and] for your children" (Acts 2:39); and baptism, like circumcision, becomes a sign of that promise received.

Of course, there are significant differences between Christian baptism and Jewish circumcision. Where circumcision is a ritual that results in a

In most congregations, the discussion about qualifications for admission to Communion is precipitated by certain very practical situations.

permanent, outward change, baptism is a ritual that results in an inward, spiritual change. Circumcision is for males only, while baptism is for men and women alike; indeed, it signifies a grafting into the Christ in whom there is "no longer male and female" (Galatians 3:28).

Despite the differences, Christian thinkers in every age have been able to speak with confidence of baptism as a sign of "the circumcised heart," in which a covenant relationship is established by God, and in which God's promise to forgive sins is made real and active in the life of an individual. It is this understanding that informs the use of the term *Baptismal Covenant* for the initiation rites in the *The United Methodist Hymnal* (pp. 32–54) and in *The United Methodist Book of Worship* (pp. 81–114).

This analogy between baptism and circumcision provides one avenue for thinking about the full participation in the community of the new covenant, including participation in the meal that nourishes the life and faith of that community. Another avenue is to return, as John Wesley did, to the sacramental theology and practice of the early church for inspiration. It seems clear that if we believe that God acts decisively in baptism, engrafting the newly baptized into Christ and into the body of Christ, which is the church, then to nullify any part of that relationship by refusing any baptized Christian Communion is theologically irresponsible. This is certainly the view expressed in the services of the Baptismal Covenant, and affirmed in the very opening statement: In baptism we are "initiated into Christ's holy Church" and "incorporated into God's mighty acts of salvation and given new birth through water and the Spirit" as a free gift of God (*UMBOW*, p. 87).[1] It is exactly these things that are renewed and celebrated each time the community of faith joins together at the Lord's Table.

INSIGHTS FROM CHILD DEVELOPMENT

Other arguments against the inclusion of small children in the celebration of the Lord's Supper are rooted not so much in theology as they are in a sense that the spiritual and intellectual life of children is not sufficiently well-developed to apprehend the vast riches of the Eucharistic meal. Of course, the easiest defense against this approach is simply to ask: "Is anyone, even the wisest of us, able to understand the Eucharist fully?" However, perhaps this question of spiritual maturity or "readiness" needs to be given more serious attention.

Although anecdotal evidence about individual children who exhibit particular attentiveness to the workings of God within them have always circulated in the church, it is only quite recently that the spiritual development of children more generally has been studied in any depth. The results have been surprising to many of us.

Most of the current research shows that the spiritual development of children begins at a very early age; indeed, most child development specialists say that the course of our adult spirituality is already being mapped out in the very first months of life. As we begin to negotiate the delicate balance between dependence and independence, trust and mistrust, acceptance and rejection, the foundations for our conscious relationship with God are being laid.[2]

These and other recent insights from the field of child development have provided a second strand of reflection on the desirability of infant Communion, calling into question the exclusion of children from what is generally seen as a primary source of spiritual nourishment simply because of their inability to articulate their spiritual experience in adult terms.

There are, of course, other aspects of church membership that may require a level of maturity that young children do not yet possess. Churches may well need to restrict voting rights, eligibility for committee work, and other positions of responsibility to those who have reached a certain age or level of responsibility. The participation of children in the administrative life of a congregation can surely be determined as local needs apply. But these are matters of negligible theological significance compared with the question of admission to the Lord's Supper.

Detaching the reception of Communion from some measure of mental or spiritual "readiness" and grounding it, like the reception of baptism, in the gracious initiative of God has other benefits as well. Many people in our congregations will never attain a high level of readiness for Communion in this intellectual sense, including those who are mentally challenged and those who suffer from senile dementia. To recognize that we do not produce the fruits of the Eucharist from within ourselves, but that they are fundamentally gifts of God, allows us to set the Communion of people with mental limitations within the overall theological integrity of the sacrament, rather than understanding it as some sort of exception.

PASTORAL AND CATECHETICAL CONSIDERATIONS

If there are good theological and spiritual reasons for admitting very young children to Communion, there are good pastoral and catechetical reasons as well. As a look at any school playground will tell you, children have a very keen sensitivity to being excluded from group activities, and for this reason exclusion from the Lord's Supper raises serious pastoral problems with small children. As Eucharistic worship becomes increasingly more central to the life of United Methodist congregations, it raises the possibility that a child's experience of exclusion from a principal act of worship may arise weekly. The reception of Communion at an early age can also be an important factor in religious education. Teachers tell us that the best and most deeply integrated learning takes place when instruction is intimately connected to experience; to tie teaching about the Lord's Supper to actual experiences of receiving the Supper is simply good pedagogy.

This is not to say that a pastor should not expect a level of seriousness toward the act of receiving Communion. It should be made clear that nothing that indicates a deliberately frivolous or irreverent attitude is acceptable. Of course, this is true of young and old alike. It is part of the teaching ministry of the church to develop and share an understanding of the presence of Christ in the Supper, which creates a disposition of devotion in all participants.

But there is more at stake here than whether children feel included or not, or whether they find the Supper a learning experience. To invite children to the Lord's Table and to expect of them serious engagement with the act of Communion, at the level of which they are capable, is to affirm their dignity as members of the community of faith. In a world where the worth of children is so often violated and denied, this simple act of acceptance can be a sign that an alternative society is being proposed—a society of fundamental equality in Christ.

If there are good theological and spiritual reasons for admitting very young children to Communion, there are good pastoral and catechetical reasons as well.

"ALL YE WHO ARE HEAVY LADEN": THE "OPEN TABLE" DEBATE

The second important issue that arises in discussions about who to admit to the Lord's Table is whether any external criteria ought to be applied when deciding who is invited to receive Communion and, if so, what those criteria might be. It is worth repeating here that the Communion rail is not the place to ask questions about the baptismal status, doctrinal convictions, or moral failings of any people who present themselves for the Lord's Supper. But each congregation and its leadership does have a responsibility to set up a normal Communion discipline, which is known to those in the congregation, so that a foundation for pastoral conversation is in place when certain kinds of situations arise.

Various categories of people may, by their regular presence at the Communion rail, raise questions about the openness of the Lord's Table. First, there are those who are baptized members of other Christian denominations who, in this highly mobile society, may attend not only the occasional United Methodist wedding or funeral but also Sunday services. Then there are the so-called "seekers," those who are actively interested in the Christian faith but who are, as yet, unbaptized. Increasingly, as interfaith relationships become more common, adherents of other religious traditions—Judaism, Buddhism, or Islam, for example—may expect to receive Communion. And finally, there are people whom the early church would have described as "notorious sinners," those who are baptized Christians, but who have caused scandal or division in the church, or who promote doctrines that are decidedly contrary to traditional Christian teaching. Let's look at these issues in more depth.

THE QUESTION OF THE UNBAPTIZED

Throughout its history, the church has taken the clear and consistent position that the Lord's Supper is for the baptized and only for the baptized. In practice, the question of unbaptized people partaking of the Lord's Supper is rarely raised by the ancient theologians. For most of our Christian forebears, it was simply unthinkable that an unbaptized person would ask to receive Communion. In the early church, those who were preparing for baptism would attend a service of Christian worship up to the point at which the Communion was celebrated; then they were required to leave the assembly. Until his or her baptism, no Christian would ever have even witnessed a celebration of the Supper, let alone have participated in it; and much of the emotional and spiritual power of Christian initiation lay in the revealing of the "mysteries" for the first time.

When the issue is raised in this early period, the restriction of the Lord's Table to the baptized is used as an incentive for timely baptism. In a famous Lenten sermon, Augustine, who recognized that there was some reluctance on the part of his hearers to receive the sacrament of baptism and the Christian discipline that attended it, used admission to the Lord's Supper as an enticement to becoming a baptized member of the church:

> Christ provides food every day, his table is the real community table. Why is it, O "hearers," that you see this table but do not approach?... Sign up for baptism! If the festival [of Easter] does not motivate you, let simple curiosity prompt you, that you may know the meaning of "He who eats my flesh and drinks my blood, abides in me and I in him" (John 6:57).[3]

For Augustine, it was the opening of the heart occurring at baptism that allowed a person to perceive the risen Christ in the elements of bread and wine.

Some Methodists turn to the writings of John Wesley in support of inviting the unbaptized to the Table. They cite his understanding of the Eucharist as a "converting ordinance" with the power to grant knowledge of Christ's mercy and an assurance of forgiveness of sin. First, Wesley rarely talks about "conversion," and in doing so he does not use the term in its later sense of a turning away from another form of religious faith (or no faith at all) to Christian belief. He is rather describing a personal assurance of a Christian faith already professed.

Second, in every case in which Wesley refers to the Lord's Supper as a "converting ordinance," he cites the example of a baptized Christian such as his mother, Susannah, who, in a famous passage from Wesley's *Journal,* is quoted as saying that it was at a Communion service that she fully understood that she had been given new life in Christ.[4] Like his early-church exemplars, Wesley would never have considered that an unbaptized person would be invited to the Lord's Table.

Many of those who argue for a radically open Table, for a situation in which no one is ever excluded from receiving Communion for any reason whatever, argue that the urgent demands of evangelization and pastoral care take priority over all other constraints. They may grant that theology, Scripture, and church history all tend toward a restriction of the Lord's Table to baptized Christians, but say that to refuse anyone Communion is to close the door on an evangelistic opportunity. This approach, it seems, is opening us to long-term difficulties.

When we look at the words of the Great Thanksgiving (*UMBOW,* pp. 36–38), we see that the affirmations we invite people to make relate directly to (and in a way depend on) the promises that God has made to the baptized. This is not to say that the Supper is some sort of reward for having assented to the baptismal promises. It is to say that in the Lord's Supper we celebrate what we have received from God in our baptism, and that on the ground of our baptism the Lord's Supper provides nourishment for further growth in faith, hope, and love. In being grafted into Christ in our baptism, we are given the ability to (in the words of the Service of Word and Table) "offer ourselves in praise and thanksgiving as a holy and living sacrifice, in union with Christ's offering for us, [and to] proclaim the mystery of faith" (*UMBOW,* p. 38).[5]

There are occasionally those who say that they find ongoing spiritual nourishment in the Supper, but who are not ready or willing to make the lifelong commitment that baptism entails. This is problematic as well. To approach the Lord's Table is, in effect, to ask to enter into a relationship with the One who invites us to that Table—and the rite of entry into that relationship is baptism. In baptism we are given both our Christian identity and Christian responsibility. For the baptized, the Lord's Supper is both liberating and demanding. It liberates us for reconciliation with one another and with God as members of Christ's body, and it demands the living out of that reconciliation in the world. To say you are not ready to commit yourself to the demands of baptism is to say you are not ready to commit yourself to the demands of the Lord's Supper. Or, stated more positively, anyone who appears regularly at the Table should be baptized as soon as possible.

Throughout its history, the church has taken the clear and consistent position that the Lord's Supper is for the baptized and only for the baptized.

WORTHY COMMUNION

If John Wesley is arguing anything in those passages about the Lord's Supper as a "converting ordinance," it is that our own sense of unworthiness after baptism should not hinder us from approaching the Lord's Table. From very early in the church's history, there has been a strong sense that the health of the body of Christ as a whole depended on the righteousness of each of its members and on the quality of their mutual relationships. In cases of notorious sin or doctrinal deviation, erring Christians were subjected to various structures of church discipline, including rigorous penitential practices, forms of ritual repentance, and (most seriously) prohibition from receiving Communion, which came to be referred to as "excommunication." This is already hinted at in 1 Corinthians 11, in which Paul is condemning rich members of the church at Corinth for humiliating poor members, and suggesting that if they were to receive Communion under these conditions, they would "eat and drink judgment against themselves" (1 Corinthians 11:29).

Unfortunately, the general sense of the link between amendment of life and the receiving of Communion led people to be increasingly anxious about their worthiness to receive the sacrament, until it became the practice for most Christians to stay away from Communion altogether because of their sense of sinfulness. In most of the Reformation churches, this led to very infrequent celebrations of Communion since considerable time was needed for people to make spiritual preparation for worthy Communion.

From the very beginning, Methodists were urged to receive Communion as often as possible, giving less thought to their own worthiness than to the abundant mercies of God available in the sacrament. John Wesley makes this case in his famous address, "The Duty of Constant Communion":

> [God] offers to endue your soul with new strength; because you are unworthy of it, will you deny to take it? What can God himself do for us farther, if we refuse his mercy because we are unworthy of it?[6]

This is not to say that people who present themselves for the Lord's Supper are not under obligation to renew their commitment to the vision of the holy life that is enacted in the breaking of bread and sharing of the cup. What is the pastor to do about people who regularly appear at the Communion rail and who are known to be involved in serious fraud, slander, or violent abuse of spouse or children, and who pridefully resist making steps toward amendment of life? For many Christian congregations these are among the most difficult situations to deal with when asking the question: "Who gets Communion?" On the one hand, to deny to anyone the redeeming grace of Christ available in Communion seems harsh and judgmental. On the other, to welcome a thoroughly unrepentant person who seems unable to see the implications of the Supper can be a source of scandal to the Christian community, and can create a serious fracture in the body of Christ.

Once again, for a pastor to turn away such a person at the Communion rail is irresponsible. But it may be that consideration of the theology of both baptism and the Lord's Supper can be the starting point for a serious pastoral conversation, which might well conclude with the decision that a particular person should stay away from the Lord's Table for some period of time for the sake of the community as a whole.

BAPTISM AND COMMUNION IN AN ECUMENICAL CENTURY

How we answer the question about who is and isn't admitted to the Lord's Table has consequences not only within our own congregations but also for our relationships across denominational lines within the larger body of Christ. Because different branches of the Christian church have established different Eucharistic practices based on divergent theological convictions, they are currently inhibited from sharing in the Lord's Supper freely across denominational lines. Indeed, the most basic form of excommunication is when the leaders of churches suspend the fellowship of Communion between their churches.

Because of this, one of the central questions for ecumenical relations has been: Under what conditions can Christians gather around the Lord's Table in unity? For the past seventy-five years this question has been explored in bilateral and multilateral conversations. Although full ecumenical agreement has not yet been achieved, many Christian bodies have worked in the past decades at something approaching consensus in this matter.

Internationally, it has been the World Council of Churches (WCC) that has facilitated this discussion. In the United States of America, a similar role has been played by the Consultation on Church Union (COCU). Consensus documents such as *Baptism, Eucharist and Ministry* (WCC, 1982) and the "covenanting" documents of the COCU member-churches have dealt with the issue of mutual Table fellowship among historically divided denominations.

While these discussions have been both useful and exciting, they have often been very painful as well. In many cases, the best that has been achieved is what is termed "interim Eucharistic fellowship," in which churches acknowledge their deep divisions but agree to recognize one another's Eucharistic ministry. Many Christians claim, however, that it is wrong to share in Communion while we remain so deeply divided, since it will be the sharing in the Lord's Supper that is the sign of our ultimate pulling down of the barriers that divide the one body of Christ. Although the Methodist churches traditionally invite to the Table all who have been baptized—whatever their denominational affiliation—a congregation may find that invitation being declined because of the canonical discipline of another church.

CONCLUSION

A close reading of both the United Methodist "Services of the Baptismal Covenant" (*UMBOW*, pp. 81–114) and the "Services of Word and Table" (*UMBOW*, pp. 33–53) gives us answers to many of the questions we have raised in this article. For example, at the end of the service of the Baptismal Covenant I, we find the following rubric: "It is most fitting that the service continue with Holy Communion, in which the union of new members with the body of Christ is most fully expressed. The new members, including children, may receive first" (*UMBOW*, p. 94).[7] This statement encapsulates the understanding of the new services about the relationship between baptism and the Lord's Supper and, in this regard, makes two things clear.

First, Christian baptism is initiation into the body of Christ, of which the local congregation of The United Methodist Church is an expression but not the totality. Second, the Lord's Supper is the profoundest expression of the meaning of baptism and of the trajectory baptism sets for us into the meaning of Christian discipleship.

> From the very beginning, Methodists were urged to receive Communion as often as possible.

In addition, we are given a clear sense in these services that both sacraments are gifts of God to us, binding us together in the body of Christ and empowering us for mission in the world. To be both serious and generous in our approach to the question, "Who gets Communion?" is to understand the significance of the sacramental life in our journey along the way of salvation toward the day when "Christ comes in final victory and we feast at his heavenly banquet" (*UMBOW*, p. 38).[8]

FOR FURTHER READING

"A Converting Ordinance and the Open Table," by John Bowmer in *Proceedings of the Wesley Historical Society* (Burnley, England: Wesley Historical Society), Volume 34, pp. 109-13.

Baptism: Christ's Act in the Church, by Laurence Hull Stookey (Nashville, TN: Abingdon Press, 1982).

Eucharist: Christ's Feast With the Church, by Laurence Hull Stookey (Nashville, TN: Abingdon Press, 1993).

Responsible Grace: John Wesley's Practical Theology, by Randy Maddox (Nashville, TN: Abingdon Press, 1994).

ENDNOTES

1 From "The Baptismal Covenant I," © 1976, 1980, 1985, 1989, 1992 by The United Methodist Publishing House; from *The United Methodist Book of Worship,* p. 87. Used by permission.

2 In his classic book *The Spiritual Life of Children* (Boston, MA: Houghton Mifflin Company, 1990), psychiatrist Robert Coles analyzes children's dreams, drawings, and modes of play. He concludes that even though a small child cannot describe in a sophisticated, analytical way the shape of the spiritual life that is growing within, that spiritual life is very real and perhaps as complex as the spiritual life of adults.

3 From *Patrilogiae: Cursus Completus* (Series Latina), by J. P. Migne (Paris, France: Garnier, 1958), Volume 38, Sermon 132, p. 734. Translated by Susan J. White.

4 See "The Journal of the Reverend John Wesley, A.M.," by John Wesley, in *The Works of John Wesley,* Volume I (Grand Rapids, MI: Zondervan Publishing House, n.d.), p. 222.

5 From "A Service of Word and Table I," © 1972 by The Methodist Publishing House; © 1980, 1985, 1989, 1992 by The United Methodist Publishing House; from *The United Methodist Book of Worship,* p. 38. Used by permission.

6 See "The Duty of Constant Communion," by John Wesley, in *The Works of John Wesley,* Volume VII (Grand Rapids, MI: Zondervan Publishing House, n.d.), p. 151.

7 From "The Baptismal Covenant I," © 1976, 1980, 1985, 1989, 1992 by The United Methodist Publishing House; from *The United Methodist Book of Worship,* p. 94. Used by permission.

8 From "A Service of Word and Table I," © 1972 by The Methodist Publishing House; © 1980, 1985, 1989, 1992 by The United Methodist Publishing House; from *The United Methodist Book of Worship,* p. 38. Used by permission.

The Distribution of Communion by the Laity to Those Who Cannot Attend Worship

LAURENCE HULL STOOKEY

Hugh Latimer Elderdice,
Professor of Preaching and Worship,
Wesley Theological Seminary,
Washington, DC

LAITY TAKING THE ELEMENTS FROM THE CONGREGATIONAL Table of the Lord to those who cannot attend the parish worship service is a recent development in United Methodism. The usual practice has been for a pastor to arrange a convenient time to conduct the sacramental service with people who are sick or who are limited in their ability to leave home. Often this has been done independently of the Eucharistic celebration on Sunday—probably on a weekday, and less frequently than the parish celebration. In the hospital or home the pastor then conducted a form of the Communion service, perhaps of reduced length depending on the circumstances. In any event, this form of the service included the act of giving thanks over bread and the cup that were not previously used by the congregation.

There is a significant difference between receiving the *same* bread and cup the congregation received, and participating in a separate Eucharistic celebration apart from the congregation. Consider the following scenarios from everyday life:

1. For some years, a group of close friends has had lunch at a local pizzeria on the first Saturday of each month. Missing from one of these occasions is Maria, due to injuries in a recent accident. The assembled friends pass around and sign a "sorry about your accident" card and delegate Karen and Joe to deliver it to Maria, along with portions of the pizza. The designated friends do this, bringing Maria greetings from "the gang" and also reporting the gist of conversations that took place so that she will be "up on the news." Although Maria could not attend, she feels connected both to the event and to all who have participated in it.

2. Juan, injured in an accident and therefore unable to cook for himself, places a phone order for pizza, which is shortly delivered to his door.

Note that the need for physical nourishment is satisfied as fully in the second instance as in the first. The difference has to do with the sense of being connected to people who have eaten the same meal as part of a familiar and significant social event. In the case of Juan, there is no sense that he is being surrounded by the care and concern of loved ones. Therefore, the pizza he received as the result of a phone order does not "mean" the same thing as the pizza brought to Maria by Joe and Karen on behalf of an entire group of close friends.

The difference in the meaning of the experiences of Juan and Maria reveals the fundamental reason for encouraging the distribution of Communion by members of the congregation at the close of the Sunday service: Such a practice enhances a sense of worship that is truly corporate and not individualistic, by maintaining regular connections between those who can and those who cannot attend the parish Eucharist. In many circumstances distribution of Communion by laity may ease the schedule of overextended clergy; however, this is a secondary benefit, not a primary purpose. Clergy should continue to make regular pastoral visits to provide spiritual counsel and mutual edification to those who are unable to attend Sunday worship. These visits should take place regardless of whether the Eucharist is celebrated or not. The analogy above is not suggesting that the pastor's visit is as insignificant as an employee delivering carryout food. All analogies have limited applicability.

The distribution of Communion by laity after each congregational observance of the Lord's Supper will seem like an innovation only if we do not remember our history. From the report of Justin Martyr we know that, at least as early as the mid-second century, after a congregation had received Holy Communion on Sunday, deacons took portions of the remaining elements to those who were absent.[1] This practice arose from a conviction that the congregation is the family of God and that all members should share significant family meals, even if they were unable to be present. We may compare this to the modern-day practice of taking portions of turkey, stuffing, cranberries, and pumpkin pie to family members who are unable to attend the Thanksgiving Day feast.

The ancient practice declined as congregations began to see themselves less as members together in God's household who by virtue of their baptism gather around the Table of their common Lord, and more as an assortment of individuals gathering voluntarily in the same location to seek fulfillment for personal spiritual needs. These are two quite different views of the nature of the church. In recent times, we have come to realize that the early pattern, much closer in time as it was to the New Testament church, contains a wealth of meaning we need to recover.

What is implied in the shift from the pastor's weekday visit with Holy Communion to the lay distribution from the common Sunday Lord's Table is nothing less than this: We seek a renewed sense of the church as a body of believers called by God and bound together in Christian faith, worship, and service. We are no longer willing to settle for viewing the church as a voluntary gathering of individuals who live largely in isolation from one another but assemble in the same building when they find this useful for meeting of private spiritual needs.

WHO OUGHT TO BE INCLUDED IN THIS MINISTRY?

This renewed sense of the church as God's household extends the scope of our usual understanding about who shall be included in the sacramental meal. Certainly, people who are sick and those who are limited in their ability to leave home will be included. But often we overlook people who cannot attend the parish service for other legitimate reasons. These include individuals whose work schedules coincide with the hours of Sunday worship and those who at these times may be engaged in other necessary responsibilities, such as caring for the sick. Certainly, frivolous reasons for not attending the Lord's Day service (preferring to stay in bed or to do the grocery shopping) should be discounted. But often we unintentionally excommunicate people who truly wish to attend. We can seek out these people through notices in church publications and through personal communication, so that they may be included in the reception of the sacrament.

We should also note that people of very diminished mental capacity are proper candidates for receiving Communion. Indeed, these individuals may particularly be in need of such visits, for in the wisdom of God the sacraments operate at levels beyond that of cognitive recognition. Pastoral experience demonstrates again and again that people who have been faithful communicants during former times when they were cognitively aware of the meaning of the Eucharist, but who now seem unable to understand the sacrament, are nevertheless refreshed or given a sense of joy when the familiar bread and cup are administered to them in the name of Christ. Well-meaning relatives or medical personnel may respond to a phone call asking about a possible future visit by saying: "It is very kind of you to offer, but there is really no need to come. She no longer has any awareness, so it would be a waste of your time." An apt reply is: "I understand your concern. Still, we find that often such people respond to the sacrament in positive ways we can neither anticipate nor explain. We would like to visit her despite her condition, if that is convenient for you."

The inclusion of the absent in the congregational Communion helps to maintain ties that otherwise would become frayed. Often those who become permanently limited in their ability to leave home are remembered by everyone at the beginning of their confinement, but over time fewer and fewer active members take a continuing interest in them. Thus these people gradually receive less and less attention in the thoughts and prayers of their sisters and brothers in Christ.

People whose work schedules require them to be absent from Sunday worship for prolonged periods of time may be forgotten entirely; for, unlike people who are sick or who are limited in their ability to leave home, their names never even appear on prayer lists in a church bulletin or newsletter. One way for a congregation to create a greater sense of cohesiveness among its members and to help everyone remember those who are absent is for everyone to whom Communion will be taken on a particular Sunday to be named and remembered in prayer as a part of the worship service.

The cohesiveness of Christ's people should also be seen as extending to those who have died in the Lord. Our earthly Eucharists are anticipations of the great feast of heaven. Death itself cannot not break the Table fellowship of God's people. Extending the Table as fully as possible on earth enables us to see more clearly the hosts of heaven who gather with us at the banquet. Thus facilitating the fullest possible participation in the sacrament incarnates the petition we sometimes sing as we leave the Table: "With our sainted ones in glory seated at the heavenly board, may the church that's waiting for you keep love's tie unbroken, Lord" (*UMH,* 614).[2]

The purpose of the preceding discussion is precisely to keep the ties of love unbroken—among the living (present and absent) and between all the saints (living and the dead), for all are bound together in the love of Christ. Achieving this awareness is worth pursuing carefully as we work out the practical aspects of extending the Table of the Lord.

The distribution of Communion by members of the congregation... enhances a sense of worship that is truly corporate and not individualistic, by maintaining regular connections between those who can and those who cannot attend the parish Eucharist.

HOW DOES A CONGREGATION BEGIN SUCH A MINISTRY?

To begin the distribution of the Eucharist as suggested in this article requires several steps:

1. Establish a comprehensive list of those who cannot attend Sunday worship but who wish to receive the sacrament.

2. Contact these individuals before each worship service during which the Eucharist will be celebrated to determine if they wish to receive the Supper. In large congregations this process may require a significant amount of work; however, consider asking one or more of the people who are limited in their ability to leave home to do the contacting rather than involving a pastor, church secretary, or worship committee member. People who are limited in their ability to leave home often feel cut off from volunteer church work when, in fact, they may be very capable of making phone calls and keeping records.

3. Once the comprehensive list has been compiled, secure and train recruits who will make the visits. It is ideal to create visiting teams consisting of at least two people. Not all of these volunteers will be available to make visits every time they are needed; therefore, it is well to recruit two to three teams for every person to be visited, unless, of course, some teams are willing to make more than one call on the same day.

Once the program is in place, those participating as visitors will be the best recruiters, as they can attest to the benefits they receive through this kind of service. Those visited will become the best interpreters of the program to others who may have reservations about it.

4. When assigning visiting teams to those unable to attend Sunday worship, be sure to create a variety of visiting options. The most "natural" assignments may not be the most useful in fostering cohesiveness across a congregation. For example, it seems logical for a brother or aunt or neighbor to take Communion to a relative or friend who is limited in his or her ability to leave home. However, while this arrangement may be convenient, it may not achieve the goal of keeping members of the congregation fully in contact with one another. Both the congregation as a whole and the person who sees her or his relatives or neighbors regularly will benefit more from a visit by people she or he would otherwise not see or even know. It may be a good idea to assign new members to individuals they have never met, precisely in order to establish contact between people in the congregation who otherwise would never encounter one another.

Similarly, it is advisable to create diversity within visitation teams. Convenience might dictate that a married couple constitute a team; however, serving Communion is not a "marital" function. It is probably better to assign a husband and wife to separate teams. Youth can be assigned to form teams with older people, and people of differing ethnic traditions or dissimilar socioeconomic backgrounds can also be profitably paired.

5. Keep teams from visiting the same person month after month. The goal is to keep attending and non-attending members as fully in contact with one another as possible across the whole congregation. Therefore, rotate the teams regularly, even if it meets with some resistance due to the lure of convenience or the appeal of familiarity. Of course, there are always exceptions. For example, someone who, due to the loss of mental capacity, remembers only a few people can easily become agitated by people he or she does not recognize. In such a case, it is wise to assign one team to this person.

6. As mentioned earlier, visiting teams should receive careful training. Training usually takes several hours, and pastors should provide the primary leadership in designing the training. Indeed, the *Book of Discipline* encourages pastors to design and conduct such training (*BOD*, ¶331.1b). While the mechanics of the visitation must be thoroughly explored (perhaps through roleplaying exercises), the theological understanding of the Service of Word and Table is fundamental. At a minimum, the commentary on pages 13 and 14 of *The United Methodist Book of Worship* together with the service on pages 51 through 53 deserve to be considered in detail.

It is likely that initially all of those being trained will be new to the program. Give careful attention to participants who may feel anxious because the process is unfamiliar to them. Once the program has been in place for some time, try to pair new volunteers with experienced ones. This allows for on-the-job training, which augments the more formal training sessions.

7. Establish clear procedures for team members to follow when unexpected personal circumstances prevent them from participating on an assigned Sunday. Such procedures help avoid situations where a team discovers at the last minute that it has to do "double duty" because another team is unexpectedly absent.

8. At the Sunday service, the bread and cup to be taken to the absent should be on the Lord's Table with the elements to be received by the congregation. After everyone has received Communion, hand portions of the bread and cup to the visiting teams. This can be done just before the closing hymn is sung. The presider can read the names of those to be visited and then offer a brief prayer on their behalf. While the closing hymn is being sung, the visiting teams can depart. This process enhances the continuity between what happens in the congregation and what occurs in hospitals and homes. That is to say, the Communion received by those who are absent from the service truly becomes an extension of the Communion received by those who are present. Work schedules may dictate that some people who are to be visited will not be at home until much later in the day; in such cases, make the necessary adjustments about when the particular visiting team should depart.

HOW IS THE COMMUNION SERVICE CONDUCTED?

The instructions and the form of the service in *The United Methodist Book of Worship* (pp. 51–53) designed for use in the hospital or the home are in line with all that has been discussed above. Note, however, that this service is designed for two different uses:

1. When the pastor makes the visit and does not bring the elements remaining from the congregational service, the full text should be followed. That means that the pastor should pray the Great Thanksgiving to consecrate the new bread and cup.
2. When laypeople serve someone with sacramental elements consecrated at the parish service, the Great Thanksgiving is omitted. This is understandable: Saying a prayer twice over the same bread and cup would destroy the sense that this is truly an extension of the congregational service. Moreover, in The United Methodist Church, only ordained clergy or others specially authorized to be pastors may preside at the Lord's Table and thus offer this prayer.

The Communion received by those who are absent from the service truly becomes an extension of the Communion received by those who are present.

However, when the Great Thanksgiving is omitted, what remains of the service is skeletal at best. The rubrics on page 51 do make some general suggestions for filling in this sparse framework; however, more specific and elaborate guidelines are in order. Below are several suggestions to consider:

- Upon entering the place where the visit occurs, state the purpose of the visit. After some initial informal words and gestures of greeting, one of the team members may clarify the purpose and begin the service with words such as these:

  > "We come today in the name of the Lord, and we come on behalf of your fellow members at [*Name*] United Methodist Church, of which you are a cherished part. Those present today gathered around the Table of our Lord to receive together the bread of heaven and the cup of salvation. Now we extend these same gifts of God to you also. In this way we express our Christian love for you and assure you of the prayers and concerns of the whole congregation."

- Tailor the service to accommodate the attention span of the person being visited. If the visit takes place in a hospital or nursing facility, keep in mind the policies of the facility and the duties of the medical staff. Whenever possible, the visiting team should read aloud Scripture passages used in the Sunday worship service. They may also give the gist of the day's sermon. (Preachers may wish to provide the visiting teams with a written summary of their sermon for this purpose.) Visiting teams may also note particular joys and concerns expressed in the congregation's prayer time.

- As circumstances warrant, pray the prayers used in the parish service. If the congregation has a printed bulletin with such items included, bring sufficient copies of the bulletin. Alternatively, use the brief "Confession and Pardon" (*UMBOW,* pp. 51–52). Sing hymns that are familiar, particularly at Christmas or Easter.

- Note that circumstances will vary greatly. In some cases, the person being visited may be in a hospital room or ward with other patients. You may want to invite patients in adjoining beds (and their visitors) to participate in the service; however, if they decline or seem uncomfortable, this may constrain how the service can be conducted. In another case, you may encounter a person who is limited in his or her ability to leave home who is physically comfortable and mentally alert, and surrounded by family members who wish to take part fully in an ample service. There may even be a piano or other musical instrument and someone ready to play it. Whatever the scenario, your team needs flexibility and good judgment in designing each service. Often, due to altered circumstances, you may actually depart from the service you had originally planned to use.

- At the appropriate time, make the transition to the Communion service proper. Open this part of the service with an invitation, such as the one on page 51 of *The United Methodist Book of Worship.* To simply and abruptly dispense the bread and cup immediately following the invitation can seem cold or trivializing at best. At worst it can suggest that the Communion elements have somehow been magically "infused" with special powers ahead of time and can now be routinely dispensed as quickly as possible. When circumstances allow, such impressions can be avoided by having a team member give a narrative such as this:

"At the Lord's Table this day our pastor took the bread and the cup. Recalling God's many acts of graciousness in the past, we gave thanks and praised God with the familiar words, "Holy, holy, holy Lord, God of power and might, heaven and earth are full of your glory. Hosanna in the highest. Blessed is he who comes in the name of the Lord. Hosanna in the highest." (Those present may join in this acclamation if they know it by memory or if the text is provided for their use.)

"Then we called to mind the gracious ministry of our Lord. In Jesus' name our pastor took the bread and then the cup and spoke the Savior's words: 'This is my body. This is my blood. Do this in remembrance of me.'

"On our behalf the pastor asked that the Holy Spirit would make this bread and cup be for us the sacramental presence of the risen Christ, who is ever living in our midst. We asked that the same Spirit would enable us to be more fully Christ's body on earth in service to the world. And we looked ahead to the great feast of heaven, of which this meal on earth is a foretaste.

"Finally, we offered together the Lord's Prayer as we do now, saying: 'Our Father...'." (Everyone present joins to pray the Lord's Prayer.)

"After receiving the bread and cup, we remembered you by name in prayer, together with the others who will also receive Communion today." (Here a team member may read the names of those to be visited.) "And now we offer to you this bread and this cup."

- Afterward, distribute the elements to everyone present who wishes to partake. The members of the visiting team, and any other people present who attended the congregational service, should eat and drink again with the person who is sick or who is limited in his or her ability to leave home. Failure to do this wrongly suggests that Communion is an individualistic reception of grace rather than a corporate act in which God's grace is shared in community.

- After everyone has partaken of the Supper, the table is put in order. You may then pray a prayer of thanksgiving after Communion and a blessing (*UMBOW*, p. 55). If need be, the visiting team may then depart, or they may remain for a period of informal conversation.

- Team members need to be clear about when and where in the church to return the vessels used as well as any remaining elements, or how to care for these otherwise. In the week following the visit, team members should remember specifically in prayer the person or persons with whom they shared the sacramental service.

TO CONCLUDE: SOME WORDS OF CAUTION

Some people who are sick or limited in their ability to leave home will readily accept sacramental visits by the laity, and will more than likely want to receive Communion with increased frequency. Others will not. In the latter case, the pastor who in the past served Communion to the person should, if possible, interpret to them the reasons for having laity serve the sacrament. Some people who are limited in their ability to leave home will resist change simply because unfamiliar practices make them uncomfortable. Others will feel strongly that they have not "really"

> United Methodists have often wrongly assumed that because only ordained or other duly authorized pastors may *preside* at the Lord's Table, only such persons can *distribute* the sacrament.

had Communion if the pastor is not present. Still others will wish to receive Communion on a less frequent basis than that practiced in the congregation. In some cases, one or more of these sources of resistance may be enough to warrant the continuation of the old patterns with a particular individual, at least for a time.

The program outlined in this article is designed to extend the Eucharistic ministry as widely as possible across the congregation. United Methodists have often wrongly assumed that because only ordained or other duly authorized pastors may *preside* at the Lord's Table, only such persons can *distribute* the sacrament.[3] Baptism, not ordination, is the rite that allows us to exercise the priesthood of all believers by sharing the bread and cup with one another after the ordained or authorized pastor has presided at the Great Thanksgiving.

The last thing that needs to happen is for Communion servers to be seen as an elite group within a congregation. Any tendency to view them as "paraclerics" will destroy the primary purpose of this form of Eucharistic ministry. Over time, those who have hesitated to become a member of a visiting team should be encouraged to take part in order to extend this form of service as broadly as possible.

Some people will serve more ably in the capacity of team member than others. Therefore, as suggested earlier, give careful thought to the appropriate pairing of team members (or to creating teams of three or more persons) so that those who are more skilled and experienced can guide the others. Where sufficient interest in participating in the program exists or can be generated, a rotation system can guard against establishing a permanent elitist cadre. It can be specified, for example, that after three years of consecutive service, a person must rotate off for at least one or two years. This can also be a graceful way of removing from active duty people who are unsuitable for continued participation.

The early stages of any new program tend to be bumpy. But experience will usually iron out initial wrinkles that cannot be anticipated even by the best planning. Furthermore, it takes time for everyone to become comfortable with new patterns. Therefore, do not jettison a program too quickly simply because of start-up difficulties. Allow the program to run at least ten or twelve months before concluding that it just won't work in your congregation. If you persevere, God may surprise you with unexpected blessings!

FOR FURTHER READING

Eucharist: Christ's Feast With The Church, by Laurence Hull Stookey (Nashville, TN: Abingdon Press, 1993). See Chapter 7 (pp. 136–43) and Appendix I (155–59).

ENDNOTES

1 See *Ante-Nicene Christian Library: Translations of the Writings of the Fathers, Volume II: Justin Martyr and the Athenagoras,* edited by Rev. Alexander Roberts, D.D., and James Donaldson, L.L.D. (Edinburgh: T and T Clark, 38, George St., 1870), pp. 65–66.

2 From "For the Bread Which You Have Broken," words by Louis F. Benson, in *The United Methodist Hymnal* (Nashville, TN: The United Methodist Publishing House, 1989), 614.

3 The former Evangelical United Brethren Church typically had "pew Communion," in which laity distributed the elements to seated worshipers. In anticipation of the 1968 merger with that body, the 1964 General Conference of the former Methodist Church agreed to allow laity to distribute the elements in the same manner. Thus the *principle* of distribution by the laity is not at all new, although its *application* to visits in homes and hospitals is recent.

Creating Space for Worship

JAMES F. WHITE

*Professor of Liturgy,
Department of Theology,
University of Notre Dame,
Notre Dame, Indiana*

THE ENGLISH THEOLOGIAN JOHN A. T. ROBINSON ONCE SAID that when it comes to worship, the building will always win. That is a pretty strong statement, but it is certainly true that the building will define the possibilities that are open to us in worship and will shape thoroughly how we experience worship. So it is necessary to take a hard look at how the church building—what we know as liturgical architecture—interacts with Christian worship.

The best way to do this is to deconstruct the building—that is, take it apart and analyze how each of the components functions to aid or to inhibit worship—then to reconstruct these components by seeing how they all fit together to create space for worship.

WORSHIP AND ARCHITECTURE

Liturgical architecture consists essentially of six or fewer liturgical spaces, each with distinct functions for the doing of Christian worship. These spaces focus on three or four liturgical centers or furnishings (such as the pulpit), which are necessary for various acts of worship. In order to analyze a church, it is necessary to have a clear view of each of these spaces and centers and how they function in the worship life of the community. Unfortunately, building committees are frequently more concerned about how a building looks than about how it works, so they often neglect this type of study. The result is often buildings that are an obstacle to much that the community aspires to in worship, and sometimes they are a clear contradiction of their understanding of themselves as a Christian community.

LITURGICAL SPACES

In recent years, we have become much more sensitive to the dynamics of assembling for worship. It is no accident that the United Methodist Basic Pattern of Worship lists "Gathering" as the first act of worship (*UMBOW,* p. 16; *UMH,* p. 3). Accordingly, we begin our discussion of liturgical spaces with the *gathering space.* Coming together in the Lord's name may be the most important single act of worship as we form a community to discern the body of the Lord (1 Corinthians 11:29). How gathering space is shaped has enormous consequences for how the community will function as the body of Christ. We come together to meet the Lord, and the first thing that happens is that we meet our neighbor.

In some climates the gathering space may be outside the church building. In others it takes the form of a narthex, vestibule, or concourse where people come together before moving into the main worship space. It also provides space for them to linger and chat after worship. Instead of making a beeline from a side entrance to a pew, people meet in the gathering space with the neighbor with whom they shall greet the Lord.

The second type of space required for all worship is *movement space*. It is obviously necessary to move to where one will sit or stand for most of the service. It may be less obvious just how much of worship depends on movement. We literally do worship with our feet. Weddings and funeral services are structured around processions and recessions. At Holy Communion, we move to the front of the church to receive the body and blood of Christ. And at almost every service, offerings are received and individuals come forward to read, sing, make announcements, and so forth.

All this means that movement space must be designed in a way that gives convenient access to whatever is happening at any time in the service. The need for movement space dictates the length of pews or other seating so that one does not have to crawl over too many participants. We have become much more sensitive in recent years to those who have physical disabilities and their needs for space to maneuver. And we all have become more aware of the importance of our own bodies as well as our minds in worship.

The largest space is usually *congregational space*. This is where most of the congregation sits or, until the fourteenth century, stood. This is where most worship is done by the whole people of God; therefore, the arranging of this space is a good reflection of how we imagine the Christian community. If the community is seen as a passive audience, then it is appropriate that people sit in a rectangular space receding from a stage-like platform for the chief "actors," the clergy. But this image of the people of God has been repudiated increasingly in recent years and replaced by a picture that views the congregation as the chief actors who are on stage themselves. "Full, conscious, and active participation"[1] has been the slogan for worship in recent decades.

In the building of many new churches, congregations are experimenting with a variety of ways of shaping congregational space to express that worship is done by the whole community. Fan-shaped spaces are quite popular, but churches have tried a wide variety of shapes. These new spaces are designed to both express the full participation of all those gathered for worship and to overcome the impression that God is located in holy space that is remote from the people of God. The arrangement of congregational space involves important decisions about the nature of the Christian community.

Baptismal space has often been neglected, but United Methodists are taking baptism more seriously than at any time in decades. Baptism involves the whole process of becoming a Christian and how this relates to being a part of the Christian community. As United Methodists focus more on the process of Christian initiation, baptismal fonts are becoming much more significant liturgical centers. This has important implications for baptismal space. Where the font is located and how it relates to other liturgical spaces involves important decisions.

In United Methodist worship, baptism is almost always a public act done in the context of Sunday worship. In general, this implies that the whole congregation participates in welcoming new Christians into their midst. The church, after all, is people not a building. The symbolism of baptism as entrance to the church *as building* is secondary to entrance into the church *as people*. Therefore, since baptism should be seen and heard by all present, the best location for the baptismal font is in front of the gathered congregation, not behind it.

The act of baptism involves a number of people arranged, as it were, in concentric circles of love around those being baptized: clergy and candidates for baptism, parents and sponsors, and the whole congregation. There must be sufficient space around the font to accommodate all these people, especially when several children or adults are being baptized at the same time.

The space about the altar-table is referred to as *altar-table space*. It is a focal point of worship, not just at the sacrament of Holy Communion but in all worship. In the past, this space has often been "fenced in" by Communion rails; many of our churches still have such rails. Methodists have often called this whole enclosed space simply *the altar*, since it was used for altar calls or altar prayers. As more and more congregations receive Communion while standing, sometimes encircling the altar-table itself, Communion rails have become less necessary.

An important function of the altar-table is that of symbolizing the unity in Christ of all those gathered. As we come forward for Communion or other acts of worship, space about the altar-table becomes very important. This space needs to be visible from all parts of the church and physically accessible to all who will gather there. To ensure visibility, this space may need to be raised a bit, as long as this does not make the space less accessible.

The final liturgical space, *choir space*, is probably the most controversial. This is because United Methodists have no clear image of the function of the choir in worship. Is the choir there to sing *to* the congregation, *for* the congregation, or *with* the congregation? Or a combination of these? How its function is envisioned will determine where the choir is to be located. A choir is meant primarily to be heard rather than seen. Thus acoustics takes priority over visibility. Indeed, a backdrop of choir members during a sermon can be highly distracting. So a less conspicuous location is preferable as long as it does not interfere with audibility.

Other problems arise, too. Choir space often must accommodate instrumentalists, which are increasing in diversity. The person conducting the choir from the piano bench or organ console must be clearly visible to the singers. A key function of the choir is to support congregational singing, which demands a location where choir members do not feel isolated from the congregation (such as in a rear balcony). The more closely the choir is related to congregational space, the more likely the choir is to reinforce the singing ministry of the whole community. However, before it can locate and shape choir space, the congregation must decide how it views the function of the choir.

LITURGICAL CENTERS

We move now to look at the essential liturgical centers, where most of the action of worship is focused. It is surprising how few and simple these centers are; and yet, churches often have erred in preferring to make things more complicated by multiplying these centers with unnecessary furnishings.

United Methodist worship tends to center on the *pulpit*. Here is where the Word of God is read and preached. It is often where the congregation is led in prayer, announcements may be made, and much of worship led. In relatively recent times, many United Methodist churches sprouted lecterns in addition to pulpits. This practice should be discouraged; the presence of a lectern and a pulpit suggests a distinction between the Word read and the Word preached. A single pulpit—our tradition through most of Methodist history—is preferable.

Unfortunately, building committees are frequently more concerned about how a building looks than about how it works.

The Bible should be clearly seen on the pulpit. This is where the Bible belongs, not on the altar-table. (A Bible on the altar-table is probably a good indication that neither is used.) The pulpit needs to be carefully placed so that sightlines are not blocked and the preacher is able to see all whom he or she addresses. It is more difficult to preach to people arranged on a 180-degree arc than with a narrower focus. Proper acoustics are essential for effective preaching, and the pulpit should be well lighted.

Another liturgical center is the *baptismal font*. As we have already mentioned, location of the space about it is important. As one of the biblical sacraments, baptism demands a significant center. Even when baptisms are not being celebrated, it is a reminder to us all of God's acceptance of us. Martin Luther felt that baptism was this world's greatest comfort, and it is certainly a form of proclamation of God's love.

This suggests that baptism deserves a prominent liturgical center, not just a candy dish. In recent years, more emphasis has been placed on the sign value of washing as conveying God's offer of forgiveness. Obviously a larger quantity of water communicates this value more effectively. Our Baptist friends have long understood the high sign value of immersion; now Roman Catholics are moving in that direction. It seems likely that we shall see larger fonts that allow baptism of infants by dipping and eventually maybe baptismal pools for immersion of adults. Sprinkling, pouring, and immersion are all allowed in United Methodist practice.

The *altar-table* is a visible sign of the unity in Christ of all present, but it also has several practical functions. It is ideally the place at which all prayer is offered. This demands that the altar-table be free-standing so the presider can face the congregation across it. It also demands sufficient height, basically the same as a kitchen counter (thirty-nine or forty inches high). The altar-table should be about the length of the presider standing with hands outstretched. Round, oval, or other peculiar shapes are hard for the celebrant to relate to.

The altar-table is a *table* because the Lord's Supper is a meal of Christ's followers gathered with the risen Lord. It is an *altar* not only because the language Christ used at the Last Supper was explicitly sacrificial but also because ever since 1745 Methodist theology has seen the Lord's Supper as implying sacrifice. The design of the altar-table can suggest both these aspects of the sacrament. The altar-table ought to be impressive, not because of its size but because of the care put into designing and building it.

These three items—pulpit, font, and altar-table—are essential for United Methodist worship. Beyond these, some items are convenient. In Roman Catholic circles since Vatican II, there has been an emphasis on the *presider's chair*. When the presider sits, he or she is delegating leadership roles to others—readers, singers, and so forth. A pastor on his or her feet for the whole service is probably monopolizing leadership roles. So a suitable place for clergy to sit is important. It may be best for the pastor to sit with his or her family when others are leading worship. At any rate, the presider's chair should not be a throne or be too impressive. Unlike the pulpit, font, or altar-table, the presider's chair makes no theological statement.

Other items—the lectern, prayer desk, tables and stands, Communion rails—often intrude in meaningful worship. None of these items is essential; therefore, before deciding what to do with any of these items, a church should consider carefully whether an item is necessary. As a general rule, the more focus there is on essentials, the stronger the statement they make. The more the focus is dispersed among a variety of items, the less impact any of them makes.

PREPARING TO BUILD FOR WORSHIP

All the worship spaces and centers mentioned in this article exist in relation to one another. Their meanings and functions are largely determined by these relationships. In every church the total worship environment is always a compromise between the spaces best suited for preaching, music, Communion, and prayer; therefore, there is no one solution. This is why it is necessary for each congregation to discover its own worship needs before it talks about architecture. If a congregation cannot delineate the priorities in its worship life together, it is by no means ready to cast this confusion in concrete.

Preparing to build begins with the theological enterprise of discovering what it is to be a worshiping congregation. Such reflection may take time, but it often has brought the renewal of the community's life together. There are many books, this one included, that can serve as a catalyst in this process. But preparing to build demands careful consideration of every aspect of worship for which the building is intended. Otherwise, we get buildings where caskets cannot be carried in or out, or where wedding processions are awkward or even impossible.

Each of the six spaces and three or four liturgical centers discussed in this article make important theological statements. The design of the centers reflects our understanding of preaching, baptism, and the Lord's Supper. The shaping of the spaces tells us how the community sees its life together and its common activities in worship. Fortunately, we can learn both from the accomplishments and the mistakes of others. A committee would be well-advised to visit other new or remodeled churches and to ask how well they have functioned in the worship of their communities. Learning what not to do when building new worship spaces is inexpensive but valuable information.

CONCLUSION

United Methodist worship is not static. Some observers see United Methodists moving to more frequent celebrations of the Lord's Supper; indeed, some congregations are already following Wesley's directive to have Communion weekly. Baptism of both infants and adults is receiving much more attention, too. On the other hand, there are United Methodists who place more emphasis on non-sacramental worship and neglect the church year. Diversity has long been a Methodist characteristic, and that will not likely diminish. Many decisions must be made locally, although informed by all the resources The United Methodist Church can offer.

FOR FURTHER READING

Church Architecture: Building and Renovating for Christian Worship, by James F. White and Susan J. White (Akron, OH: O.S.L. Publications, 1998).

Meeting House Essays, by various authors, in nine volumes (Chicago, IL: Liturgical Training Publications, 1991–1998).

ENDNOTES

1 From "Constitution on the Sacred Liturgy" in *The Documents of the Vatican II,* edited by Walter M. Abbott, S.J. (New York, NY: America Press, 1966), p. 144.

> It is necessary for each congregation to discover its own worship needs before it talks about architecture. If a congregation cannot delineate the priorities in its worship life together, it is by no means ready to cast this confusion in concrete.

21

SARA WEBB PHILLIPS

*Pastor, Discipleship First
United Methodist Church,
Evanston, Illinois*

The Role of Artists in Worship

Then Moses said to the Israelites: See, the LORD has called by name Bezalel son of Uri son of Hur, of the tribe of Judah; he has filled him with divine spirit, with skill, intelligence, and knowledge in every kind of craft, to devise artistic designs, to work in gold, silver, and bronze, in cutting stones for setting, and in carving wood, in every kind of craft. And he has inspired him to teach… [The LORD] has filled them with skill to do every kind of work done by an artisan or by a designer or by an embroiderer in blue, purple, and crimson yarns, and in fine linen, or by a weaver—by any sort of artisan or skilled designer.

(Exodus 35:30-35)

PRIMITIVE PEOPLES DREW ON THE WALLS OF CAVES. ANCIENT cultures carved statues. The medieval church designed Gothic cathedrals. In human experience, something drives us to express in tangible ways our response to life and faith. The ancient Hebrews felt compelled to decorate the Temple with designs in gold and precious metals, with an intricately carved ark, richly colored fabrics, and elaborate priestly vestments. Their impulse was to offer the best of creative expression to God.

So it continues with people of faith today. Worship space and liturgy is filled with witness to the arts, helping congregations to express tangibly the mystery and majesty of God. Indeed, interest in the arts and worship is growing. One of ten major developments during the 1990's noted by futurist John Naisbitt (along with co-author Patricia Aburdene), is that art is replacing sports as the chief avocation in America; and non-verbal arts are growing the most.[1] Whether by visiting arts festivals or taking art classes, many people are realizing through the creativity that the arts draw forth the deep connection between body and spirit. Contemporary Christians, responding to God's call in their lives, are bringing the art they have to offer to their worship.

What is the role of the artist in connecting worship with the varying art forms? How does the artist enable worship without overshadowing the liturgy with performance or dominance of image? How does the artist provide leadership as one who enables the congregation to be participants not spectators? This article offers practical suggestions about how United Methodist worship leaders can think about worship and the creative work of artists in ways that help our churches employ the artistic gifts of the community.

Worship Matters: A United Methodist Guide to Ways to Worship (Volume I) © 1999 Discipleship Resources. Used by permission.

THE PRESENCE OF ART IN WORSHIP

Few places in our society are more comprehensive in displaying the work of artists than churches. The building designed by architects invites us to worship; so do the windows as they filter the light through the work of the designer of stained glass. The woodcarver's work is present in pews, altar rails, Table, and font. Banners, vestments, and paraments display the talent of the textile artisan. The silversmith and the potter's work are evident in Communion ware, candleholders, and cross. Paintings on the wall, photographs on the bulletin, and flowers arranged on a table tell of an artisan's impact. Often there is wood or stone sculpture as part of pulpits and baptismal fonts.

The service itself most likely uses skilled organists, pianists, and other musicians. It includes reading of literature (Scripture, prayers, and poetry), and possibly drama and dance (as well as movement in standing, kneeling, and sharing the peace). Thus, in church we find ourselves immersed in, surrounded by, and dependent on the arts to communicate the holiness of the space and moment pointing us to God. Often, the church is not even aware of how deeply the artist has contributed to religious expression. We need to claim this intricate connection as a gift to be celebrated.[2]

The arts is an elusive term and, as noted above, quite encompassing. *Artist* is just as evasive. These terms are even more difficult to define in relationship to worship. For example, if an artist is someone who is good at "art," what makes art "good"? When we consider the relationship of art to worship, is art appropriate for worship because the art is good in itself, or should it employ explicitly religious themes?

We might respond that art used in worship is appropriate if it has to do with things of faith. However, just because the artist has chosen a topic that is historically or sentimentally religious does not necessarily make it good art for worship. While the secular artist might be able to pursue a purely aesthetic goal, the liturgical artist will produce art that evokes prayer, praise, and reflection on the holy. That is to say, liturgical art has a distinctive purpose: to express the truth of the holy in such a way that we are drawn more deeply into the mystery of God.[3]

Historically, Protestants have interpreted this mystery with such a focus on the transcendence of the divine (God is above and beyond us) that God's immanence (God is near us) has tended to be overlooked. The Protestant Reformation emphasized the words of the Bible, preaching and prayer, and minimized visual images. Too much emphasis on art seemed vaguely idolatrous, or at least trivial.

In the mid-twentieth century, Protestant churches began to take notice of liturgical reforms of Vatican II, which began modern worship renewal within the Roman Catholic Church. That assembly of broad leadership within Catholicism focused on many aspects of art within the liturgy: environment and space, drama, dance, reading, vestments and paraments, and music. The arts were emphasized as crucial to providing a context for worshiping in all the majesty and splendor that is due God. With twentieth-century reforms, the whole church of Jesus is recovering the embodied gospel. In its various forms, liturgical art "incarnates" the life, message, suffering, death, and resurrection of Christ. It is with such responsibility that worship planning teams and artists approach with gifts to offer to the liturgy.

The artist's role helps us reclaim the "inner eye" to see into the reality of God's incarnation. It is like the classic story of the little child who asks

> The artist's role helps us reclaim the "inner eye" to see into the reality of God's incarnation.

the sculptor as he works on a block of granite, "What are you doing?" "Making a horse," the artist replies. "How do you know?" The artist answers, "I see it. It's just there." Art and its producers can help us learn to see that God is "just there" in the work around us.

Through art's revelatory and sacramental power, it, like theology, is concerned with how to make visible the invisible. The artist helps express and shape our moral imagination, enables us to identify religious and moral questions, and influences the way we interpret these questions. The arts free worship from captivity to words and enables worship to take place through action and symbolism.[4] Visual art is liberation theology for the eyes; the aural is liberation theology for the ears.[5] The artist as theologian expands human experience to know the divine.

THE ROLE OF THE ARTIST

The role of the liturgical artist is to represent the community of the church through artistic expression in worship. Therefore, the liturgical artist does not function autonomously (even while recognizing that to produce their work artists cannot be too constricted). What building committee would turn over plans of sanctuary design to an architect without much discussion of the theological understanding of worship space or the congregation's purpose in mission? (Sadly, many have.) How could banner design or paraments be made without considering the mission, the chancel structure, or the nature of the community and its people?

I know of the work of a vestment designer who creates and sews beautiful albs and stoles. She has, however, made some vestments with unicorn designs on them. Her reasoning was that women have to create fresh symbols apart from the inherited patriarchal symbols. I know enough of feminist theology to recognize that rethinking tradition is no simple matter. Yet I could not help wondering whether a congregation would be able to connect the meaning of unicorn imagery with the God we know from the Scriptures; or might the congregation instead understand this image as a fairy tale or even a pagan myth. Even our vestments must speak to the community's purpose as the people of God who are disciples of Jesus.

Three concerns are crucial to the role of the artist in worship: (1) integration of the arts with worship planning; (2) congregational participation in the art as a criterion in company with the quality of the art; and (3) education in art appreciation within the congregation.

INTEGRATION

Since liturgy itself is an art form, all the pieces that compose the liturgy must contribute to the whole worship experience. Thus, worship planning is critical to the involvement of the arts. Each contribution, from the music to the preaching to the visual effect of the worship space, must meet the critique of this planning, in order that there be a cohesiveness to the worship. This worship planning, whether done by pastoral and/or trained staff or lay planning teams must include the artists who are contributing to the service.

Furthermore, the work of the artist must be submitted to the critique of the planning teams. How does the artist's work enhance worship? Is it an honest expression of that community? Does it challenge or confirm the theological understandings of that community and its practice of worship?

Is it in good taste? The theology of aesthetics is what is at stake here; the "beauty" of the art for worship cannot be overlooked. Liturgical art serves to enable worship by the community and is not for the personal edification of the artist.

Any work offered for worship requires discipline as well as creativity. An artist may have the inspiration or gift of the Holy Spirit, but that gift must still be evaluated by the church—what Saint Paul calls the spiritual gift of discernment. The need for discernment certainly applies to commissioned pieces of art or space design as well. The artist must have a clear vision of what is being requested. It is not enough to say to the hymn writer, "Write a hymn for the start of our Sunday school program." Who is the target congregation: children or the entire community? How important is education in relation to the rest of the church program? Should the hymn be oriented toward Sunday school activities or discipleship in the world?

Some artists have had the frustrating experience of having their commissioned work received less than enthusiastically—even rejected—due to insufficient conversation about the work's purpose and the aesthetic expectations. This conversation, however, must also be sensitive to the freedom of the artist, in order to allow full expression of the creative imagination the artist brings.

PARTICIPATION

Another significant consideration of the role of liturgical artist is the creative tension between the quality of the art and the participation of the community. Artists can stimulate the creativity of other people so that they, too, are drawn into the production of the art form along with the professional artist.[6] For example, the textile artist could do the overall design and color scheme of a liturgical banner. Then the gifts of those in the congregation could be used to cut, place, and sew—all under the careful eye of the artist. The dancer might draw others (indeed the whole congregation!) into simple movement, reserving skilled pivots and broader gestures for disciplined dancers. The trained musician brings expertise in reflective and accompanied music; there is no substitute for such skill. Such musicians can also stimulate the interests and gifts of a congregation's children and youth through involving their instruments, as appropriate.

A difficult but critical issue for the artist is to maintain the quality of the work or performance without hindering the participation of people who are untrained. For example, the choir director maintains a delicate balance in relation to the tension between performance and participation. To do choral pieces well requires rehearsal, and to do rehearsal requires commitment on the part of the choir. How much can one expect of volunteers? Thus the director may also need skills in community building, volunteer recruiting, supporting—and, as many directors will confirm, cheerleading and handholding—to move a choir toward confidence in their ability to serve God through music. Yet choral music in worship is not a performance per se, but an offering on behalf of the entire congregation. The stress lies in holding an expectation of quality for performance while always recognizing that God transforms the gift within the hearer.

Too many times, sloppy work or presentation is blamed on the fact that the presenters are not professional artists. Often, however, the problem has to do with the lack of commitment and discipline of the

> The art of worship is liturgical, and its purpose is to engage the congregation in the work of worship, whether reflectively or actively.

volunteers to give their best to God. How many times have children sung in front of a congregation before they were ready—before they have learned the tune, text, or behavior befitting liturgy? Quality art requires time for preparation or rehearsal. That insight alone offers the congregation an alternative to our "fast-food" culture: Art slows our pace to ponder the things of God, for God.

The issue of artistic quality will always be difficult. One may be able to distinguish clearly between a trained musician and a beginner, a felt banner and a tapestry, an amateurish play and a seasoned production. Nevertheless, the defining line is that the art of worship is liturgical, and its purpose is to engage the congregation in the work of worship, whether reflectively or actively.

EDUCATION

Artists play an important educational role in the life of the church. Using the arts calls for disciplined looking and listening on the part of the congregation, just as the artist must be disciplined to channel creativity into art form. The liturgical artist would be wise to involve him or herself in educating the congregation to understand the arts, but we must remember that many worshipers must first be drawn into an eagerness to receive God's Word. Only then will the congregation come to understand the sights, sounds, and symbols as expression of knowing or experiencing the living God. For example, banners or paraments during the season after Epiphany may contain symbols of a star, crowns, and colors of black, brown, red, yellow, white. But until people know the story of the wise men and how the foreign magi open the Christ event to all nations and races, the symbols will only be decoration. Another example would be the symbolic nature of the texture of materials we choose. Advent's satin, shiny purples, blues, and golds can convey the royalty of Christ, once one understands the prophetic message of a coming King. One could more fully understand the rough textures of Lenten raw silks and burlap when connecting the season with the way of the passion.

Cyril Richardson gave good educational guidelines when he outlined the three distinctives of liturgical art: It connects with tradition; it is communal; and it has religious power.[7] In a real sense, all education of the church shapes the artistic understanding of the congregation. Broader and deeper biblical understandings and historical studies help connect symbols and stories with visual effects. In the same way, liturgical art can give life and fresh meaning to the Bible and to theological concepts.

The community's participation in the preparation and/or selection of art invites the work to have integrity in representing the people who will benefit from it. Although art affects different people in different ways, true religious art will move its observer in some profound way so as to come away with an encounter with the Holy.

It takes time and effort for this understanding to be developed, but nevertheless, it is well worth it, as people come to see God "just there" in the work of the art and the artist and in our world.

CONCLUSION

Ultimately, the role of artists in worship is more than to provide imaginative, decorative, inspiring works in whatever medium he or she prefers. Rather, their role is to provide works that draw us to God and through which God can be known and glorified.[8]

A friend of mine recently recounted his experience of dealing with cancer. He wrote of his trials and frustrations and fear to his pastor. The pastor replied, "Turn it into art!" At first this reply was confusing, but then my friend recognized it for the wise counsel it was. Over time, the disease took the form of poems that expressed the anxiety and alienation and even healing that was being experienced.[9] "Turn it into art!" is a challenge to the church to offer praise to God by becoming co-creators with God.

Art is not on the periphery of worship; it is not an ornament.[10] It is the medium through which we are drawn to God and through which God speaks to us. Artists who understand that their role goes beyond the form of their art will serve God and the church well.

For Further Reading

Full Circle: A Proposal to the Church for an Arts Ministry, by Nena Bryans (San Carlos, CA: Schuyler Institute for Worship and the Arts, 1988).

Planning Blended Worship: The Creative Mixture of Old & New, by Robert Webber (Nashville, TN: Abingdon Press, 1998).

Toward a Theology of Beauty, by John Navone and Robert Stefanotti (Collegeville, MN: The Liturgical Press, 1996).

Voicing Creation's Praise: Towards a Theology of the Arts, by Jeremy S. Begbie (Edinburgh: T & T Clark, Ltd., 1991).

Walking on Water: Reflections on Faith and Art, by Madeleine L'Engle (Wheaton, IL: Harold Shaw Publishers, 1980).

Organizations dealing with religion and the arts:

- American Academy of Religion. For membership information, contact: Membership Services, Scholars Press, P.O. Box 15399, Atlanta, GA 30333-0399. Phone: 404-727-2345. Internet: *http://www.aar-site.org/AAR*
- American Guild of Organists. Contact: AGO National Headquarters, 475 Riverside Drive, Suite 1260, New York, NY 10115. Phone: 212-870-2310. Internet: *http://www.ahohg.org*
- Center for the Arts and Religion, Wesley Theological Seminary, 4500 Massachusetts Ave., NW, Washington, DC 20016-5690. Phone: 202-885-8608. Internet: *http://www.wesleysem.org/car.htm*
- Sacred Dance Guild. Contact: Carla Kramer, Membership Director, Sacred Dance Guild, 2558 Delaware Street, Wickliffe, OH 44092. Phone: 440-585-1676. E-mail: Rkram@aol.com. Internet: *www.us.net/sdg*
- The Fellowship of United Methodists in Worship, Music, and Other Arts, 159 Ralph McGill Blvd., NE, Room 501C, Atlanta, GA 30308.
- The Schuyler Institute for Worship and the Arts, P.O. Box 790, 2757 Melendy Drive, Suite 15, San Carlos, CA 94070. Phone: 650-595-2433.

Endnotes

1 See *Megatrends 2000,* by John Naisbitt and Patricia Aburdene (New York, NY: Avon Books, 1990), p. 50.

2 See "The Arts in the Seminary: Recognizing the Obvious," by Wilson Yates, in *The Arts in Religious and Theological Studies* (ARTS), One /Three, Summer 1989 (United Theological Seminary of the Twin Cities), p. 1.

3 Thanks to James White, who pointed me to Cyril C. Richardson's article, "Some Reflections on Liturgical Art," in *Union Seminary Quarterly Review* (Volume VIII, Number 3, March 1953), pp. 24-28. This article discusses the place of liturgical art in worship.

Ultimately, the role of artists in worship is more than to provide imaginative, decorative, inspiring works in whatever medium he or she prefers. Rather, their role is to provide works that draw us to God and through which God can be known and glorified.

4 See *Blended Worship: Achieving Substance and Relevance in Worship,* by Robert E. Webber (Peabody, MA: Hendrickson Publishers, 1996), p. 108.

5 Thanks to musician Kevin McKelvie, who reminded me that art is more than just for the eyes.

6 It is not my purpose in this article to define who an artist is. To do this, one will need to ask questions such as: Does the phrase *professional artist* refer to the person who makes his or her living through art, or does it refer to the quality of the person's product? There are many individuals who can produce good work without being professional.

7 Thanks to James White, who pointed me to Cyril C. Richardson's article, "Some Reflections on Liturgical Art," in *Union Seminary Quarterly Review* (Volume VIII, Number 3, March 1953), pp. 24-28. This article discusses the place of liturgical art in worship.

8 The collection of articles in this book gives attention and background to several art forms in worship: the role of leadership, creating effective worship space, and body movement in gestures. Volume II of *Worship Matters* highlights the work of musicians, readers, dancers, media, visual arts, and altar guilds, as well as how these can be addressed in multicultural and small-church settings. Individuals who are artists in worship can consult those pages to find out more about their particular liturgical roles.

9 As recounted by Dr. Alva Caldwell of Garrett-Evangelical Theological Seminary, of his pastor, Rev. Bill Killian.

10 Don Saliers made this comment in 1978 in connection with art and worship in a lecture delivered at Candler School of Theology, Emory University, Atlanta, Georgia.

Using Media in Worship

THOMAS E. BOOMERSHINE

Professor of New Testament, United Theological Seminary, Dayton, Ohio

22

A S THE CHURCH EXPLORES THE EVOLVING RELATIONSHIP between electronic media and worship, it needs to consider at least the following issues:

- the history of earlier media systems in Christian worship;
- the relationship between communication systems and cultural formation;
- an integral approach to electronic-communication technology in Christian worship.

It is in the context of reflection on these issues that congregations can begin to identify the challenge of the use of media in worship.

A HISTORY OF MEDIA IN WORSHIP

In the history of cultural communication systems, three basic systems have emerged: oral, written, and electronic. When a new cultural communication system emerges, the old system continues but is modified in the context of the new dominant system. For example, oral communication continues as a primary means of communication in the worship of literate cultures, but the role of storytellers and the character of sacrifice is radically modified. The lector/preacher replaces the storyteller, and the symbolic sacrifice of the Eucharist replaces the sacrifice of animals. The history of worship can be seen as a highly complex and varied integration of communication systems into the worship of God.

Worship in an oral, tribal culture is centered in storytelling, festivals, and animal sacrifice. The oral memory of the people is steadily reinforced by participation in prayer and the recital of the central stories of the tribe. This happens in the daily worship of the tribe in prayer or ritual gestures in the morning, at meals, and during the regular storytelling in the evening.

A central element of personal and corporate worship is the sacrifice of animals and agricultural products. Prayers and stories are chanted so that the sounds of musical stories and songs are the atmosphere of oral cultural life. The festivals of the yearly cycle are the occasion for the recital of the great epic stories of the tribe, dancing and feasting, and the sacrifice of many animals. Thus, oral communication—face-to-face speaking, communal singing, ritual action—has always been the primary communication system of worship.

Since the development of writing in the fourth millennium (3900–3500 B.C.E.), the patterns of worship in oral culture have been gradually

Worship Matters: A United Methodist Guide to Ways to Worship (Volume I) © 1999 Discipleship Resources. Used by permission.

modified as different aspects of the communication system of literacy have been integrated into worship. At the core of this development has been the integration of books into worship. The reading of Scriptures, the singing of songs from hymnals, and praying with prayer books have profoundly changed the character of worship. Furthermore, the styles of worship have been dramatically altered according to the levels of literacy in the worshiping community. One can experience the different styles of literate cultural worship in the differences between the worship of "pentecostal" or "holiness" churches (in which the congregation uses no books), on the one hand, and the worship of Lutheran or Episcopal churches (in which the congregation uses three or four books), on the other.

In general, one can estimate the degree of integration of written media in worship by

- the number of books a worshiper uses during worship;
- the size and character of the worship bulletin;
- the number of manuscripts and books used by the leaders (liturgy, sermon, prayers);
- the level of literacy of the preacher.

The buildings constructed for worship in literate culture have been altered from the open-air character of temples for the conduct of sacrifice to the book-centered buildings of sanctuaries and education buildings.

Worship music has been transformed by the integration of the new musical instruments that have been developed in literate culture. In oral culture, the dominant musical instrument is the drum, with some form of guitar and flute providing harmony and melody. In literate culture, the organ and the piano have become the primary instruments. The complexity of the music of these instruments is inextricably connected with the development of systems for writing and reading music.

Finally, images have become central to worship. In Orthodox and Roman Catholic worship, icons, stained glass windows, statues, and paintings have served as the means for telling sacred stories, centering prayer, and directing attention to God. In even the most iconoclastic Protestant communities, the images of the sanctuary, the pulpit and lectern, the Table, and the Bible have been an integral part of the environment of worship. And in the majority of Protestant churches, stained glass windows, central images over the altar, and various symbols are important elements of the worship space.

When seen in this context, many of the major controversies in the history of the church over the role of icons, organs, buildings, and books have been about the role of media in worship. The rich complex of worship styles in the various branches of Christian worship can be described in terms of the ways in which the communication media of books, images, musical instruments, and architecture have become an integral part of worship.

MEDIA AND CULTURAL FORMATION

A dimension of the conflicts about media in worship has been the relationship of media and culture. Communication systems and culture interact to shape and form each other. It is possible to identify characteristic elements of oral, literate, and electronic culture, but it is also clear that different cultures form and shape communication media in different ways. Thus, the Arab Islamic cultures of the Middle East have interacted with both literate and electronic communication systems in very different ways than the predominantly Christian cultures of Europe and the United States of America. It is impossible to sort out the complex dimensions of cause and effect—both communication systems and the various elements of culture. In the same manner, the roles of media in worship are both shaped by and shape culture.

The controversies about media in worship have often been intense sources of conflict and division in the history of the church (for example, the iconoclastic controversies and the conflicts over instrumental versus vocal music). These are also controversies about cultural values and ways of being in relation to God. Thus, the characteristics of Byzantine culture—icons, large hanging lamps, ornate golden symbols, bearded priests in black robes—that have shaped many of the Christian holy sites in Israel and the styles of worship there seem utterly foreign and alien to Western culture and its styles of worship. These complex interactions of media and culture are part of the past and the future of media in worship.

INTEGRATING ELECTRONIC MEDIA

The development of electronic communication systems in the twentieth century has already had a significant impact on worship. Electronic sound systems have become an integral part of the sanctuaries of many churches. This has made it possible for women, whose voices are generally softer and more difficult to hear in large spaces, to become leaders of worship with a degree of effectiveness that would not have been possible in pre-electronic worship centers. Electronic organs (both cheaper and easier to install than the earlier technology of pipe organs) have made it possible for many sanctuaries to have organ music. Another function of electronic communications has been to place electric clocks in key places where the preacher can see the time. The lighting of sanctuaries by electric light has had an impact on worship at all times of the day and especially at night.

However, in the late-twentieth century, the use of electronic media in worship has been limited to the electronic extension of the voices of worship leaders, to organ music, and to providing candle and lamplight. This use of media expresses the predominant understanding that has shaped the use of electronic media by the church. It has viewed media in worship as an *instrumental* means of extending a message or accomplishing a task.

Thus, an audio amplification system or an electronic organ is an electronic *instrument* that makes it possible to deliver the same kind of sound as in the past—a voice or an organ—but more effectively. Electronic light has many advantages over candles and kerosene lamps for the instrumental task of lighting a sanctuary for worship. In this understanding of media, the role of electronic media is to be the means for more effectively delivering the same elements of worship as in the past.

The history of media in worship makes it clear that this is only the first step in the development of the relationship between media, culture, and worship. Over time, new technologies of communication and culture become an integral part of worship and reform the character of worship. These new technologies become, in turn, a factor in the reformation of culture.

A clear instance of this is the reformation of worship that took place in the aftermath of the invention of the printing press that caused the media revolution of mass printing and distribution of documents. The

> In order to provide an integral context for people who live in electronic culture to worship God, it is necessary for the church to integrate electronic media into its worship.

centrality of the sermon, the emergence of congregational singing of hymns, and the use of prayer books were all an integral part of the new styles of worship that emerged in print culture. These developments in the worship of the church also had an impact on the reformation of the economic and educational systems of feudal culture and on the role of printing and education in the emerging cultures of the sixteenth century.

In order to provide an integral context for people who live in electronic culture to worship God, it is necessary for the church to integrate electronic media into its worship. And in order to maintain continuity with its traditions, the church needs to do this in a manner that preserves as many of the worship traditions of the church as possible. Some of the central elements of media in the worship of the church in electronic culture are new electronic technologies.

SCREENS

Just as placing the Holy Book at the center of the sanctuary was the symbolic center of media in worship in print culture, so placing a screen at the center of the sanctuary also will be an important symbol in electronic culture. The role of the screen is to show images that are related to the elements of the worship service. Such elements can include the words of hymns, videos, film clips, photographs, icons and pictures from the traditions of Christian art, and also computer-generated graphics and images from the Internet. The graphics may be printed words such as outlines, definitions of terms, related biblical texts, and Hebrew and Greek words. But they may also be newly created graphics that will visually concretize or supplement elements of the sermon, the history or experience of the congregation, or the Scriptures that are being recited.

The challenge is to use the screen not solely as an instrumental means for displaying the face of the preacher but also as an integral dimension of new forms of the sermon and prayer. Screens can potentially be used as an integral dimension of every aspect of worship, from the call to worship to the benediction. Screens can facilitate singing, prayer, Scripture recital, sermon, Eucharist, post-Communion meditation, mission connection, and announcements.

MUSIC

Perhaps the most controversial role of electronic media in worship nowadays is the transformation of congregational music. The "praise song" led by a "praise team" is a new form of congregational music. Accompanied by a band composed of guitars, drums, a synthesizer, and various solo instruments such as a saxophone, flute, trumpet, or trombone, this form of congregational singing is often more participatory than the forms of congregational singing accompanied by organ or piano.

With the words projected on a screen, the congregation is able to look up and sing together without reference to a hymnbook. This form of congregational music is very young and will, it is hoped, develop a much more varied and spiritually profound musical tradition. The challenge will be to integrate the organ and the rich tradition of the hymns and songs of the church into an electronic worship environment. A further dimension of the new music will be the emergence of new forms of prelude and postlude music that will provide a context for prayer and meditation prior to and following the service.

SCRIPTURE LESSON

The Scripture lesson has become the deadest part of worship, especially in high literate churches in which the disembodied reading of the Scriptures in a virtual monotone has become normative. The Scripture lesson in the worship of the electronic culture can be the occasion for making the Scriptures a vivid and compelling dimension of worship.

The memorization and recital of the Scriptures with accompanying images and music is a new form of the Scripture lesson that can greatly enrich worship. In effect, this form of Scripture lesson embodies the Scriptures, and connects—through the images and music—the original character of the Scripture with contemporary culture.

THE SERMON

The sermon can be transformed by the integral use of electronic media. The exegesis of the meaning of the text in its original context can be deepened and broadened by being linked to images and materials from the cultures of the past, the present, and the future. The meaning of the biblical tradition now can be made vivid by integrating clips from contemporary music, film, and TV.

The sermon itself can be reconceived as both a time for teaching and as an opportunity for retelling and connecting with the central stories of the Christian tradition. Electronic culture is a secondary oral culture in which elements of oral culture such as storytelling can be reintegrated into worship.

LINKING

With the possibility these days of linking directly to the Internet, it is possible to establish links in worship with congregations and mission projects all over the world. The worship of each local congregation can be connected with other churches around the world.

CONCLUSION: THE CHALLENGE OF ELECTRONIC MEDIA

The potential roles of electronic media in worship are at an early stage of development. Most of the churches that are using electronic media in worship are culturally conservative, using the media as a way of reinforcing the political and economic cultures of the nineteenth century. The liberal churches have been extremely conservative in their use of electronic media in worship. The challenge for the conservative churches is to use electronic media in ways that will help to transform electronic culture in a healthy manner rather than to simply reinforce traditional culture. The challenge for the liberal churches is to integrate electronic media into worship in a manner that will preserve maximum continuity with the traditions of the past and help to form a new global culture of peace and justice.

At one level, the challenge of electronic media for the church is the need to sacralize this new technology by the transformation of its role in culture. As in the past, the integration of new technologies into worship changes worship, but it also changes the technology.

Finally, however, the issue is whether we can find ways to offer our new technologies to God as a fitting and appropriate offering of ourselves.

> **As in the past, the integration of new technologies into worship changes worship, but it also changes the technology.**

In as far as we have identified ourselves with a communications system—as we clearly have with writing—the offering of our literary liturgical creativity to God has been both fitting and appropriate. The challenge for the future is to be open to the ways in which God may be seeking to enable us to do this with electronic media.

FOR FURTHER READING

A Father and Two Sons, Videocassette/CD-ROM (New York, NY: American Bible Society). Phone: 212-408-1200.

Christian Worship and Technological Change, by Susan White (Nashville, TN: Abingdon Press, 1994).

Out of the Tombs, Videocassette/CD-ROM (New York, NY: American Bible Society). Phone: 212-408-1200.

Out on the Edge: A Wake Up Call for Church Leaders on the Edge of the Media Reformation, by Michael Slaughter (Nashville, TN: Abingdon Press, 1998).

Story Journey, by Thomas E. Boomershine (Nashville, TN: Abingdon Press, 1988).

The New Era in Religious Communication, by Pierre Babin and Mercedes Iannone (Minneapolis, MN: Augsburg Fortress Publishers, 1991).

The Visit, Videocassette/CD-ROM (New York, NY: American Bible Society). Phone: 212-408-1200.

The Power of Sign-Acts

23

DON E. SALIERS

*Parker Professor of
Theology and Worship,
Candler School of Theology,
Emory University,
Atlanta, Georgia*

THE WORDS WE USE IN CHRISTIAN ASSEMBLY DEPEND GREATLY for their meaning and point on the nonverbal dimensions of worship. This is certainly clear from Scripture. The words Jesus used in the upper room, "This is my body, given for you," had power because he took bread into his hands, after having raised his hands in praise and thanksgiving to God, and broke it into portions that he then gave to the disciples to eat. The words and the gestures were thereafter forever fused together into what we now call a "sign-act." Thus ritual actions such as blessing, anointing, washing, giving and receiving the kiss of peace, and others mentioned in the New Testament combine saying and doing into potent signs of grace. Christian worship, from the very beginning of the Way of Jesus, was permeated and communicated by such sign acts.

SIGN-ACTS AS HUMAN AND DIVINE

We do well to consider both the human and divine dimensions of sign-acts in Christian worship. On the one hand, sacraments such as baptism and the Lord's Supper employ human means of communication. The water bath involves hands and touch and words; the Eucharist involves hands and touch, taste, and words. What the sacraments communicate requires the incarnate human bodily presence and action. On the other hand, we claim that the sacraments communicate more than what is visible, audible, and tangible; they communicate God's grace and mercy. Thus the human actions designated by the Christian tradition, derived from God's fullness in Jesus Christ, point beyond themselves and take part in the divine reality imparted to those who receive.

Watching people say hello and goodbye at airports or other places of meeting and departure is instructive. We say much more with our bodily gestures and postures than our words alone can convey. I am deeply impressed with how touch and embrace, lingering waves of the hand, and a small child's wordless "bye-bye" have the power to touch family members and even the stranger who is observing. In worship, the language of touch and gesture and movement is even more crucial, since we deliberately use the vocabulary and the grammar of these human acts to participate in Word and Sacrament. Exchanging the peace of Christ, the presiding gestures at the Lord's Table, the touch of the server's hand in Communion, the laying on of hands for prayer, for blessing of the old or

Worship Matters: A United Methodist Guide to Ways to Worship (Volume I) © 1999 Discipleship Resources. Used by permission.

the young, for commissioning and for ordination—all of these carry far more meaning than we ordinarily think they do. So in planning and celebrating the Christian gospel and the mystery of God's self-giving, we must attend to the ways in which Jesus Christ touched and gestured his grace to others.

In recent times many have called attention to how "body language" often contradicts what people say, or betrays what in our innermost being we are actually feeling or thinking. So one may speak words of greeting—"Welcome; how nice to see you"—while actually not perceiving another as welcome. In such a case, we say that the person is only "going through the motions." Yet, the outward motions are part of a sincere welcome, too. So it is the fusion of inner intention, disposition, and attitude with the gesture that is required for the power of such actions to convey what we find to be praiseworthy in a host. We know from the inside, so to speak, of our own "hiding" behind the words; but we also know the joy and truth of gestures.

THE ESSENTIAL SIGN-ACTS OF CHRISTIAN WORSHIP

I propose that there is a basic set of gestures that are essential to Christian worship over time. Some of these belong to those who lead; some belong to the whole assembly.

First, the gestures of welcome and hospitality are sign-acts. These may take many forms depending on the cultural context of the worshiping community. Greeting in the name of Christ can be restrained or exuberant, but the welcoming is necessary in word and gesture. The whole atmosphere of our gathering to celebrate the promises and grace of God in Word and Sacrament is established and communicated in how we welcome friend and stranger alike. Welcoming gestures combine with attentive eyes and ears to make the words potent: "Welcome to this place."

Second, the gestures of prayer, ranging from postures of kneeling or standing, with hands folded or raised, to nonverbal praying with eyes wide open are sign-acts. All too often we settle for one or the other. But different occasions and contexts for prayer invite a range of postures and gestures. Especially noteworthy is the recovery of the presiding minister's gestures while praying the Eucharistic prayer at the Table. With hands uplifted, palms upward, the ancient gesture of the "orans" (praying) invites the whole assembly to pray with the celebrant in thanking and praising God for creation and redemption. The very meaning of *Eucharist*—giving thanks for God's good gifts—is given nonverbal expression in this biblical gesture, highlighting the significance of the whole action sequence at the Table: taking the bread and cup, blessing God (with the raising of hands and hearts), breaking the bread, and communing.

Third, gestures of blessing are sign-acts. Worship offers human beings the blessing of divine grace, mediated through human means. Thus, the laying on of hands for healing, the extending of the hand in blessing over the bread and cup in invocation, the touching of hands and foreheads in anointing for ministry and for the confirming seal of baptism all show forth the "action" character of these sacramental moments. The power of forgiveness and blessing flow through prayerful human touch in every rite of reconciliation.

Fourth, the kiss of peace, recently recovered from the early church and the witness of the New Testament and a focal point for the shared love of Christ, is a sign-act. Not only are we, in Wesley's words, to "offer Christ," we are to recognize Christ in one another. So whether in a more formal handshake or a robust embrace (depending on the community's tradition and ethnic background), the kiss of peace as a sign-act may occur at several points in worship: as a greeting, as a "sealing" of prayers, as an act of reconciliation in preparation for the Eucharist, or at the conclusion of the service before moving out in ministry.

Fifth, setting the table for Communion, or preparing the worship space (as in the "stripping of the altar" or the "hanging of the greens"), is a sign-act. These sign-acts convey the sense of preparing a place for contemplation or new engagement with the holiness of God. Observing the worship space change in color, texture, and intensity at the hands of other members of the congregation can offer some of the most moving dimensions of sign-acts. When the Table has already been well prepared, the celebrant and assistants at the Table may then pour the fruit of the vine into chalices, and may break the bread with words about Christ (or in silence). These become integrated into the whole sign-act of the sacrament itself, adding bodily dimensions to what is prayed and sung.

The act of pouring water and fruit of the vine into vessels, the principal sacramental actions of baptism and Eucharist, is both a practical action necessary to the water-bath and the meal and making visible what Christ offers us in the common elements from the earth. The act of pouring itself, when done with integrity and compassion, symbolizes the very nature of the sacrament: God's love in Christ poured out for us. So pouring is not an ornament, but is an essential gesture in which the whole assembly is prompted to "see and hear," to "taste and see" the goodness of God.

Processions are also sign-acts. Sometimes these are by special ministries such as the choir, symbolizing and energizing the opening praise of a service. At other times, such as on Palm/Passion Sunday, the whole assembly takes part in the procession. Movements of the children's choir, or the sending forth of deacons and/or laity to take Communion to those unwillingly absent from the service can be significant processions. Each has its own character, but the point of procession is the movement of God's people in the ever-present dance of gathering and dispersing to serve the members of Christ's body, week by week, year by year.

John Wesley was intent on pointing out that there are many "means of grace," but the chief ones that give focus to our identity as Christians are found in the principal sacraments of Eucharist and baptism. Sacraments are verbs, not nouns. That is, they are complex words and actions that convey and effect the reality of God's self-giving—the central mystery of faith to which they point. Each of the gestures and acts outlined above are part of, and proceed from, the principal sacraments of baptism and Eucharist, and from the audible sacrament of the Word and song. I would certainly not hesitate to include foot-washing, acts of reconciliation and forgiveness, burial, healing, and marriage covenants within the field of force of sacramental meaning.

CONCLUSION

All the sign-acts of Christian worship are oriented toward "receiving" the grace of God in Christ. All the sign-acts are also the means by which we come to understand and to discern one another as "living reminders"

Christian worship, from the very beginning of the Way of Jesus, was permeated and communicated by sign-acts.

of Christ. It is in and through the sign-acts that we are formed in how we are to be in the world of everyday. Worship is thus a genuine "rehearsal" of becoming who we are in Christ, and of a continual "schooling" in his gestures toward the world: hospitality, blessing, healing, feeding and being fed, consoling and admonishing, forgiving and supporting, acting justly toward one another, and commending life and death to the presence of God.

Today United Methodists, along with many other Christians, are moving toward a more mature practice of the sign-acts that shape and define Christian existence in the world. They carry our humanity and divine grace. These are the very sign-acts God has given us in the incarnation of Jesus Christ.

FOR FURTHER READING

Liturgical Gestures, Words, Objects (selections from *Assembly* in honor of Mark Searle), edited by Eleanor Bernstein, CSJ (Notre Dame, IN: Notre Dame Center for Pastoral Liturgy, 1995).

Strong, Loving and Wise: Presiding in Worship, by Robert W. Hovda (Collegeville, MN: The Liturgical Press, 1981).

The Lord Be With You: A Visual Handbook for Presiding in Christian Worship, by Charles D. Hackett and Don E. Saliers (Akron, OH: O.S.L. Publications, 1990).

Touchstones for Liturgical Ministers, edited by Virginia Sloyan (Washington, DC: The Liturgical Conference, 1978).